Avebury

DUCKWORTH ARCHAEOLOGICAL HISTORIES

Series editor: Thomas Harrison

Also available

Pompeii

Alison Cooley

Tarquinia

Robert Leighton

DUCKWORTH ARCHAEOLOGICAL HISTORIES

Avebury

Mark Gillings
&
Joshua Pollard

Duckworth

First published in 2004 by
Gerald Duckworth & Co. Ltd.
90-93 Cowcross Street
London EC1M 6BF
Tel: 020 7490 7300
Fax: 020 7490 0080
inquiries@duckworth-publishers.co.uk
www.ducknet.co.uk

A catalogue record for this book is available
from the British Library

ISBN 0 7156 3240 X

Typeset by Ray Davies
Printed and bound in Great Britain by
Biddles Ltd, King's Lynn, Norfolk

Contents

To

Mum and Dad (JP)
Mum, Dad, Flo and Luke (MG)

Acknowledgements

We would like to thank the following for assistance when it was needed the most: David Field for making available copies of the English Heritage surveys of Avebury; Ros Cleal for making available photographs of the Gray and Keiller excavations, discussing Avebury matters and providing tea and biscuits; and John Evans for information and discussions regarding the pre-henge environmental evidence.

We have also benefited enormously from discussions with Julian Cope, James Dyer, Hella Eckhardt, Brian Edwards, Dave Edwards, Lucy Franklin, Pete Glastonbury, Anthony Gouldwell, Rosina Mount, Deirdre O'Sullivan, Rick Peterson, Mike Pitts, Andrew Reynolds, Dave Robinson, Sarah Semple, Jeremy Taylor, Aaron Watson, Dave Wheatley, Alasdair Whittle and Ruth Young.

Finally we would like to thank Deborah Blake at Duckworth for her patience.

Keep going back into the history of stones, and the people begin to fall away. Go back far enough, and there are only stones.

Tobias Hill, The Love of Stones (2001)

Illustrations

Plates

(between pages 116 and 117)

ix

Figures

Illustrations

Tables

1. Introducing Avebury

The most extraordinary work in the world.
Stukeley (1743), 14

How do you begin to write about a site such as Avebury? One could start by describing it in the rather cold, analytical terms of traditional archae-ological narrative. For example:

Situated in the Upper Kennet Valley of north Wiltshire, southern England, the Avebury henge comprises a 420 m diameter enclosure with four entrances, an internal ditch and external bank. Within the interior is a perimeter circle of c. 100 standing stones, which in turn encloses two smaller stone circles, themselves containing internal stone settings. Megalithic avenues lead from two of the entrances, connecting the henge to other timber and stone construc-tions. The monument was constructed in a series of stages during the late Neolithic and early Bronze Age (c. 3000-2000 BC).

This certainly communicates the structural essence of Avebury, but tends to downplay its key qualities. It is certainly a type of prehistoric monu-ment that archaeologists have grouped into the general class 'henge', but this obscures the fact that there is no other site, henge or otherwise, quite like Avebury. You could perhaps instead focus upon precisely this unique-ness and difference, remarking first upon the sheer physicality, presence and scale of the monument. It is, after all, the largest stone circle in Britain, the banks, ditches and huge standing stones dwarfing visitors as they weave their way around the monument (Plate I). Alternatively, you could stress its status as a designated World Heritage Site – one of the planet's unique cultural resources. Another approach would be to high-light the presence of a substantial portion of the modern village of Avebury actually *within* the perimeter of earth and stone, stressing that Avebury is very much a lived monument rather than relic fossil of some bygone age. Another point of entry would be to emphasise the sense of mystery it invariably engenders: why and how was it built, and what was it for? These are mysteries that have fuelled archaeological and popular imagi-nations alike since the discovery of the monument in the seventeenth century, drawing in researchers and filling bookshelves. A final tactic may be to focus upon the extraordinary history of the monument: constructed between *c.* 3000 and 2000 BC; 'discovered' by the antiquary John Aubrey in 1649; recorded in detail by William Stukeley in the 1720s; and restored in the 1930s to its perceived former glory by the marmalade magnate and playboy Alexander Keiller.

As archaeologists are engaged in a series of new excavations and surveys in and around the monument, a pioneering World Heritage Site management plan is launched, activists daub the stones in paint, and modern day druids and mystics revere the stones, we are faced with a plethora of understandings and interpretations of the site. What should be clear by now is that writing about Avebury is no straightforward task, as Avebury is simultaneously all of the things listed above: a unique prehistoric monument; a managed cultural resource of international stature; a lived and worked modern landscape; the catalyst for innumerable ideas, theories and explanations; and the locus for a number of questions which, despite over three centuries of investigation, remain stubbornly unanswered.

Negotiating Avebury

The uniqueness of an encounter with Avebury today can best be summed up by the word *informality* (Gingell 1996). Avebury is not only a monument that you can read about in dry, dusty, academic texts, examine on any one of a hundred websites, or gaze at from behind a sturdy wire fence. You can go and quite literally immerse yourself in Avebury, ponder its mysteries, wander around its features and run your hands across the cold surface of the stones – whether visitor, enthusiast, archaeologist or druid. The informality of Avebury is everywhere evident, from the unobtrusive tourist facilities to the way in which visitors are encouraged to encounter the site. Rather than being herded along a carefully signposted and proscribed 'official' route around the features, fenced off from the stones themselves, they are instead left to wander, experience and *engage* with it in their own time, following their own pathways.

And yet it is important to realise that underlying this relaxed informality, Avebury is a site in a constant state of flux and negotiation. While there is little of the overt political argument, debate and occasionally open conflict that has characterised the recent history of Stonehenge, Avebury is very much a contested space (Bender 1998). The tensions at Avebury arise in part from its tripartite nature (archaeological monument, international cultural resource, and a living, working village) and the attendant need to balance the requirements of research and preservation, management and promotion, and the impact the policy of openness and informality has on the everyday lives of the village's inhabitants.

1. Introducing Avebury

A recent example is the concern expressed that plans to improve and enhance visitor facilities and reorganise the World Heritage Site will upset the balance, resulting in the effective overloading and destruction of the village and the fossilisation of the present landscape around Avebury through reversion to pasture (Fielden 1996, 506; Edwards 2000, 76). Yet it is perhaps ironic that the alternatives tendered, such as moving all visitor facilities to a nearby town (Fielden 1996, 507), will be equally disruptive to Avebury's unique character of informality. Despite claims to the contrary, Avebury does not represent the unique survival of a small patch of an otherwise lost bucolic village England (Edwards 2000, 72).

A further example arose in 1999 with the rediscovery of a group of stones on the line of the Beckhampton Avenue (Gillings et al. 2000). Faced with having to decide what to do with these newly discovered megaliths once archaeological recording was over, local opinion was firmly divided. Some wanted the stones re-erected, the field in which they were found turned to pasture, and the avenue restored to some notional former glory. Others were vehemently opposed to such a reconstruction on the grounds that it would result in the loss of arable farmland that was doing no harm to the monument and result in even more visitors disrupting day-to-day life. The stones were reburied.

Other tensions arise from the site's very informality. This is perhaps best illustrated by the events that took place in June 1996, when a group of eight stones on the West Kennet Avenue were covered with a series of abstract painted glyphs and motifs. The assembled list of suspects was extensive – mindless vandals; disenfranchised ice-cream vendors; New Age pilgrims; people out to discredit such New Age pilgrims. Conspiracy theories abound. In June 1999 one of the same stones was completely covered in a thick coating of red and green paint while another was daubed with the words 'genetically modified' and 'cuckoo' (*Guardian*, 19 June 1999, 12). This act was claimed by an anonymous group of artists but widely attributed to anti-GM protestors.

In highlighting these inherent tensions and contradictions, the point we would like to make is that far from reflecting peculiarly modern concerns, it can be argued that such negotiations have characterised the entire history of the site. It is our contention that rather than a recent distraction from some deeper, more essential quality that makes Avebury unique, it is this constant engagement and negotiation that makes it the monument we encounter today.

Knowing what was there

The fame of the area has run far ahead of basic archaeological understanding.

Whittle (1993), 30

In archaeological terms, there is a tendency to think of Avebury as 'done'.
Detailed plans and descriptions exist dating back to the seventeenth
century, and many excavations have taken place, culminating in the
campaigns undertaken in the first half of the twentieth century by Harold
St. George Gray and Alexander Keiller (Gray 1935, Smith 1965). Along
with Stonehenge it has earned the status of a World Heritage Site – at the
time of writing one of only 529 such cultural monuments in the world – it
has its own museum, and has been partially restored and renovated to
reflect its 'original' state. However, the paucity of detailed archaeological
knowledge can be illustrated by Burl's estimate (1979, 75) that only 6% of
the interior has been excavated. Likewise, although there exist a number
of plans and antiquarian accounts of the monument drawn up prior to the
almost complete destruction of the stone settings in the seventeenth to
nineteenth centuries, the apparent detail such records hold is invariably
illusory, as the partial sources upon which they were assembled, the
underlying motivations of the authors and internal contradictions, errors
and speculations are revealed (Ucko et al. 1991). As the authors of the
most detailed recent discussion of the archaeological and antiquarian
record of Avebury rightly claim, the available archaeological evidence from
the site 'remains haphazard, almost incidental, and focused upon the
standing stone monuments and earthworks alone' (ibid., 158). As we shall
see, even within the 6% studied through formal excavation, the results are
far from conclusive and often frustratingly unclear. Ambiguity is ever
present.

The fabric of the monument

Our understandings of Avebury are based upon a combination of very
limited excavation, antiquarian records of varying consistency and quality
and, in more recent years, ad hoc campaigns of aerial and geophysical
survey. The results of working within such a piecemeal archive are most
visible when an attempt is made to offer a coherent description of the
archaeological remains present at the site (Fig. 1). However authorita-
tively presented, any attempt at such an enterprise inevitably comprises
a blend of four types of information (Table 1).

4

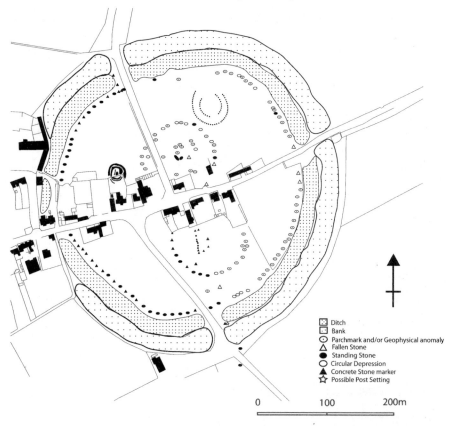

Ditch
Bank
Parchmark and/or Geophysical anomaly
Fallen Stone
Standing Stone
Circular Depression
Concrete Stone marker
Possible Post Setting

0   100   200m

1. Composite plan of Avebury. Reproduced by permission of Ordnance Survey on behalf of the Controller of Her Majesty's Stationery Office, © Crown Copyright 100043105.

Table 1. Knowing Avebury

Confirmed features	*Certainties*	Located through excavation, or still extant
Recorded anomalies	*Ambiguities*	Located through survey and excavation
Suggested (suspected) features	*Speculations*	Based upon inconsistent, incomplete or ambiguous data
Expected (yearned for) features	*Fictions*	Generated by preconceptions and desires

To make the task even more difficult, the relationship between these classes of information is fluid rather than fixed, with features slipping effortlessly from class to class according to personal preference, changing fashions within the discipline, new discoveries or some combination of all of the above. A good example of this is the Beckhampton Avenue. To the

5

antiquary William Stukeley the existence of the Avenue was a *certainty* (stone settings were recorded), though its course was a *speculation* (the surviving record was patchy) which embodied aspects of *fiction* (it curved to form the tail of a snake). To some later antiquaries such as Lukis, the very existence of the Avenue was seen as little more than a *fiction* (Lukis 1881-3), whereas others saw it as a *certainty* (King 1879). More recently, many archaeologists (e.g. Ucko et al. 1991) regarded it as part *speculation* and part *ambiguity*. Its existence as a *certainty* was only proved through excavation in 1999 (Gillings et al. 2000), bringing the circle fully around. As will become clear in the following discussion, the case of the Beckhampton Avenue is far from unique.

In the following sections the main features of the monument are discussed with reference to the certainties, ambiguities, speculations and fictions. A full description of the physical features of the monument can be found in Isobel Smith's definitive account of Alexander Keiller's excavation (Smith 1965), from which we have drawn much of the material presented here.

Location

The monument is located in the Upper Kennet Valley of north Wiltshire, an area of chalk upland that forms the westernmost extension of the Berkshire Downs (Fig. 2). The site lies upon a low saddle or ridge of middle chalk, at a height of 160 m OD, close to the seasonal watercourses and springs that provide the source of the River Kennet. It is bounded to the south and east by the gently rolling high ground of the Marlborough Downs. The site does not exist in isolation, but stands in the centre of a remarkable concentration of Neolithic and early Bronze Age monuments (Whittle 1993, Pollard & Reynolds 2002).

The bank

The first feature that comes into view as one approaches Avebury is the enormous earthwork bank bounding the monument (Fig. 3A). This is a colossal construction in its own right. Approximately 420 m in diameter, the bank stands to a height of over 5m above the present ground surface, and is 23-30 m wide at its base. Excavation has shown that the bank is composed of a core of irregular piles of loose chalk rubble, in places held back by informal retaining walls of large chalk blocks, with possible evidence for further timber revetting at the bank ends (Smith 1965, 194-5). This in turn is sealed by a weathering deposit of finer chalk rubble and soil. The top of the bank is uneven and irregular, excepting the length in the north-western sector restored in the 1930s by Keiller, where a decision

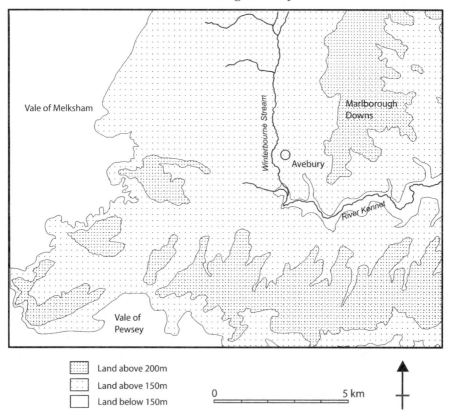

Land above 200m
Land above 150m
Land below 150m

0   5 km

2. General location of Avebury.

was taken to sculpt the bank into a regular form (ibid., 188). The traditional explanation for this marked irregularity has focused upon a combination of uneven post-depositional settling and compaction of the finer rubble and soil components of the bank material, and the irregular way in which the ditch (the source of the material for the bank) was dug. The irregularity of the bank's final form could thus be seen as a by-product of the irregularity of the work undertaken by individual gangs excavating adjacent segments of the ditch (e.g. Malone 1989, 107). More recently the suggestion has been made that the irregularity of the bank may have been a deliberate architectural feature (Gillings & Pollard 1999, 185; Watson 2001, 304), a point we shall return to in Chapter 3. Towards the entrances the bank becomes progressively larger and wider, creating a series of impressive entrance terminals. This is most evident at the north entrance, where along with the enlargement and swelling of the bank terminals, excavation revealed that the causeway itself had been deliberately scarped

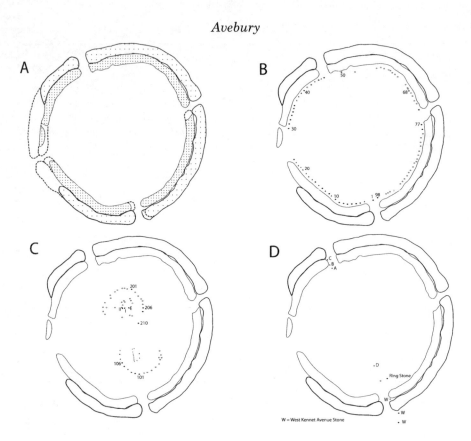

3. The prehistoric components of the henge (A – the earthworks; B – the outer stone circle; C – the inner stone circles; D – the remaining stone settings).

and sunk by over a metre to further emphasise the size and imposing qualities of the bank at this point.

Of particular interest is the recent suggestion that the bank is of more than one phase of construction. Although not identified in the section cut by Gray, excavations across the bank undertaken by Henry Meux in 1894 (Gray 1935, 104), and by the Vatchers in 1969, recorded the presence of a much smaller primary earthwork sealed within the core of the later bank. This first phase bank is around 9 m wide and 2.5 m high, and was composed of a turf core with chalk rubble capping, itself sealed by a well developed turfline (Pitts & Whittle 1992, 206). Beyond its existence, we know nothing more about this earlier feature, and it can only be assumed that the later bank follows its course (Plate V).

The ditch

Within the circuit of the bank lies the ditch. This configuration of external bank and internal ditch is seen as diagnostic of a class of earthwork enclosure termed a 'henge', dating to the later Neolithic (*c.* 3000-2200 BC) and largely peculiar to the British Isles (Harding 2003).

Today, the ditch is still an impressive earthwork: about 21 m wide at the top and 3.7 m deep (Smith 1965, 193). However, a considerable amount of silting has taken place, and the sides of the ditch have weathered back far from their original profile. Excavations undertaken by Harold St. George Gray between 1908 and 1922 revealed that the ditch was originally steep-sided, 7-10 m deep, 2.4-5.1 m wide at the base and perhaps 9-10 m wide at the top (Gray 1935). The bottom was flat but rather irregular, with occasional 'submerged' causeways extending as solid ridges of chalk across the ditch floor (ibid., 116). From his excavation of the eastern terminal of the southern entrance it appears that the ditch became deeper and wider as it approached the entrance with evidence of more careful and regular construction, for example the end of the ditch butting the causeway being neatly squared off. This appears to mirror the elaboration and enlargement of the bank seen at these points (ibid., 117-18, 123). Keiller's small excavation on the inner edge of the ditch in the south-west quadrant revealed a curious step in its upper profile, a feature also noted by Gray. Filled with chalk rubble, this has been tentatively interpreted as an earlier, shallower ditch through which the final ditch profile was cut (Pitts & Whittle 1992, 210). This shallower ditch *may* relate to the construction of the primary phase of bank noted above.

Despite the regular circularity indicated on a number of antiquarian plans (e.g. Plate XV), the circuit described by the bank and ditch at Avebury is far from circular. It is noticeably flattened to the south-west and north, and bulges somewhat to the north-east. Ironically, prior to reliable quantitative survey in the twentieth century, one of the most accurate plans of Avebury's circuit was one of the first, that drawn by John Aubrey for his *Monumenta Britannica* (1665-97) (Fig. 17). As will be seen in our discussion of the inner stone settings, this is not the only Avebury circle that fails to live up to its name.

The original entrance locations

The circuit of bank and ditch is broken today by four entrances. Although the precise locations of the original southern and western causeways have been displaced, all four entrances are thought to be original. This argument is based on excavated evidence (north, west and south); the presence of connecting stone avenues (west, south); and structural elaboration through the widening, outward swelling and increased height of the bank terminals (east and north) (Smith 1965, 194-5).

Between the sixteenth and nineteenth centuries the earthworks around the entrance causeways were subject to a variety of disturbances, ranging from quarrying and construction, to road remodelling and tree planting. Despite this, the excavations carried out by Gray and Keiller illustrated clearly the relationship between the modern day entrances and the original causeways into the monument. At the northern entrance, the bank and ditch have been cut back some 12 m from their original terminals to accommodate the modern Swindon road. To the south, the modern road runs across the infilled ditch of the western terminal, while the bank at this point was extensively quarried in 1762 (Ucko et al. 1991, 172). On the opposite side of the road the bank has been extended to the west by some 11 m. At the western entrance the modern road likewise appears to run over the edge of the infilled ditch. This part of the earthwork has suffered more than most with large-scale levelling of the bank taking place between 1683 and 1696 in order to create a platform for a barn, and again in the early 1720s (Smith 1965, 181).

The outer circle

Within the arc of the ditch and closely following its circuit is the outer circle of standing stones (Fig. 3B). In the excavated and restored western portion of the monument, the spacing of these stones is not regular, varying between 7.3 and 14.3 m, with an average spacing of 11 m. The precise number of stones making up the outer circle is not known, the most authoritative estimate being the 98 suggested by Smith (ibid., 196), which has subsequently formed the basis for the accepted archaeological numbering of the Avebury stones. It is important to emphasise that this remains only an estimate, arrived at from projecting the average 11 m spacing encountered in the *excavated* western half of the outer circle, to the remaining *unexcavated* portion of the monument. In doing so it does not take into account any possible irregularity in stone spacing or deviation from its perceived line adjacent to the ditch edge, both of which are hinted at by a recent comparative analysis of antiquarian plans and geophysical surveys (Ucko et al. 1991, 209). Of this notional 98 stones, 30 are visible today, either standing or recumbent, with the locations of a further 16 marked by concrete pillars. Of this total only 19 were visible prior to Keiller's excavation and reconstruction of the western half of the circle (Smith 1965, figs 67 and 68). As will be discussed in detail in Chapters 7 and 8, the missing stones met a variety of fates during the later life of the monument, being either buried, burned, broken up, dragged away, blown up, or some combination of the above.

1. Introducing Avebury

At this point it is useful to take a look at the stones themselves. They are all unmodified, naturally shaped blocks of sarsen: a very hard, locally occurring sandstone. The stones vary markedly in their shape and size, though those in the north-west quadrant are on average slightly smaller and more regular than the stones making up the south-western part of the circuit. Some have an angular, geometric form while others are rounded, their surfaces curving in an organic mass of folds and creases. The smallest are less than a metre in maximum dimension, while the largest exceed 6 m. The stones also vary in their surface texture, some are smooth, some rough and others pitted with fossil root-holes. They also range in hue from almost white-grey through to a dull orange-red (Pollard & Gillings 1998, 150-1). Although there is no evidence for their being artificially shaped, some carry marks from earlier use as axe polishing stones (Smith 1965, 223), and others encase fragments of fossil bone and shell. Within the outer circle, the largest stones visible today are the truly monumental blocks flanking the northern and southern entrances to the henge, the surviving examples standing over 4 m in height (Plate X). The remainder are less substantial, but still large enough to dwarf the human body, ranging between 2.0 and 3.9 m high (Pollard & Gillings 1998, 155).

Originally Stukeley had claimed the existence of a second, concentric outer stone circle, largely on the basis of a single stone setting he recorded in the north-west quadrant and the position of the isolated 'ring-stone' near the southern entrance. An excavation undertaken by Keiller to locate the former failed to find any evidence for its existence, though it has subsequently been pointed out that due to a misunderstanding of the scale of Stukeley's plans the excavation was carried out in the wrong place (Ucko et al. 1991, 206). Progressive geophysical surveys have located no trace of a second outer circle and over time even Stukeley, its most conspicuous advocate, appears to have changed his mind about this feature (ibid.).

The inner circles

Enclosed within the outer circle are two further stone circles, located in the southern and northern halves of the monument (Fig. 3C). At around 100 m in diameter these smaller circles are still impressive features in their own right. Positioned on a ridge of high ground running north-south across the interior of the monument, they each comprise sub-circular rings of sarsen enclosing further megalithic settings. The stones making up these inner circles are, in general, larger than those of the outer circle, reaching an average height of 3.4 m. In both cases the central features within these inner circles have suffered from large-scale and thorough disturbance, not least by the uncoordinated diggings of early antiquaries,

11

and only a relatively small number of stones survive in their original positions.

Smith postulated an original circuit of 29 standing stones making up the southern inner circle (Smith 1965, 198), though the caveats applied to her outer circle estimate apply equally here. In the centre of the circle Stukeley recorded an enormous stone that had long since fallen. He described this as an 'Obelisk', roughly circular in section, some 2.5 m in diameter and 6.4 m in length. Excavations undertaken by Keiller bore out this description, identifying a 6.4 m long line of burning pits associated with the destruction of the stone and its original socket (ibid.). The socket suggested that when standing the stone would have exceeded 5 m in height. Also evident were a series of prehistoric pits located to the immediate north-west, intermingled with the remains of a possible cremation burial, the post-settings for the village maypole and flagpoles erected during village fetes. It is interesting to note that Gray had earlier mused that 'a traditional "sanctity" still lingers around this spot' (Gray 1935, 109n3).

Excavations undertaken in the area to the west of the Obelisk revealed a curious setting of smaller sarsens, reddish in colour and forming a linear arrangement running for 31 m on a roughly north-south axis. At either end of the long axis a stakehole was discovered, perhaps relating to the laying-out of the line, or forming components of an earlier fence line. Although it was thought that the linear setting might describe one half of a rectangle enclosing the Obelisk (Smith 1965, 251), subsequent geophysical survey has failed to identify any continuation of the feature. It might be regarded as an independent stone row pre-dating the southern inner circle, or a façade fronting the Obelisk (Fig. 4, below).

As with the outer circle, Stukeley had originally claimed that the southern inner circle was a double concentric setting, citing the existence of a single surviving stone and the destruction pits of others to support his claim (Stukeley 1743, frontispiece). Although a single stone setting was located by excavation to the south-west of the Obelisk (stone D), inset approximately 10 m from the perimeter of the inner circle, further excavation and geophysical survey show this to be an isolated feature (Smith 1965, 198; Ucko et al. 1991, 219) (Fig. 3D). Stukeley appears to have mistakenly identified stones of the linear setting as elements of a conjectured internal circle (Smith 1965, 199).

The second inner circle is situated immediately north-west of the southern one (Fig. 4, above). Recent geophysical surveys and parchmark evidence have confirmed that the setting of standing stones here is far from circular, enclosing what can best be described as an 'egg' shape with its long axis aligned north-east/south-west (Ucko et al. 1991, 221; Bewley et al. 1996, fig. 2). This is a distortion that many early surveyors of

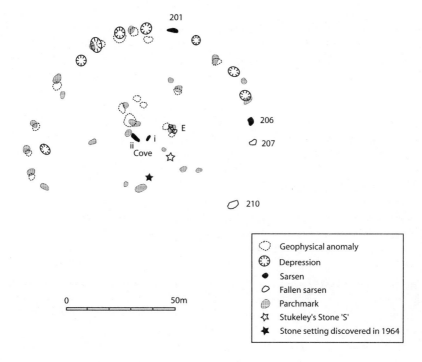

4. The inner stone circles (above: the northern inner circle; below: the southern inner circle).

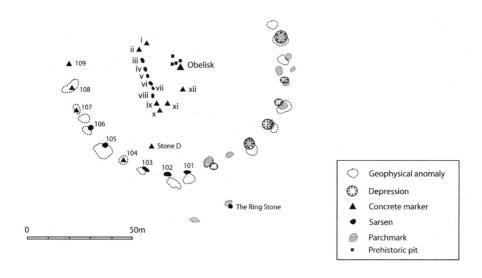

13

Avebury failed to identify, leading to considerable variation in their plans (Ucko et al. 1991, 221). Once again, the northern inner circle has suffered considerable depredation, with only four perimeter stones surviving to Keiller's day. Unlike the southern inner circle, excepting a small-scale investigation of a single recumbent stone by two of Gray's workmen in 1922, it has seen little in the way of modern archaeological excavation. Stukeley's notional 30 stones and Smith's estimate of 27 must once again be offset against a survey record which suggests some irregularity in stone placement around the perimeter of this feature (Bewley et al. 1996, fig. 2). A recent comparison of antiquarian records, geophysical survey results and excavation data concluded that 28 stones originally stood in this setting (Pollard & Gillings 1998, fig. 5).

Slightly offset from the centre of the circle are the remains of a truly monumental three-sided sarsen setting, open to the north-east (Plate IX). Known as 'the Cove', following terminology devised by Stukeley, this box-like structure encloses an area of *c.* 40 m². While unique in its scale and particular format, similar coves are known from other later Neolithic monuments, such as the henges of Arbor Low in Derbyshire, Stanton Drew in Somerset, and Mount Pleasant in Dorset, as well as on the Beckhampton Avenue at Avebury (Burl 1988). Two stones remain of the Avebury Cove, those making up its south-eastern and south-western sides. The former is some 2.4 m in breadth and stands 4.9 m high; while excavations in 2003 demonstrated that the latter originally stood over 5.5 m high and is 4.9 m wide. Weighing around 100 tonnes, the western stone ranks among the largest megaliths in Britain. There have been various claims that a capping stone surmounted the Cove, in effect creating a roof for the box, and that there existed a flat 'altar' stone facing the opening (Ucko et al. 1991, 227-32). However, both may be little more than wishful antiquarian thinking. There is certainly no evidence that either existed and future excavation is unlikely to shed further light as post-medieval building, episodes of stone destruction and numerous antiquarian sondages dug in the nineteenth century around the base of the stones, have created much disturbance here.

Between the Cove and the perimeter of this circle three stone settings were recorded by Stukeley, again leading him to conclude that a second concentric stone circle was present. Although two of these stones had disappeared by the time of Gray and Keiller's fieldwork, their presence on several nineteenth-century plans of the monument, coupled with the chance discovery of a former stone setting in a water-pipe trench dug in the 1960s, led Smith to argue in favour of Stukeley's second internal circle (Smith 1965, 223), a view subsequently supported by a number of researchers (e.g. Burl 1979, 151, fig. 7). More recent geophysical survey and aerial photographic evidence has suggested that these stone settings are not part of a circle at all but instead form the fragmentary remains of a complex and ill-understood setting of sarsens around and adjacent to the Cove. Some of these have recently been reconstructed as a façade-like setting immediately to its north-east (Pollard & Gillings 1998, 153).

The remaining stone settings

In addition to the outer and inner 'circles', there are other groups of stone settings within the henge (Fig. 3D). An isolated stone was recorded by Stukeley to the south-east of the southern inner circle, between its perimeter and the south entrance. Although destroyed shortly afterwards (between 1724 and 1812: Burl 1979, 186), its presence was subsequently confirmed by the excavations of Keiller (Smith 1965, 202). This stone was described by Stukeley as being relatively small and perforated with a natural hole. Interpreting this as a tethering point for sacrificial victims, he named it the 'Ring-stone'. Although often presented as a free-standing feature (e.g. Burl 1979, Malone 1989), parchmark evidence recorded in 1996 suggests a second stone setting may have existed some 20 m to the west (Bewley et al. 1996, fig. 2). If so, the Ring-stone was originally one of a pair of standing stones lying between the large sarsens flanking the southern entrance and the perimeter of the southern inner circle; perhaps forming a formal entrance into the latter. Keiller's excavations in this area during 1939 appear to have just missed the putative second stone.

Further enigmatic settings were discovered during Keiller's excavations around the northern entrance. A very substantial socket ('stone-hole A') was discovered 3.7 m to the south-west of stone 46 of the outer circle, and slightly offset from the arc of that feature. To the north-west of this setting excavations revealed two further sockets ('stone-holes B and C') running along the edge of the ditch terminal (Smith 1965, 203). Taking these features as indicative of an earlier sarsen setting that was dismantled to make way for the earthwork and outer circle, Keiller postulated the existence of a third 'inner' circle (Keiller 1939; Burl 1979, 163-4). Although some researchers still argue for a third, dismantled circle (Burl 2000, 322-3), subsequent excavation and geophysical survey have failed to provide any evidence for such a feature (Piggott 1964; Ucko et al. 1991, 227). Stone-holes B and C might more plausibly belong to an early entrance feature, while the status of A remains uncertain. Stukeley claimed that another standing stone was present in this area, located on the edge of the ditch terminal flanking the eastern side of the north entrance. Subsequent excavation failed to locate the feature and reservations have been aired concerning the veracity of Stukeley's record in this area (Ucko et al. 1991, 208-9; Smith 1965, 203).

Possible timber settings

Although it is the earthworks and megalithic settings that have captured the imaginations of visitors, antiquaries and archaeologists alike, there exists some evidence for the presence of prehistoric timber structures within the monument. The clearest indication comprises a single substantial post-hole, located on the eastern side of the south causeway, on the berm (level space) between the bank and ditch (Fig. 5). Excavated by Keiller, this was found to be 1.6 m across and over 1.0 m deep, and supported a post some 0.6 m in diameter (ibid., 204). Due to the lack of extensive excavation in this area it is not known whether this is an isolated, free-standing feature or part of a larger setting. A prehistoric date does, however, seem likely (see Chapter 2). More recently, in the far north-east of the monument, tucked in the area between the northern inner circle and the outer circle, geophysical survey has revealed two

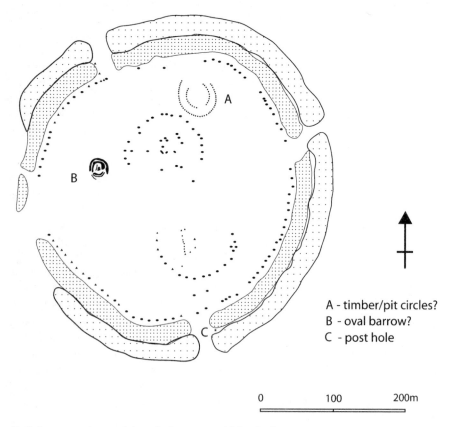

A - timber/pit circles?
B - oval barrow?
C - post hole

0   100   200m

5. Other putative prehistoric features within the henge.

16

concentric rings of anomalies, 30 and 50 m in diameter respectively (Ucko et al. 1991, 227, pl. 69). Their discovery has led to suggestions of the existence of a late Neolithic multiple timber circle in this part of the henge. Confirmation of whether the feature is real or not, or made up of post-holes rather than stone sockets or pits, must await excavation.

An oval barrow?

The final putative prehistoric feature within the henge was first revealed as recently as 1995, taking the form of a parchmark in the north-western quadrant of the monument (Fig. 5). Subsequently confirmed by geophysical survey, this lies in the area between the northern inner circle and the stones of the outer circle. It takes the form of a double-ditched sub-rectangular enclosure, some 25 m in diameter, enclosing a small central feature (Bewley et al. 1996, 641, fig. 2). Morphologically, it resembles closely the middle Neolithic oval barrow at Barrow Hills, Radley, Oxfordshire (Bradley 1992), though in the absence of any confirmatory excavation it could equally be much later, possibly Roman or Anglo-Saxon.

The village

Today the prehistoric features of the henge lie within the network of roads, buildings and garden boundaries that make up the eastern half of Avebury village (Fig. 1). Like so many rural settlements, the village has a long history. Shallow earthworks in areas of pasture correspond to the arrangement of fencelines and field banks carefully recorded on early estate documents and dutifully inscribed upon the plans of the early antiquaries. Others, such as those recently detected by geophysical survey, appear to hint at earlier boundary ditches and alignments (Bewley et al. 1996). Stretching between the western and eastern entrances of the henge is an irregular mix of surviving village buildings, and platforms and earthworks left when buildings were demolished during the 1930s by Keiller, and as recently as the 1960s by the National Trust, in an attempt to clear what was perceived as intrusive clutter from the centre of the monument. What remains is a miscellaneous collection of buildings ranging from timber-framed houses of the sixteenth and seventeenth centuries through to brick-built farm labourers' cottages of the late nineteenth century. The range of styles is quite typical for a north Wiltshire village, and charts the development of late medieval and post-medieval vernacular building traditions, from timber to stone, and then to mass-produced brick and tile. Although belonging to a more recent past than the enigmatic settings of stone and earth, features of the village are far from insignificant, providing an important archaeological indicator of the unique symbiosis that existed between village and henge. It is perhaps axiomatic of Avebury that our archaeological knowledge of them is at best partial (Edwards 2000).

Moving beyond the earthwork – the avenues

It is important to acknowledge that the physical fabric of the monument does not stop at the far edge of the bank. Whether reflecting direct observation or artistic elaboration, the earliest plans of the monument by Walter Charleton and John Aubrey show pairs of large flanking stones outside each of the entrances (Ucko et al. 1991, pls 5 and 6). We know that in the case of the southern and western entrances such settings did exist, related to two megalithic avenues, comprising lines of paired standing stones that march out across the surrounding landscape to create a tangible, physical link between the henge and other prehistoric monuments and features in the vicinity (Plate III).

From the southern entrance, the West Kennet Avenue stretches for approximately 2.5 km down towards the River Kennet and then on to Overton Hill, linking Avebury to a late Neolithic circular stone and timber setting known as the Sanctuary (Cunnington 1931; Pollard 1992; Pitts 2001). To the west, the Beckhampton Avenue covered a distance of at least 1.3 km, linking the henge to a pre-existing earthwork enclosure. The stones in these avenues were on average smaller than those making up the main circles of the henge: the majority being 2.4-3.7 m high, though there is evidence that the stone size increased towards the avenue terminals (Ucko et al. 1991, 187; Gillings et al. 2002). The spacing of the avenue stones is remarkably consistent, with the transverse interval ranging from 14 to17 m and the longitudinal spacing between the stone pairs from 21 to 30 m. The main variation comes at the junction between the West Kennet Avenue and the Sanctuary, where there is a progressive reduction in both the transverse and longitudinal spacings (Cunnington 1931, pl. 1). Stukeley claimed an authoritative 100 stone pairs for each avenue (Stukeley 1743, 37), but this may reflect little more than an innate desire to see symmetry. Owing to a combination of widespread destruction and limited archaeological fieldwork, there remains some ambiguity over the precise course followed by each of the avenues, and as a result the number of stones involved.

In his excavation of the West Kennet Avenue, Keiller claimed that there existed slight depressions running down the sides of the feature, creating the impression that the central area between the stones was raised (Ucko et al. 1991, 189). Excavations on the line of the Beckhampton Avenue revealed no such features and more recent geophysical evidence for the West Kennet Avenue suggests precisely the opposite, with less eroded chalk bedrock running along the edge of the stone lines (ibid., 189). Such erosion, if it is there, could of course relate to the presence of later trackways or agricultural activity against the line of the avenue.

Both avenues have suffered from the ravages of later agricultural activity, building and concerted programmes of stone destruction. It is a sobering thought that only two large stones remain today to mark the Beckhampton Avenue – the adjacent Longstones, known locally as Adam and Eve. This feature was already severely dilapidated by the time Stukeley recorded it in the 1720s (Stukeley 1743). Along with a handful of stones left marking its course, the main feature comprised a cove, similar to that in the northern inner circle at Avebury. Stukeley believed this to be located at the notional midpoint of the avenue, but we now know that it marks its terminal. The majority of the stones seen by Stukeley were destroyed shortly after his visits, leaving only Adam and Eve to mark its former existence. The very lack of any conclusive evidence for the Beckhampton Avenue led many subsequent antiquaries and archaeologists to question its existence, not to mention the sanity of Stukeley and the reliability of his record (e.g. Piggott 1985). In 1999, geophysical survey and excavation vindicated Stukeley, locating its course in Longstones Field to the south-west of Avebury, exactly where he had identified it (Gillings et al. 2000) (Plate II).

The exact relationship between the avenue and Avebury itself has been lost beneath the modern village that clusters around the west entrance to the henge, and the vast majority of its course has yet to be investigated. However, recent work in the area of Stukeley's Beckhampton Cove has revealed that the original terminal to the avenue is of at least two phases of construction (Gillings et al. 2002). We know the avenue ended some 1.3 km south-west of Avebury at a point where it crossed the ditch of an earlier enclosure. This was marked by a T-shaped setting of large sarsens perpendicular to its long axis that was subsequently dismantled and the cove constructed in its place. The latter comprised a slightly splayed rectilinear setting of four massive stones, *c.* 15 x 10 m, aligned north-west/south-east. As with the Avebury Cove, the stones of this feature were large, the one remaining stone, Adam, standing 4 m high and weighing upwards of 60 tonnes (Cunnington 1913). From the evidence of excavated stone sockets and the one remaining avenue stone, Eve, the sarsens increased dramatically in size as they approached the terminal. Stukeley was unequivocal in his belief that the avenue continued beyond this point, originally ending adjacent to a group of round barrows on Fox Covert another kilometre to the west – 'a most solemn and awful place' (Stukeley 1743, 36). The chance find of a stray buried stone near the present Beckhampton roundabout, and on Stukeley's postulated course, seemed to lend support to his claimed westerly continuation (Smith 1965, 217; Vatcher 1969; Vatcher & Vatcher 1980, 41-2). However, excavations undertaken in the summer of 2003 confirmed the avenue's end at the Longstones Cove.

Returning to the West Kennet Avenue, this suffered considerably less from episodes of post-medieval stone destruction than the Beckhampton Avenue, being identified both by Aubrey and Stukeley, the latter compiling a detailed record that was subsequently confirmed by excavation and geophysical survey (Smith 1965, 206-9; Ucko et al. 1991, 186-94). However, once again the precise relationship between henge and avenue has proved difficult to elucidate. Despite numerous small-scale excavations in the area of the southern entrance, Keiller had difficulty in delineating with any certainty its precise route as it made its final approach to the henge. The excavated evidence suggests a marked dog-leg in its course over the final 120 m (Smith 1965, 208). It is almost as if the avenue was not originally heading towards Avebury at all, but turned sharply at the last possible moment to link up with the henge (Fig. 6). It is worth noting that the precise severity of this dog-leg is unknown as a result of the rather ambiguous nature of the excavated evidence; some claimed stone-sockets perhaps being earlier or later pits (ibid., 208; Wheatley & Earl 2002). Following this kink, the line of the avenue appears to have passed through the entrance to link up with the large entrance stones of the outer circle. The Ring-stone and its newly identified partner could represent a further continuation of the avenue up to the perimeter of the southern inner circle. As an aside, it is interesting to note that the last stone pair of the Beckhampton Avenue before it entered the earlier enclosure also incorporated a perforated stone – an interesting symmetry perhaps?

From Avebury the West Kennet Avenue ran south-east, incorporating an area of earlier occupation at the foot of Waden Hill (Smith 1965, 210-16). At the midpoint of the avenue Stukeley claimed to be able to recognise the remains of another cove, but the fact that the suggested location of this feature falls beneath the modern road makes it unlikely that its existence can ever be confirmed. There are, nonetheless, hints of changes in the avenue's format along its mid-section as it approaches the hamlet of West Kennet. Geophysical survey suggests it is reduced to a single line of stones after the well-mapped 1000 m length leaving Avebury (Ucko et al. 1991, pl. 62), while excavations in 2002 and 2003 on the line immediately to the south-east of this have revealed a gap in the avenue's length. Here its course crosses a dry valley and enters a natural sarsen field. It may well be that the creation of artificial settings of stone was considered unnecessary by the avenue's builders because of the presence of natural sarsens here.

The avenue resumes its normal format of paired stone settings as it starts to climb out of the valley in the area of West Kennet House and the present A4. In recording the final stretch as it approached the Sanctuary, Aubrey noted a sharp kink in its course, very reminiscent of the dog-leg subsequently recovered through excavation at the Avebury end. Excava-

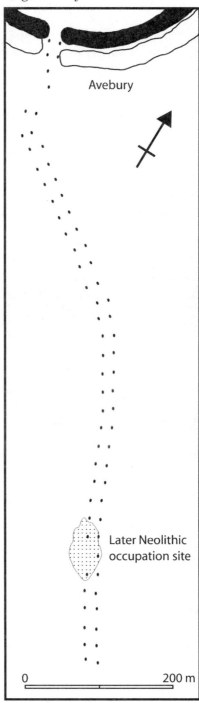

6. The northern third of the West Kennet Avenue as it approaches the Avebury henge.

Avebury

Later Neolithic occupation site

0   200 m

tions undertaken at the Sanctuary in 1930 revealed that the avenue changed its form markedly at this point, the lateral spacing decreasing and the original double row being replaced by triple lines of stone (Cunnington 1931, 306), whose surviving remains were perhaps rationalised by Aubrey into a kink (Fig. 10). This raises the tantalising possibility that a similar complexity marks the Avebury terminus of the Avenue, leading to the rather confused excavation plan recovered by Keiller.

Other entrances, other avenues?

As mentioned earlier, on the seventeenth-century plans of antiquaries such as Aubrey and Charleton (e.g. Ucko et al. 1991, pls 5 and 6) external pairs of sarsens are shown flanking each of the four entrance causeways. On the basis of this, some researchers have tentatively suggested that Avebury may originally have had four avenues – one for each entrance (ibid., 184). Although these features do not appear upon the early eighteenth-century plans of Stukeley, we know how badly denuded the Beckhampton Avenue was at this time and can only guess at what else may have been lost in the few decades separating the records of Aubrey and Stukeley.

Unravelling the remains in time and space

This then is Avebury as it can be encountered today. It should have become clear that in the description offered above no attempt has been made to unravel the chronological sequence or meaning of the various features and components of the monument. This is in part a deliberate attempt not to anticipate the narrative we will be developing in later chapters, and in part a reflection of the fragmentary nature of the evidence. We have also avoided lengthy discussions of the principal episodes of fieldwork and recording that have taken place at the site, though the unique importance of individuals such as Aubrey, Stukeley, Gray and Keiller will become clear as our narrative progresses. Our final omission has been any concerted effort to place the monument within the context of its surrounding landscape. No archaeological site exists in isolation, and Avebury is far from an exception, lying at the centre of one of the most remarkable concentrations of Neolithic and early Bronze Age archaeology in western Europe. Although through necessity brief, reference will be made to this broad context throughout the following chapters in an attempt to place Avebury within its contemporary world. Those keen to explore the Avebury landscape in more detail are directed to recent detailed accounts by Whittle (1993) and Pollard and Reynolds (2002).

2. Avebury before Avebury

As is so often the case with life-stories, the very earliest years are often the most uncertain, with accounts based more upon impressions than on any concrete record of events and circumstances. This is certainly the case with Avebury, where the ephemeral nature of pre-henge activity, the paucity of reliable dating evidence and the general lack of modern excavation on any significant scale all make it difficult to unravel the earliest events with much certainty. As a result this chapter, perhaps more than any other, is reliant upon subtle details within the available evidence, informed not only by the archaeological work that has been undertaken at Avebury, but also by analogy with a range of other sites in the wider region.

We begin our account in the early Holocene landscape, during the later Mesolithic (c. 7000-4000 BC), but focus largely on events following the onset of the Neolithic (c. 4000-3800 BC) when a dramatic series of developments occurred in the ways in which people lived and understood the world. It is during the latter period that we see the first sustained occupation of the Avebury landscape, evidence of cultivation and the keeping of domesticated livestock, and the appearance of long mounds, enclosures and other ceremonial monuments.

In our discussions of the Neolithic in the following two chapters we make reference to the chronology established by Whittle (1993) for the Neolithic of the Avebury area. This is summarised in amended form in Table 2 and consists of six discrete phases. Whittle's chronology is useful for two reasons. First, it is based upon the evidence of radiocarbon dating. Secondly, by breaking down the period into blocks of typically 400 years it provides a more refined sequence than the conventional divisions into early and late Neolithic, which are rather crude, each encompassing as much as a millennium. Since there is currently little evidence of Neolithic activity in the region during his phase A (the last centuries of the fifth millennium BC), many of the events described in this chapter span phases B-D, i.e. the period c. 4000-2800 BC.

Table 2. Whittle's chronology for the
Neolithic of the Avebury area (with amendments)

Phase	CAL BC (1 sigma)	Environment	Avebury	Environs
A	4354/4245-3999/3826	Woodland. First clearances.	Early clearance?	Limited occupation.
B	3999/3826-3698/3542	Scattered small clearances. Animal husbandry.	Some occupation.	Simple barrows and shrines?
C	3698/3542-3361/3109	Mosaic of clearance. Limited plough cultivation and cereals, animal husbandry.	Continued occupation. Oval barrow?	More sustained occupation. Long mounds and causewayed enclosures.
D	3361/3109-2916/2782	Trend to scrub and woodland in places.	First phase earthwork and early stone settings?	Blocking of West Kennet long barrow begun by this phase.
E	2916/2782-2564/2457	Renewed clearances.	Main earthwork at E/F border. Stone settings?	Simple circles. Sanctuary, Silbury at E/F border.
F	2564/2457-2133/1959	Trend to open country. Pigs. Some cultivation.	Outer circle and other stone settings. Avenues.	Palisade enclosures. Blocking of WK completed. Early Beaker burials.

The earliest inhabitants of Avebury

It is difficult to know quite when Avebury became a recognised *place*, but we are aware from finds of Mesolithic flintwork that it was occasionally visited in the three or so millennia before 4000 BC. Several later Mesolithic flint tools have been found in and around the area later occupied by the henge, including a possible microlith from under the bank (Smith 1965, fig. 76, F190) and a tranchet axe from close to the southern entrance (Wiltshire Sites and Monuments Record). While these may represent little more than chance losses by highly mobile hunter-gatherers moving through the region, a more sustained presence is implied by a localised scatter of later Mesolithic flintwork 300 m to the west of Avebury. Revealed during small-scale excavations on low ground adjacent to the Winterbourne stream, this dense scatter of flint-working debris and burnt flint included 14 narrow-blade microliths (Evans et al. 1993, 151-3). An environment of dry woodland existed here at the time of occupation, which could fit anywhere between 6800 and 5700 BC on the basis of a single luminescence date. The working of flint, creation of fires and repair or replacement of tools might imply occupation over several weeks, or repeated returns to a short-stay camp over a long period of time (Whittle 1990, 106).

Further Mesolithic activity in the wider environs of Avebury is attested by largely isolated finds of flint tools from Windmill Hill, Horslip, South Street, the site of the Falkner's Circle and elsewhere (Whittle 1990, 106-7; Pollard & Reynolds 2002, 21-6) (Plate III). There is also a possible flint extraction site on the downs at Hackpen Hill to the east of Avebury (Holgate 1988, table 1). Even taking into account the scatter adjacent to the Winterbourne, this hardly constitutes evidence of dense and repeated Mesolithic exploitation of the landscape. If anything, the centre of the Avebury region seems to have been quiet and little used during the period (Whittle 1990). The Upper Kennet Valley perhaps formed a very marginal component of the overall territory employed by these hunter-gatherer communities.

Excavations undertaken at Cherhill, 6 km to the west of Avebury (Evans & Smith 1983, 111), and Hungerford, 20 km further down the valley to the east, suggest that the main base-camps were located outside the immediate Avebury area (Whittle 1990, 106). The former comprised a surface spread of flint artefacts and occupation debris: worked flint, animal bone (wild cattle, pig and deer), charcoal and some fragments of sarsen stone. The composition of the flint assemblage suggested that this may have acted as a base, or more likely hunting-camp, for a largely mobile community where the carcasses of animals killed and butchered elsewhere were further processed. The material recovered was deposited over the course of a number of repeated visits, with individual occupation episodes relatively short in duration (ibid, 105). A notable characteristic of these repeated occupations was the lack of any deliberate interference with the forest, though this is attested in other regions (Simmons 1996). Indeed, the only structural feature accompanying the artefact spread was a shallow hollow (Evans & Smith 1983, 111).

How should we view the relative absence of Mesolithic activity in the environs of Avebury? It could be that the area offered few advantages for more sustained occupation, perhaps possessing little ecological diversity and not attracting large herds of wild animals. Whatever the reason, we should not read the absence of occupation as indicative of the absence of significance. There are other regions in southern England which show little evidence of a Mesolithic human presence yet became important places during the Neolithic, their early significance marked by the occurrence of large ceremonial post settings. Stonehenge provides one instance, where four massive 'totem-pole' posts dating to the eighth millennium BC occupied the area immediately north of the later monument (Cleal et al. 1995, 43-7). To the south, amid the massive earlier Neolithic enclosure complex on Hambledon Hill in Dorset, two similar post settings were also found to date to the eighth millennium (Healy 2004). Once again, this is a location that is otherwise largely devoid of Mesolithic activity.

Similar settings could exist at Avebury. Previously unconsidered, a prime contender is a substantial post-hole revealed during Keiller's excavations in the area of the southern entrance (Smith 1965, 204). Situated on the berm between the bank and ditch, and set to the east of the entrance itself, it is in an odd position in relation to the architecture of the henge (Fig. 5). While essentially undated, the location of this post-hole strongly suggests that it belongs to a pre-henge phase. Tapering, 1.6 m in diameter at the top and over 1.0 m deep, with a post-pipe suggesting it held a timber *c.* 0.6 m in diameter, it bares a striking morphological similarity to the Stonehenge Mesolithic post-holes. An early Mesolithic date for this remains a tantalising possibility, though one that may only be resolved through further excavation of this area in a search for additional post-holes.

The early Neolithic in the Avebury region

It was during the fourth millennium BC that Avebury began to take shape as a unique location within the landscape of the Upper Kennet Valley. This coincides with the series of major social, material and ideological changes that marked the advent of the Neolithic in the British Isles. Potentially encompassing a fundamental shift in the relationships that existed between individuals, social groups and the natural world, the period is often characterised by the appearance of domesticates (both plants and animals), and the use of new items of material culture, most noticeably pottery and polished stone axes. With these went new productive technologies and social relationships. In many areas the Neolithic also marked the first sustained episode of interference with the natural world, through more extensive clearance, cultivation and the construction of monuments. Underlying and driving these transformations were new cosmologies – ways of conceptualising the world and the place of people within it (Thomas 1991, 1999a; Whittle 1996).

It is important to acknowledge that this process of 'Neolithicisation' was not a single, uniform phenomenon. Regional differences in material culture and lifestyles are evident from quite early on (e.g. Sharples 1992; Peterson 2003a). Taking Britain as a whole, these changes appear to have been the result of a piecemeal combination of population movement, indigenous enculturation and the spread of ideas. As a result of the lack of any large-scale, established Mesolithic exploitation of the area, it has been argued that within the Avebury region the onset of the Neolithic coincided with the arrival of incoming groups, either from a neighbouring area or much further afield (Whittle 1990, 107). Whatever the process, the appearance of Neolithic lifestyles here may not have been particularly early, and may have taken several generations to become fully established.

By the second half of the fourth millennium BC (phases C and D) occupation was quite extensive within the region. Traces of settlement itself are relatively ephemeral, comprising surface scatters of worked flint and occasionally pottery, remnants of middens, pits, and post and stake settings. The absence of any solid 'domestic' architecture is taken to indicate varying degrees of settlement mobility, from semi-sedentism to seasonal transhumance (Whittle 1997b; Edmonds 1999; Pollard 1999). Areas of earlier Neolithic occupation have been investigated on Windmill Hill to the north (Whittle et al. 1999, 2000), and Cherhill (Evans & Smith 1983), Hemp Knoll (Robertson-Mackay 1980) and Roughridge Hill (Proud-foot 1965) to the west. Though different in their scale and format, these sites are linked by common material assemblages of worked flint, plain pottery cups and bowls, the butchered remains of domesticated animals (principally cattle, with sheep/goat and pig), wild and cultivated plants, and cereal processing equipment such as sarsen querns and rubbers. The formal burial of midden material in specially dug pits is also a feature of these sites; a practice widely documented during the early Neolithic, and perhaps bound up with ideas of symbolic renewal as well as the commemoration and 'decommissioning' of areas of occupation (Edmonds 1999, 29; Thomas 1999a, 87; Pollard 2001).

If the character of early Neolithic settlement implies (perhaps erroneously) a fleeting relationship to place, more lasting connections to particular locales in the landscape were developed through the creation of monuments. A series of long mounds and large earthwork enclosures were constructed in woodland clearings; almost invariably in places which already possessed long histories of activity (Pollard & Reynolds 2002, 59-62; Whittle et al. 1999). There are around 30 known megalithic and non-megalithic long mounds in the region (Barker 1985). Many of those with stone chambers, as at West Kennet to the south (Piggott 1962) and Millbarrow to the north of Avebury (Whittle 1994), were repositories for large collections of human bone, representing around 50 individuals in the case of West Kennet (Plate III). Although it is tempting to think of these constructions as 'tombs', marked differences in their format and associated deposits show that their roles and meanings were more varied. Those long mounds covering stone chambers with substantial mortuary deposits are largely restricted to the east of the region, while some earthen mounds on the 'high down' to the south and west enclose the remains of wooden chambers in which only a few individuals were buried. Easton Down, with the remains of four individuals (Whittle et al. 1993), and Oldbury Hill with three (Cunnington 1872) provide good examples. In contrast, there are several earthen long mounds in the centre of the region, notably Horslip,

South Street and Beckhampton Road (Ashbee et al. 1979), which show no sign of being linked to funerary practices. Cattle skulls were found under Beckhampton Road and a curious sarsen cairn under South Street, reflecting the use of long mound architecture in the marking and commemoration of a range of relationships with places and animate and inanimate constituents of the world.

More or less contemporary with the long mounds are a series of large earthwork enclosures, created on conspicuous hilltops fringing the region. Three have been recognised so far: on Windmill Hill to the north, and Knap Hill and Rybury overlooking the Vale of Pewsey to the south. Only 2 km to the north-west of Avebury, and constructed in a large forest clearing that had been the focus for earlier episodes of occupation and cultivation, Windmill Hill is the largest of these sites (Smith 1965; Whittle et al. 1999). In terms of its scale, regional importance, and the level of participation in its construction and use, it may be regarded as the precursor to Avebury. The enclosure is made up of a series of three concentric interrupted ditches, the outer some 360 m across at its widest point and enclosing an area of 8.5 ha. Excavations here have produced massive quantities of earlier Neolithic animal bone and material culture. People coming to the enclosure brought with them animals, cereals, tools, pottery and stone artefacts – everyday things. During their stay they undertook many of the activities associated with daily life such as food preparation and consumption, as well as undertaking more specialised tasks such as the exchange of goods and the preparation and treatment of the dead (ibid.). The enclosure almost stands as the early Neolithic world in microcosm. The gathering together of people would have allowed news and stories to be spread, allegiances and affiliations to be formed and existing ties confirmed and strengthened. Occupation may have taken place on some scale, but this was most likely not a permanent settlement.

Windmill Hill's special status is also hinted at by its liminal location on the edge of the region, and by the remarkable series of deliberate deposits found in its ditches. Enormous quantities of animal bone (including partial and full carcasses), pottery, flint and other materials were carefully placed in the ditches. Fragmentary human remains were also present; often laid alongside the bones of cattle, perhaps stressing the close relationship people had with their herds and the importance of animals in cycles of feasting and exchange. Differences in the kinds of deposit occurring in the three ditch circuits – more human bone in the outer, partial cattle burials in the middle, and midden debris in the inner – almost seem to map out relationships between socialised and unsocialised realms, people and their domesticated animals, and different states of being (Whittle et al. 1999).

As with contemporary long mounds, the location of the enclosure was not coincidental but drew powerfully upon the existing history of human engagement within this area of forest clearing, weaving its genealogical and mythical past into a new understanding and embodiment of the lived world (Kirk 1998, 115). The form of the enclosure perhaps echoed the shape of an ancestral clearing, or mirrored the concentric arrangement of forest-fringed settlement and garden plots (Evans 1988, 93). The carefully placed deposits of midden material in the ditches in turn referenced traditions of deposition in pits dating back to the earliest Neolithic occupations. The enclosure stood as a powerful symbol of cooperation and collective endeavour (Edmonds 1999). This was a place of shared construction and occupation, a place where diverse groups of dispersed, mobile people gathered at certain key times of the year and celebrated shared aspects of everyday life.

Seeing the trees for the wood

The early Neolithic landscape of southern Britain has been described, quite aptly, as one of forest and clearings, pathways and places (e.g. Tilley 1994; Edmonds 1999). It is important to emphasise the *difference* of this early landscape from the grassed and gently rolling chalk downland of the Avebury area we see today. Palaeo-environmental evidence from a number of sites, including Avebury itself, has permitted a fairly detailed reconstruction of the early Neolithic environment (Evans 1972; Evans et al. 1993; Smith 1984). At the beginning of the Neolithic (phases A and B) it was densely wooded, a landscape heavily dominated by trees. Along with the trees, three other prominent physical characteristics were present: clearings, pathways and stones.

The forest comprised a mixture of tree species including hazel, elm, oak, alder and lime (Evans & Smith 1983, 107). In traditional archaeological interpretation, there has been a tendency to leave discussion of woodland to that – little more than a statement of its constituent species. It was portrayed as a functional backdrop to human life, a source of continual adaptive challenge against which human activity such as clearance and cultivation was pitted. It was also discussed in purely economic terms, for example its capacity as a resource base, a ready source of food, energy and raw materials to be exploited and plundered (Austin 2000, 63). If such approaches can be neatly summarised, it is in their tendency to see the wood entirely at the expense of the trees, ignoring the latter as meaningful components of the lived world of these early Neolithic communities.

To the inhabitants of this landscape the forest was more than simply the physical backdrop to their lives, a set of challenges to overcome or resources to win. As a number of recent anthropological and archaeological studies have emphasised, trees can and do play a much more active role in the social life of the people who live among them, being central to their concerns, myths and values (Evans et al. 1999; Jones & Cloke 2002; Cummings & Whittle 2003). Through the events that take place in and around them, or their texture, colour and shape, individual trees can become the loci for stories, myths and legends. The longevity of the life-cycle of the tree is also important, mirroring that of people yet spanning many human generations. As a result certain trees may come to mark special places within the forest, serving as narrative devices in transmitting knowledge and providing tangible links to a past of ancestors and spirits (Basso 1996).

Clearings

Punctuating the dense forest were areas of clearance, and at any one time it would have been dotted with new clearings and a succession of older patches slowly sinking back into the forest. Clearings can result from a number of natural causes, ranging from wind-throw, lightning strikes and fire, through to tree-death and the action of beavers (Brown 2000, 49). A typical natural clearing is small, with a diameter of around 80 m. If left untended it takes around 60 years (or a little under three human generations) for a clearing to re-grow and regenerate back to the original forest canopy (ibid., 60). Within each clearing would have been a very distinctive architecture created by the tangle of fallen trunks, root balls, and broken or burned stumps. Taking perhaps centuries to rot away, these would have contributed to the character and appearance of each clearing, giving each a unique and recognisable signature.

While some natural clearings dating to the Mesolithic undoubtedly persisted, their conceptual role may have subtly changed with the advent of the Neolithic. The deliberate clearance of areas of forest, coupled with the seasonal movement of domesticated animals, would have created a richer and more diverse mosaic of clearings than those produced by natural factors alone. This would have been through the addition of clearings that were artificially created then deserted, along with natural and artificial examples that were seasonally grazed and maintained by specific groups. Anthropological studies have shown how such clearings can rapidly become more than a simple agricultural resource base to the groups engaged in their creation and maintenance. Instead they can come to embody in a very physical and spatial way more abstract cultural institutions such as kinship, sharing and cooperation. In his work with the inhabitants of the village of Santa Clara, located within the dense forest of the Amazon, the anthropologist Peter Gow quickly realised that to the people of the village the surrounding landscape was not simply an economic resource or the spatial by-product of episodes of clearance and desertion. Instead the lives of the community were intimately bound up in the patterns of clearance that could be identified. Each year every married man was expected to clear a new garden plot in the forest for his family, and then with his wife plant food crops there. As gardens remained productive for more than a single year, each couple soon generated more gardens scattered around the village than they could work. As gardens became neglected and secondary forest growth began to take them over, the products became free to anybody willing to harvest them. However, the garden itself was still referred to as the old garden of the original couple. These activities resulted in a mosaic of vegetation zones around the village, which were seen not as the mere detritus of people's productive activities, but instead as a powerful physical embodiment of kinship relationships that are quite literally bound up in the pattern of clearings in the landscape (Gow 1995).

The purpose of this example is not to suggest any direct analogy, but instead to attempt to communicate the richness of cultural under-standings that may attend something as ostensibly practical as a clearing. While the pattern and status of the artificial clearings of the early Neo-lithic communities may have been read in terms of genealogies and relations between specific groups, the already extant mosaic of *natural* clearings had to be explained. Falling outside the genealogical ties of the known clearings, new natural clearings, born from the violence of storms and lightning, may have been associated with supernatural forces. In contrast, overgrown natural clearings may have been indis-tinguishable from similarly neglected human clearances and associated with the work of mythical people, or spirits and ancestors outside the living group.

An encounter with a clearing would have been a locus for questions. Who created it? How far had it overgrown since they last passed by? When was it last visited and by whom? Clearings were also places of chance encounter where groups could exchange artefacts, pass on news and trade stories (Edmonds 1999, 23-4). In the dense treescape, where the furthest view is to the next set of trunks, they also afford better views, not least of the sky. Likewise they create much lighter environments for social activi-ties than the shade and gloom of the full canopy (ibid., 49). There may also have been less attractive qualities to clearings. As well as attracting game and gatherings of people, some clearings may have been perceived as the abode of less benevolent spirits, drawn by the views of the heavens or talk and singing. Other clearings may have become associated over time with the ghosts of those who worked and died there, potent places to be avoided by the living (Gow 1995, 53-4). Such clearings may have been sources of bounty, but only to be used carefully and judiciously.

Pathways

To varying degrees early Neolithic communities were mobile, with some people being engaged in seasonal or perhaps longer rounds of movement that might take them beyond the region (cf. Montgomery et al. 2000). Even daily routines, such as the fetching of water or fire-wood, would have involved movements over short distances through the forest. Daily life was then a perpetual series of encounters with the trees of the forest and the scattering of clearings that punctuated it, linked by old, well-trodden pathways and tracks. Knowledge of these pathways and the 'correct' way to employ them would have been the only sure way to navigate and move through the treescape, reaching desired clearings while avoiding those subject to taboos. As a result, the learning of these routes through experience, stories and repeated encounter would have comprised an important element of an individual's developing social life.

Stones

Along with the forests, the Avebury landscape was also home to the dramatic sarsen boulder streams that were deposited under periglacial conditions during the late Pleistocene (Plate IV). Sarsen is a very hard form of Tertiary sandstone, and occurs in tabular and more irregular 'boulder' form in a range of sizes, from fist-sized lumps to enormous slabs over 6 m in maximum dimension (Bowen & Smith 1977, 187; Geddes 2000, 60-4).

In much the same way as trees and clearings, there has been a tendency within the archaeological literature to portray large stones and boulders in rather prosaic terms (e.g. Smith 1984; though see Pollard & Reynolds 2002, 71-4). They are seen as either a hindrance to agriculture (something to be cleared and removed) or a resource (something to be broken up and utilised). Opposed to these rather narrow understandings, a growing body of anthropological study has begun to reveal how communities can draw upon the properties of rocks, for example their hardness and durability, as potent symbolic resources (Bloch 1995). Unlike the fluctuating cycle of human birth, growth and death, stone endures. In addition, rocks themselves are frequently attributed with a form of life and agency, being capable of movement and action (Kahn 1990, 51). Indeed, John Aubrey, in his seventheenth-century record of Avebury, noted how the local people believed that sarsen stones grew out of the ground, 'a view to which they adhere most pertinaciously' (Aubrey, quoted in Long 1858, 29).

The sarsen blocks and boulders originally formed an extensive cover on the downs, concentrated mainly on the valley floors and gentler valley sides (Gingell 1992). As a result of centuries of stone removal and destruction it is hard today to envisage the full extent of the original sarsen spreads. In a mid-nineteenth-century account, the antiquary William Long described the view of the sarsens from the brow of a hill near Avebury as 'winding like a mighty stream towards the south', commenting that similar stones in the side valleys added to the sense of 'a stream of rocks, e'en now flowing onward' (Long 1858, 30). While such a view would have been impossible in the thick forest of the early Neolithic, the sheer density and linear arrangement of stones would have engendered frequent and repeated encounters between people and these sarsen rivers, within clearings and as they moved through the forest.

As with certain trees, the more massive and interestingly shaped, coloured, textured or grouped stones would have entered folk memory and myth as potent entities in the forest. Likewise, within the natural clearings, sarsens, like fallen tree trunks and other debris, would have been an integral part of the architecture of the place contributing to each a personality and configuration of its own. Certain stones acquired associations and individual histories that affected the way in which early Neolithic communities engaged with them (Gillings & Pollard 1999). Even small stones could engender respect, as with the tiny boulder carefully incorporated into the structure of the Beckhampton Road long mound; while a similar monument at South Street, 1.5 km west of Avebury, was built over a discrete cairn of cleared sarsens (Ashbee et al. 1979). Other sarsens became integral elements within the early Neolithic taskscape, acting as foci for the working of stone. A number of slabs used in the construction of the chambers of the West Kennet long barrow bore surface traces of stone and flint axe polishing (Piggott 1962, 19). These polishing zones are inaccessible on the stones as erected and must have been created over a long period of time prior to their incorporation in the monument. One such *polissoir* still lies in its original position within cleared downland 3 km east of Avebury on Lockeridge Down (Fowler 2000, 66-8).

Avebury in the fourth millennium BC

All these elements – clearings, paths and stones – seem to have come together at Avebury. Perhaps the physical setting of this particular locale provided it with a significance that was to lead, by the early third millennium BC, to its progressive monumentalisation. There is certainly reason to think that the area later occupied by the henge represented an important location within the wider landscape of the Upper Kennet Valley. It rests within an undulating 'basin', overlooked by the higher ground of Windmill Hill, Waden Hill and Avebury Down. It is bisected by an obvious north-south route alongside the Winterbourne as it works its way towards the head of the River Kennet; and an east-west route from the high

Marlborough Downs to the east and a passage from the chalk to the clay vales to the west, via present-day Cherhill. Avebury also lies close to the centre of the region as defined by the distribution of earlier Neolithic long mounds, and occupies a liminal position between zones dominated by monuments with megalithic and non-megalithic chambers. It was a place that was both central and transitional. At this nodal point within a network of paths, whose antiquity could have extended back to the Mesolithic, people undertook a variety of activities during the fourth millennium BC. Occupation and cultivation are readily attested, while periodic gathering and perhaps ceremony might be inferred.

Traces of fourth-millennium BC activity at Avebury are ephemeral and difficult to characterise. They remain only partially investigated, and in places are disturbed by several thousand years of later building and occupation. Nonetheless, they do show an early Neolithic presence at Avebury, prior to the construction of the earthwork and stone settings. At least five separate areas of earlier Neolithic activity can be identified within or close to (within 0.5 km of) the henge. To the west there was further occupation close to the Winterbourne on the same spot, and perhaps therefore in the same surviving woodland clearing, as that used during the later Mesolithic. Earlier Neolithic pottery and a flint assemblage reminiscent of that from the pits at Hemp Knoll, with a leaf-shaped arrowhead, scraper and serrated flakes, were recovered from a distinctive buried brown soil. No structural features were discovered, though the concentration of finds looks to be part of a midden spread associated with short-lived occupation in an environment of woodland clearance and grassland (Evans et al. 1993, 151-3). To the south of Avebury there is a scatter of worked flint, pits and midden deposits alongside the eastern slope of Waden Hill (Smith 1965, 210-16; Thomas 1955). It is tempting to see this linear spread of material as strung out along a path that would, several centuries later, be formalised through the construction of the West Kennet Avenue. Traces of earlier occupation would become important markers in the landscape around which later episodes of settlement and monument building were structured (Pollard in press).

At Avebury itself, excavation of the buried soil under the bank and within the interior has revealed spreads of earlier Neolithic pottery, flint and animal bone, most likely reflecting intermittent visits and occupation. Associated ceramics, which range from carinated bowls to Peterborough Wares, suggest the chronological span of this is likely to be wide, from the early fourth millennium to the opening years of the third millennium BC (Whittle phases A/B-D). This assessment of the date range is broadly supported by three radiocarbon dates relating to pre-enclosure activity, which span the mid-fourth to mid-third millennia BC (Pitts & Whittle 1992). Early Neolithic activity was certainly extensive at Avebury, being attested by surface spreads of artefacts and indications of clearance and cultivation from the buried soil profile under the bank in the south-east, south-west and north-west quadrants (Gray 1935; Passmore 1935; Smith 1965, 224-6; Evans et al. 1985). Over 100 sherds of pottery and 200 pieces of worked flint were recovered from these contexts. The flint includes 'middle Neolithic' chisel arrowheads, along with familiar components such as scrapers, a knife and serrated flakes, while the 'small splinters of flint' from the buried soil in the south-west quadrant (Gray 1935, 130) sound like micro-debitage from *in situ* flint-knapping.

Rather than forming one continuous 'site', it is more likely that these spreads of material represent a series of individual or interlinked scatters. Key-hole excavations through the bank provide little indication of their full extent, but the limits of another concentration of earlier Neolithic flintwork and pottery (plain bowl and Peterborough Ware) within the interior of the henge are easier to define. This was spread across an area *c.* 50 x 90 m within the zone later occupied by the southern inner circle. Its distribution may even correspond to the original size and shape of a clearing. The scatter includes characteristic blades and narrow flakes, part of a polished flint axe, and other retouched and utilised pieces (Smith 1965, 227-8; information from Alexander Keiller Museum). Unusually, a number of flakes seem to come from the thinning of axes or other large bifacial tools. Four small pits, filled with a fine dark brown soil and containing small amounts of worked flint, were revealed under the densest part of the scatter (ibid., 201) (Fig. 4, below). They are essentially undated but reminiscent of the kinds of earlier Neolithic pit digging and deposition commonly associated with the formal abandonment of occupation sites (Thomas 1999a, 64-74; Pollard 2001).

The clearest sequence of pre-henge activity is provided by analysis undertaken by John Evans and others of the buried soil in the south-west and north-west quadrants. Though separated by 200 m, a similar environmental succession and series of events is recorded: beginning with early Holocene woodland, clearance at some stage during the early Neolithic, then cultivation, followed by the formation of grassland (Evans 1972, 274; Evans et al. 1985; Evans & O'Connor 1999, 202-4). Cultivation included the use of an ard plough, uncommon on sites of this date; though evidence for contemporary or slightly earlier deep cross-ploughing was revealed under the earthen long mound at South Street, 1.5 km to the west of Avebury (Ashbee et al. 1979, 282). This early cultivation at Avebury was undertaken within short-lived garden plots rather than formally maintained field systems. These plots were soon abandoned and the area then became one of 'ungrazed, or lightly grazed, impoverished grassland', characterised by a dense vegetation mat and heavily decalcified soil (Evans et al. 1985, 310). Patchy scrub may also have existed in the vicinity, as hinted at by charcoal of hazel, hawthorn and horse-chestnut found under the south-east section of the bank during excavations in the early twentieth century (Gray 1935, 130).

Superficially, such evidence seems straightforward: it demonstrates that people visited this place during the earlier Neolithic, they made and used flint tools, used and broke pots, lit fires, cultivated plots of land and later left areas to become grassland. It reflects the comings and goings of dispersed and mobile communities, taking advantage of a location or group of clearings that were known and perhaps regularly visited. A simple reading would be of various episodes of short-lived settlement, continuing up to and maybe beyond the point when the first elements of the henge were constructed. This is probably close to the truth, but we have to acknowledge that our understanding of the full range of activities that might be grouped under the labels 'settlement' or 'occupation' remains very poor for the Neolithic. 'Settlement' can involve many dimensions – different residential groups, longer-scale occupation or temporary meetings, and it might be structured around special events such as rituals, exchanges and political gatherings. People might come together to live in a specific place for a variety of reasons, and not simply because of the material resources that were on offer. If we are honest, there is no single or normative base-line of Neolithic 'settlement' activity against which the Avebury evidence can be assessed. Indeed, some ways of living during the Neolithic may even be beyond present-day analogy.

A sense of the inherent complexity in interpreting these events can be gained through an assessment of the buried soil sequence. Even an activity as prosaic as plough cultivation is open to alternative perspectives. Traditionally associated with subsistence, in certain locales the initial cultivation of cereals may have served a more symbolic function (Fairbairn 2000). Cultivation could be linked to factors such as rebirth and fertility, and might even provide a metaphor for death, regeneration and continuity (Tarlow 1995). It could have held a primarily social role, drawing together groups of people to specific areas of the land at certain fixed times of the year for sowing and harvesting.

As products of cultivation, the role of cereals themselves was multifarious, encompassing both subsistence and symbolic functions, with their specific cultural value changing between areas and contexts, and different times (Fairbairn 2000, 110-15). Even interpreting the onset of grassland conditions following cultivation is not entirely unproblematic. The formation of a thick vegetation mat implies an absence of grazing that is difficult to reconcile with the site's location in a heavily utilised landscape (John Evans, personal communication). If animals were being kept off this area was there something special about this place? Was tall ungrazed grassland itself a form of 'memorial', commemorating earlier clearance and cultivation – another way of marking places and important past events?

Whether regarded as value-laden with ancestral or mythical associations, auspicious or neutral, there must have been something about this location that would make it appropriate as the site for one of the greatest Neolithic monuments in Europe. When this process of transformation ('monumentalisation') through the construction of earth and stone structures began is not easy to pin down. Arguments have been advanced for seeing some of the stone settings as early, but as we shall see in the following chapter these claims rest on unstable foundations. However, there is one structure that may prove to belong to the latest fourth or earliest third millennium BC (phase D). To the west of the northern inner circle a recently recognised cropmark suggests the existence of a double-ditched, sub-rectangular enclosure, some 25 m across and enclosing a small central feature (Bewley et al. 1996, 641, fig. 2) (Fig. 5B). While it could represent a much later monument, even a Roman shrine, a very close analogy – in terms of size, morphology (double-ditched with a central pit) and even orientation – is provided by a middle Neolithic oval barrow at Barrow Hills, Radley, Oxfordshire (Bradley 1992; Barclay & Halpin 1999). The Radley barrow was found to cover a double burial dating to c. 3300-2900 BC and is one of several broadly similar 'short' long barrows in the Thames Valley, comparable examples being known from Drayton St. Leonard and North Stoke (Barclay et al. 2003, 229-30).

Summary: a clearing in the forest

In many regions of Britain and Scandinavia, the centuries following 4000 BC marked a change with what went before. Technologies of animal domestication and plant cultivation were introduced, along with new items of material culture and an understanding of the potential to mark time, place and relations with the sacred through the creation of durable earthen, wooden and stone constructions. This may have been facilitated, or helped to bring into being, new social and ideological relations, or it could have drawn upon long-established values that were reworked to accommodate new material conditions and ways of living. Being marginal to the main areas of Mesolithic exploitation, the transition to a Neolithic world in the Upper Kennet Valley was probably more marked than in many other regions. There was more sustained occupation, deliberate forest clearance augmenting that achieved through natural processes, some cultivation, and the region became the setting for the construction of numerous long mounds and enclosures. Yet for all these apparent differences we can envisage links with what went before. An essentially mobile population frequented pathways and clearings, some of which had their origins in an episodically visited Mesolithic landscape. We can envisage a shared 'sense of place'; and it is perhaps through this that people were drawn back to one particular location overlooking the Winterbourne that would eventually be transformed into the Avebury henge.

3. Rings of Earth and Stone

A landscape in flux

The third millennium BC witnessed a remarkable increase in the scale and tempo of monument construction in and around the Avebury clearings, most likely accompanied by a concomitant increase in the scale of settlement (Pollard & Reynolds 2002, ch. 3). It is during this period that the most prominent features of the henge took shape: notably the vast circles of stone and their inner settings, the huge enclosing earthwork and the two megalithic avenues.

It is important to realise from the outset that these were not isolated developments. A host of other monuments, remarkable in their own right, were being constructed within the Avebury landscape during the same period (Plate III). Prominent among these are two spectacular structures that were constructed during the second half of the third millennium BC to the south of Avebury, in the valley bottom adjacent to the River Kennet: the gigantic mound of Silbury Hill and the extensive complex of palisaded enclosures at West Kennet (Whittle 1997a). Constructed in a series of stages, Silbury would eventually become the largest artificial mound in prehistoric Europe, while the West Kennet enclosures employed over 2000 tree trunks to create a complex series of palisades that stood as much as 8 m high (Whittle 1997a, 154). Lesser constructions include the smaller stone circles at Clatford (Piggott 1955, Meyrick 1955) to the east, Winterbourne Basset to the north (David et al. 2003), and the Falkner's circle 800 m to the south-east of Avebury (Long 1858, 39-40). Known largely through antiquarian accounts, little survives of these, and only the latter has seen any modern excavation. Further transformations of the Avebury landscape were effected in the early second millennium BC, through the creation of a series of substantial round barrow cemeteries (Woodward & Woodward 1996).

As well as monument construction, the third millennium BC also witnessed marked changes in the environment of the Upper Kennet Valley. At the beginning there is progressive woodland regeneration in certain areas, particularly on the high down to the south and in the environs of earlier monuments (Whittle et al. 1993). In contrast, the valley bottom around Avebury saw more intensive clearance and a marked opening up of the landscape (Smith 1984, Evans et al. 1993). What is more, the deposition of colluvial and alluvial soils in the valley bottoms suggests that by the latest third millennium BC the scale of cultivation had also increased.

It is in this dynamic context that the remarkable henge at Avebury was constructed.

Bringing Avebury into being

In this chapter we explore in detail how the Avebury henge came into being. Central to this discussion is a particular way of seeing Avebury. This is as a gradually evolving project rather than a coherent monument conceived at the outset and designed to serve a single, distinctive role (Barrett 1994, 13), and as a result we would argue that Avebury has more in common with Gormenghast than Haussman's Paris. As we will illustrate, Avebury was arrived at more through a gradual process of what might be termed 'becoming' than the physical realisation of a complex, predetermined blueprint. As a result, the final form of the monument might best be thought of not as an *end*-product but a *by*-product: an accretion of different material expressions and manifestations of a developing set of understandings and explanations of the world.

Despite the fact that when we look at Avebury today we tend to see a 'whole' comprised of a series of components, it is important to acknowledge that the structures present do not reflect or symbolise a series of specific, fixed understandings (representative of a particular moment in time or juncture), layered one atop the other. Avebury is not a palimpsest. Instead every addition and modification to the overall fabric of the monument in turn fed back into the very thoughts and explanations that engendered it. Thus, far from simply memorialising or fixing ritual practices or ideas about the world within it, the acts of monumentalisation that together make up Avebury served to subtly alter those very same ideas. This process has been elegantly summarised by the anthropologist Mary Douglas using the metaphor of language: 'there can be thoughts which have never been put into words. Once words have been framed the thought is changed and limited by the very words selected. So the speech has created something, a thought which might not have been the same' (Douglas 1966, 65).

It is for this reason that understandings of Avebury will always be inherently 'slippery' and open to alternative claims and interpretations. Any single original meaning will be difficult to discern and pin down for the simple reason that there probably never was any one static reading of the monument. Further, it is important to realise that rather than representing any disjuncture or radical departure from the happenings discussed in Chapter 2, the dramatic events of the third millennium BC we will describe should be seen as a development and elaboration of them. One thing that is clear from the studies of Avebury carried out to date is that the architecture of the monument was created out of existing material conditions and practices, in other words it made explicit reference to what went before.

At this point we would like to stress that we are not suggesting that the process of creating Avebury was haphazard or somehow accidental. There is clear evidence of purposeful design and planning in terms of individual projects such as the Cove, the earthwork and the outer stone circle. Indeed we would argue that there was eventually an attempt to create an architectural unity from what were originally disparate construction projects. This was achieved through drawing together different monumental constructions into an architectural 'whole', principally through the construction of megalithic avenues. However, this came towards the very end of the Neolithic. Instead we want to encourage a different way of seeing and thinking about monumental constructions such as Avebury that has less to do with planning and building in any modern sense and more to do with the gradual unfolding and elaboration of what was a special and resonant place.

These are undoubtedly complex notions, but they are central to any adequate understanding of the becoming of Avebury in the later Neolithic. Let us illustrate with an example. In Chapter 2 it was argued that knowledge of ancient pathways that once criss-crossed the forests may have played an important role in the socialisation of individuals. With the clearance of the forest, the original paths may no longer have been the only visible or accessible routes from a given location to another. As a result their utilitarian importance may have gradually diminished. Despite this, the symbolic relevance of these ancestral tracks as routes not only from place to place, but as the pathways guiding an individual's life-journey into the community, may still have been crucially important. As the significance of the routes traced out by these paths was no longer emphasised by their role in everyday movement, memory of them may instead have been fossilised through ritual acts of procession. No longer bordered by the thick growth of the forest, this in turn may have required that the precise routes of certain pathways be formalised through the erection of megalithic avenues. However, as soon as an avenue was erected and the route of a pathway fixed, the memory of other routes not so immortalised was allowed to fade. In addition, the lines of stone permitted no negotiation or deviation, and served to draw a distinction between those within and those without, factors that in turn have to be accommodated within the very acts of formal procession that gave rise to the erection of stones in the first place. And on the process goes.

Structure of the discussion

This is a detailed chapter, and in reading it the ways of thinking about Avebury outlined above should be firmly borne in mind. In the discussion that follows we look first at the chronology of Avebury during the third millennium BC – in effect what was constructed and when – before going on to look in detail at the process of construction itself. We will then examine the reasons why the various structures were erected, the meanings they may have held and the activities that took place within and around them. The chapter finishes with a consideration of the attempt to 'bring together' the various components towards the end of the Neolithic through the creation of the Beckhampton and West Kennet Avenues.

The dating game

Our knowledge of the chronology of the individual components making up the Avebury monument remains woefully inadequate. This results, on the one hand, from the relative paucity of modern excavation within the henge, and on the other from the very scant assemblages of reliably datable material recovered during excavations, particularly from the stone settings. In terms of absolute dates, there currently exist 14 radio-carbon determinations for the henge as a whole and of these only ten appear to relate to episodes of construction (Pitts & Whittle 1992, Cleal & Pollard 2004). A further eight radiocarbon dates relate to pre-enclosure activity and occupation outside the henge. Of the numerous distinct features present at the site, there are no dates for either of the inner circles and settings, the avenues or the primary bank (Pitts & Whittle 1992, 206). To compound this, with the exception of one example, all of the dated material derives from excavations undertaken in the first half of the twentieth century, before the routine application of radiocarbon analysis. This raises questions concerning the precise stratigraphic provenance of some of the samples and their post-excavation treatment. Compare this with the 54 reliable dates from Stonehenge (Bayliss et al. 1997) and the magnitude of the problem facing students of prehistoric Avebury becomes obvious.

Despite these limitations, a number of dating schemes have been put forward for the late Neolithic and early Bronze Age developments at Avebury (see Appendix A). These can be grouped on the basis of whether an essentially unitary, or short timescale is envisaged, or a much more extended period of construction. In effect, the choice is between an Avebury that was constructed in one 'go', as a complex, multi-component monument, as opposed to a monument that is the end product of a gradual process of negotiation and elaboration.

3. Rings of Earth and Stone

The first of the closely-argued short chronologies was offered by Isobel Smith on the basis of pottery finds and Avebury's physical relationship, via the West Kennet Avenue, to the nearby site of the Sanctuary (Smith 1965, 244-9). The contemporaneity of the construction of the earthwork and stone settings at Avebury was argued largely on the basis of two assumptions. The first was that blocks of lower chalk found in the packing of stones in the southern inner circle must have derived from the digging of the ditch. The second was that Beaker burials found at the foot of stones were contemporary with their erection rather than later additions (Smith 1965, 246-9). As a result Avebury was dated to the latest Neolithic/early Bronze Age, around 2000-1850 BC using a pre-calibration chronology. Similar short-chronologies have been suggested by other authors. For example, Wainwright (1989, 110) saw the stone circles, West Kennet Avenue and the Sanctuary stone circles as a unitary structural scheme belonging to the latest Neolithic, though perhaps representing a 'lithicisation' of a pre-existing earthwork. Taking account of the impact of radiocarbon calibration (cf. Renfrew 1973a), both Burl (1979) and Malone (1989) placed Avebury within the period 2600-2300 BC, though there were marked differences in the detail of the sequences proposed, Burl giving primacy to the inner circles, Malone to the earthwork.

The first of the long chronologies was proposed by Pitts and Whittle (1992). This followed the results of the first programme of radiocarbon dating that had been undertaken for the site. On the basis of analysis of the ten dates obtained, in conjunction with a critical appraisal of the archaeological sequences that could be reconstructed from the early excavations, they suggested that the construction of Avebury could span upwards of a millennium, c. 3400-2200 BC (ibid.; Pitts 2000, 279). Once again, with slight variations in the proposed sequence, this long timescale has subsequently been adopted by others. In a revision of his earlier interpretation, Burl (2000, 319) sees the construction of Avebury's various components running from c. 3400 to 2400 BC, beginning with the Cove, then the inner circles, then the earthwork and finally the Avenues – an inside-out view. Thomas argues the opposite (1999a, 212-13) giving primacy to the earthwork, with the primary bank constructed sometime after 3000 BC, the main earthwork at 2700 BC and the stone settings coming much later at 2350 BC. A pre-stone timber phase is considered possible, and the West Kennet Avenue and stone circles of the Sanctuary are placed contemporary with the megalithic settings within Avebury (Thomas 1999a, 213).

With some modifications, we opt for a similar long chronology and sequence to that posited by Thomas. That it bears similarity to the suggested phasing at Stonehenge (Cleal et al. 1995) is perhaps not coincidental: as pre-eminent ceremonial centres within their respective regions, both monuments share features in common, from the use of sarsen stone to the nature of the deposits in their ditches. Competitive emulation may even have driven parallel developments. The justification for this scheme needs explanation, and we therefore present the evidence in some detail, beginning first with the earthwork, then the stone settings and finally other putative components.

When was the earthwork enclosure created?

It is clear from sections dug through the bank of the henge that the present earthwork is an elaboration of an earlier construction (Pitts & Whittle 1992). A primary bank of turf and chalk rubble stood over 9 m wide and around 2.5 m high; dimensions comparable with the outer bank of the earlier Windmill Hill enclosure (Smith 1965; Whittle et al. 1999). That it stood for a significant period of time as an independent structure, rather than acting as a temporary laying-out line for the much larger bank that was to follow, is attested by a thick, mature soil that had time to develop on its surface before it was buried beneath the later structure (Plate V). Wholly enclosed within the later bank, the locations and number of entranceways through it are unknown. However, its presence in sections cut through the bank in both the south-east and south-west quadrants of the henge suggests that its course was respected by the later earthwork and as a result can be inferred directly from it. Since much of the bank comprised chalk rubble, there must be an associated ditch or series of quarry pits, though these have so far proved elusive. The most economical explanation is that the course of the primary ditch was followed by that of the later earthwork, the massive scale of later 're-cutting' effectively eradicating it. However, a marked step in the upper profile of the later ditch, seen in the excavations of both Gray and Keiller in the south-west quadrant, could be the remains of this feature (Gray 1935, pl. XXXVII; Pitts & Whittle 1992, 210).

Finds of diagnostic artefactual material from under the bank and radiocarbon dates for the later earthwork phase provide a chronological bracket for the primary bank and ditch. Ceramics from the buried soil include Ebbsfleet and Fengate varieties of Peterborough Ware, which on current evidence look to span the mid-fourth to earliest third millennia BC (Gibson & Kinnes 1997), with associated chisel arrowheads belonging more to the later end of that range. Given that the later earthwork – the bank and ditch as visible today – can be placed in the mid-third millennium BC (see below), and that a thick turfline had time to develop over the primary bank, a date for the first-phase earthwork of 3000-2700 BC plus or minus two centuries seems logical. An early date of around 3000 BC would make it more or less contemporary with the phase 1 earthwork at

Stonehenge (Cleal et al. 1995), though the scale of the Avebury enclosure would set it in a class of its own.

A date range for the construction of the later bank and ditch can only be realistically established through radiocarbon dating. Small and weathered, the limited number of pottery sherds from the primary ditch fills are likely to be residual and derived from much earlier episodes of occupation (Smith 1965, 228-9). That pottery was not deliberately deposited on the base of the ditch in the same way as at Woodhenge, Durrington Walls and other henges (Richards & Thomas 1984, Pollard 1995) reflects either a sense of appropriate action or, more contentiously, the possibility that the earthwork was created during a locally aceramic period. Fortunately, deliberate deposits of antler and worked bone were made during construction and immediately after completion of the bank and ditch, and these have provided material for a series of radiocarbon dates. Of five available dates relating to the construction of the second-phase earthwork, one is from the bank and four from the ditch; all derived from antler picks used in the construction process (Pitts & Whittle 1992, Cleal & Pollard 2004). These are in broad agreement and fall within the range 2630-2460 BC.

Which came first, the earthwork or the stones?

If a degree of ambiguity still surrounds the dating of the earthwork, it is nothing compared to the can of worms that is opened once we turn to the stones. While the relative chronology of one or two of the stone settings can be established through structural relationships, usually the only means of dating the erection of megaliths is via associated material in the stone sockets: in terms of either direct artefactual dating, or the presence of organic materials in a primary context suitable for radiocarbon determination. Here we are confounded by the 'cleanliness' of many of the stone sockets, which were normally not the focus for the deliberate deposition of artefacts.

A basic question is which came first, the stones or the earthwork? A common-sense response, at least in terms of the rationality of the modern west, is to argue for the sarsens, as the presence of the ditch would have proved a hindrance in transporting and erecting the stones (e.g. Gibson 1998, 37, 55; Smith 1965, 248). Smith in fact argued for broad contemporaneity between the outer circle and earthwork (ibid., 248), with stones being set up immediately prior to the digging of adjacent sections of ditch. As we shall see below, the reverse may in fact be true.

Then there is the question of the relative sequence of the different megalithic components: the outer and inner circles, the innermost settings and the avenues. Here there is even greater uncertainty, and consequently numerous variations are possible. The logic of progressive elaboration and evolution, beginning with innermost features such as the Cove, which then become enclosed by the inner circles, and in turn the massive outer circle, is seductive. However, such schemes fail to take account of the potential 'messiness' of the stone architecture. This is best seen with features such as the linear setting and stone D within the southern inner circle, the Ring-stone and anomalous sockets at the northern entrance, none of which fit neatly into the larger architectural components. To compound this, as with Stonehenge, there is also evidence that some stones were re-set (see below). Taken together these factors suggest the possibility of much more contingent and *ad hoc* addition and reworking of the sarsen fabric of the monument. As a result we may never be able to establish an absolute and definitive sequence and chronology for the Avebury stones.

At the time of writing, radiocarbon dates are available only for stones of the outer circle (Pitts & Whittle 1992; Cleal & Pollard 2004). Two of these, on charcoal, give spans in the first millennium BC, and therefore relate to much later prehistoric activity (see Chapter 4). To compound matters, the three remaining dates hardly overlap. The earliest, from stone-hole 41 of the north-west quadrant, spans the early to mid-third millennium BC, but might be treated with suspicion since it is on charcoal from wood of an unknown age. More reliable is a date range of 2600-2000 BC on pig bone from the base of stone-hole 44, which seems to provide the best indication of the true age of this part of the circle. This leaves a recently obtained date on human bone from stone-hole 41 spanning much of the earlier Bronze Age (*c.* 2000-1700 BC). This particular socket was unusual in having two levels of packing material, the lower effectively serving to raise the base on which the stone was set (Smith 1965, 221). It would appear that at this location a larger stone was substituted at some stage by a smaller one, and that the late radiocarbon date relates to this re-setting.

At the very least, these dates strongly imply that the outer circle is unlikely to pre-date the second-phase earthwork, though it could be contemporary or, more probably, a century or two later. This is supported by Smith's observation that only one stone (stone 44) shows evidence of having been set up from the ditch side (ibid., 248n). Of course, following a pre-determined line established by the earthwork, there is no reason why the outer circle could not have been constructed in stages.

Recalling the situation with stone 41, the socket for the Ring-stone, isolated between the outer and southern inner circles, was also observed to have a curious double base. The stone itself was found resting on top of a basal layer of sarsen and lower chalk, within what was originally a deep socket intended for a much larger stone (Smith 1965, 202). While there is no indication that this re-setting occurred as late as that of stone 41, the erection of nearby stone D (another 'anomalous' component) is neatly dated by sherds of Beaker sealed beneath clay packing (ibid., 227). The implication that certain stones were re-erected and others originally set up as late as the established early Bronze Age is an intriguing one. It presents a much more dynamic image of selected reworking than is often acknowledged, and warns against seeing the megalithic components of Avebury as static and unchanging constructs. This is a familiar story in the context of contemporary timber monuments, as for example at the nearby Sanctuary, where recent excavation has provided clear evidence of repeated, perhaps even annual, post replacement (Pitts 2001). It also recalls the dynamic sequence of reworking seen with the megalithic settings at Stonehenge, belonging to much the same period (Cleal et al. 1995).

Dating the stone settings

There is thus potential for considerable chronological depth. While the latest stone settings at Avebury can be assigned to the early Bronze Age, there are claims that some of the earliest might belong to the fourth or early third millennia BC (e.g. Burl 2000; Pitts & Whittle 1992). It is not inconceivable that some may even pre-date the enclosure. The contenders include three sockets (A-C) discovered during the excavation of the northern entrance in 1937, the Cove and Obelisk, and miscellaneous internal components such as the linear setting in the centre of the southern inner circle. Each of these needs to be considered in turn. Sockets A-C were thought by Keiller to describe part of a pre-enclosure 'northern circle' that was dismantled when the bank and ditch were created (Keiller 1939) (Fig. 3D). This postulated circle was effectively disproved through targeted excavations directed by Stuart Piggott in 1960 (Piggott 1964) and later geophysical survey (Ucko et al. 1991, 227). The structural status of the three sockets remains unknown, but they clearly come early in the sequence of development of the stone settings. Wedged between stones 45 and 46 of the outer circle, the stone held in the southernmost socket, A, must have been taken down before this section of the outer circle was constructed. Likewise B and C look to be partially truncated by the weathering ramp of the western terminal of the ditch flanking the northern entrance (information from records in the Alexander Keiller Museum, Avebury). It is unlikely that they were placed here after the upper profile of the ditch began to weather back, implying that they either pre-date the second-phase enclosure or were set up soon after the ditch was dug.

The erection of other stones has been linked to the digging of the ditch via the presence of blocks of lower chalk in their socket packing, the argument being that lower chalk was only exposed in the lower levels of the ditch and that this rapidly became inaccessible once primary silting had commenced (Smith 1965, 248). The stones in question comprise the linear setting in the southern inner circle and the Ring-stone. Against this synchronicity argument is the observation that suitable blocks of lower chalk could easily have been obtained from exposures elsewhere in the region (Pitts & Whittle 1992, 210), and that the incorporation of this material may have been part of a deliberate strategy to draw components of the wider landscape into the fabric of the henge (see below). Nonetheless, there are other grounds for favouring an early date for the linear setting at least. First, it is very different in scale and character to any of the other stone settings, making use of small blocks of reddish sarsen, rather than the large slabs of grey stone otherwise ubiquitous. The sockets of these stones also contained sherds of Peterborough Ware and quantities of fresh flintwork that would not be out of place in a middle Neolithic assemblage. However, given that the sherds were small and weathered, they could easily be residual material from an episode of pre-henge occupation – i.e. they need not date the erection of the stones. The jury must remain out.

As central features within the complex, the Cove and Obelisk have been seen by some as original foci around which the inner then outer circles were created. Pitts and Whittle (1992) have drawn attention to the similarity between the massive pillar-like setting of the Obelisk and early Breton menhirs, hinting at an early Neolithic date for the former; while Burl (1988, 2000) holds to the view that the Cove belongs to a transitional category of monument between earlier Neolithic chambered tombs and later Neolithic stone circles. As tempting as analogies with Breton menhirs are, they belong to a much earlier and quite distant world, the first being created perhaps a thousand years before the inception of the British Neolithic (Patton 1992). While accepting the capacity for local inventiveness, it is difficult to find analogous evidence for the setting up of isolated standing stones during the earlier Neolithic. Most such stones date to the later Neolithic and early Bronze Age.

Much the same doubt hangs over Burl's early dating of coves. These do not form a particularly coherent category of monument, and their morphological similarity may well derive as much from localised responses to a desire to create small, enclosed spaces in stone, as from any unitary architectural blueprint. Few coves have been the subject of modern excavation, but those at Site IV, Mount Pleasant (Wainwright 1979), and Beckhampton (Gillings et al. 2000) can both be dated with a fair degree of confidence to the late Neolithic (around 2600-2300 BC). As an aside, it is worth pointing out that in terms of its geometric arrangement, the postulated form of the settings inside the northern inner circle at Avebury, with the Cove, façade and outliers (Pollard & Gillings 1998, fig. 5), does bear close similarity to that inside Site IV, Mount Pleasant. The late date tentatively suggested for the Avebury Cove need not conflict with Burl's pertinent observation that it may copy the chamber format of earlier megalithic tombs (Burl 2000, 31-3). It does, however, cast doubt on any simple evolutionary development from such constructions.

To summarise, there remains much ambiguity over the dating and sequence of the stone settings. A few are potentially early, though none need pre-date the primary earthwork; while the erection of isolated stones and reworking of others went on into the early Bronze Age. There may be a more intense and focussed period of 'lithicisation' during the mid-late third millennium BC – seen perhaps with the creation of the outer circle, the Cove and Obelisk, and also the two avenues and Sanctuary stone circles (Pollard 1992) – but further programmes of excavation and dating are needed before this can be confirmed. Comparison with developments at Stonehenge might be tentatively made, where the most intensive period of stone construction occurred during Phase 3, spanning *c.* 2600-2000 BC (Cleal et al. 1995; Bayliss et al. 1997).

Other components

In Chapter 2 attention was drawn to two other elements within the henge: a large post-hole in the area of the southern entrance, and an oval cropmark in the north-west quadrant. Both are poorly understood, but it was inferred that the former might belong to an enigmatic class of Meso-lithic post settings while the latter could be a middle Neolithic oval barrow. The remaining non-stone feature within the henge is the geo-physical anomaly to the north of the Cove, which consists of two concentric rings of pits, 30 and 50 m in diameter respectively (Ucko et al. 1991, 227). These do not seem to be stone sockets, but instead the positions of either open pits or large post holes. Without excavation the precise status of this setting remains uncertain, but it is tempting to speculate that it repre-sents a pit-circle henge similar to that at Monkton Up Wimborne, Dorset (Green 2000, 77-84), or a late Neolithic multiple timber circle. If it corre-sponds to either of these types of structure it has enormous implications for our understanding of the constructional sequence at Avebury. The earliest timber circles in southern Britain appear around 3000 BC (Gibson 1994), and although they were originally thought of as precursors to stone circles, it is best to think of the two monument forms as contemporary developments. Like stone circles they are found freestanding and as components of larger monuments. When found within larger structures, they are usually a primary component; rarely do they appear to have been added to an existing monument (Gibson 1998, 27). If the geophysical anomaly *is* a timber circle it could be one of the earliest structures at the site. However, the Avebury anomaly appears to display a slight flattening of its circuit where it runs closest to the edge of the northern inner circle (Ucko et al. 1991, pl. 69), strongly suggesting that the stone settings were already extant when this feature was constructed.

Constructing Avebury

So far we have dealt with Avebury at a rather abstract level, principally addressing issues of chronology. But to talk, for example, of the outer stone circle coming after the second-phase earthwork, or the Cove being late in the sequence, is to gloss over the sheer scale and physicality of the henge, and the human labour and endeavour that was invested in its creation. Even when broken down to the level of constituent projects, the creation of the earthwork and stone settings was an enormous undertaking on a scale scarcely seen before.

In response to the human toil that went into Avebury's creation and the sheer scale of the resultant features, generations of archaeologists have resorted to their calculators and adding machines in an attempt to work out how long such an endeavour would have taken. Estimates rarely agree. Richard Atkinson calculated 1.5 million 'man-hours' would be needed for the Avebury earthwork alone, Startin half a million (Wainwright 1989, 158). Again for the earthwork, Burl's estimate of 750 people over four years can be compared with Pitts' 300-400 people over 25-35 weeks (Burl 2000, 324; Pitts 2000, 191). Fun though such exercises are, the sheer number of variables present makes anything other than idle speculation impossible. Whether six months or four years, what is clear is that this was a major communal undertaking, involving a large number of people for a considerable length of time. Workload figures also hide the human dimension: the sense of shared achievement engendered through the act of labour; the bonds established; the friendships broken through argument; and the physical traces that the work would leave on people's bodies in the form of scars and injuries, the smearing of chalk dust, mud and sweat. Digging deep into the chalk and moving and erecting massive sarsens was dirty and sometimes dangerous work. Accidents must have occurred, and these undoubtedly left some people disabled, while others may have been killed.

Perhaps as a legacy of seeing monuments like Avebury as planned entities, there has been a tendency to view construction as a means to an end, rather than an act significant in its own right. This is unfortunate since it shifts focus away from the social practices that support building projects, and the way in which construction is constitutive of social relations. Not only do people make buildings, but buildings (monuments included) make people. Wainwright has talked about building henges as a 'method of integrating different parts of an embryonic society in a single undertaking' (1989, 30). While reference to a supposedly 'embryonic society' smacks of evolutionary social models and begs the question of what came before 'society', the emphasis on building as a process that encouraged inclusion and cohesion is welcome. Each of the projects that contributed to Avebury required first an element of vision, but also consensus and a willingness on the part of people to contribute. Perhaps some people were drawn by existing bonds and obligations, while others simply relished the opportunity to become involved and may have travelled from afar to do so. Acquiring and co-ordinating the resources required would not have been an easy task, and responsibilities had to be negotiated and allocated. Since those taking part could simply up and leave, interest in the project would have to be sustained or periodically reanimated, perhaps through powerful speeches offered by elders, or the prospect of further episodes of feasting and celebration. Perhaps construction was always a punctuated process, occurring in short bursts over a long period of time; some projects never seeing completion.

Participation in construction was likely to be varied – including men, women and children – it gave people new roles and identities, and connected them to this place. There would be those involved in raising pigs or collecting plant foods for feasting that would sustain the labour; those involved in preparing timber and ropes to haul stones, making baskets to move chalk, or collecting antlers for use in digging the ditch and sockets; as well as those more directly involved in creating the earthwork and erecting stones. Participation was constitutive in other ways. Just as in the building of medieval cathedrals, creating Avebury involved a set of practices that produced people with skills and brought about a 'massive transformation of the organisation of labour, resources and knowledge' (Turnbull 2000, 78). What is clear is that in as much as it was guided by those networks and relations that already existed, it also served to create new social and economic relationships, and knowledgeable practices.

In other ways making Avebury changed things. Construction irrevocably altered the landscape. Creating the enclosure permanently separated a formerly open space from its surroundings, hiding it behind vast walls of chalk, while the acts of uprooting and moving sarsens scarred adjacent valleys and downs and took away familiar landmarks.

Construction, then, was an important act, both in terms of the effect it had on those taking part, and in terms of bringing about a monumental transformation of place. Marking the transition from one physical state to another, it can even be regarded as a rite of passage, and therefore more of an active ritual than a prosaic technology. It is therefore not surprising that in many traditional societies the building of houses and monuments is regarded as a ceremonial activity in itself, hedged around with observances, offerings and spiritual blessings (e.g. Waterson 1990). From the physical character of the site's architecture and the presence of deliberate deposits, we know that the creation of the different components of Avebury was accompanied by similar acts.

Creating the earthwork

Today it is difficult to comprehend the full scale of this task. An estimated 200,000 tons of chalk was prised out of the ground using an array of stone, wood and bone implements (Plate VI). Pre-eminent among these appear to have been antlers, 44 examples of which were found placed upon the base of the ditch where it was excavated by Gray (e.g. Gray 1935, 126-7). With the crown used as a rake and the beam a pick that could be used to prise out blocks of chalk, these instruments bore the brunt of the construction work (Pitts 2000, 186) (Plate VII).

There has been a tendency to view the creation of the ditch of the earthwork in strictly functional terms, whether serving to demarcate a perimeter or acting as a quarry for chalk needed to create the bank. But such a perspective is surely reductionist. Carving a series of steep pits and trenches up to 10 m deep into the chalk was a special act, and one that might have been regarded as both symbolically and physically dangerous. It was an act of inversion, taking materials deep out of the ground and using them to create a new horizon against the sky and surrounding hills. The ditch is therefore of interest, both for the information it provides about the technology of digging and for the social information it may have 'encoded'. Like the ditches of earlier causewayed enclosures, it was initially dug as a series of pits and arcs rather than more continuous lengths. Variations in depth and width were very evident in Gray's excavations of the ditch in the southern part of the henge, where the remnants of former causeways of un-dug chalk were occasionally encountered between individual sections (Gray 1935, 116, 121-2). Different pits and lengths of ditch may have been the responsibility of different work groups, which themselves could correspond to distinct social units such as families or kin groups (cf. Startin & Bradley 1981 for similar claims in relation to causewayed enclosures). Thus the completed ditch could come to symbolise different identities within a broader unity.

The form of the ditch is also unusual, being exceptionally deep and narrow. This makes it different from the other Wessex henge enclosures against which it is often compared: Durrington Walls, Marden and Mount Pleasant. In fact, the shaft-like profile of the Avebury ditch has more in common with the rings of pits and shafts making up the enclosure circuits of certain Dorset henges such as Maumbury Rings (Bradley 1975) and Wyke Down (Barrett et al. 1991). This precipitous profile may have been chosen for optical effect, serving to enhance a sense of vast depth. It would also have been unstable, weathering and silting rapidly.

Paul Ashbee has recently (2004) made the interesting observation that those cutting such a deep, narrow ditch would have been fully aware of how quickly the sides would weather back and the primary chalk rubble fills form. Put simply, it was dug with the knowledge that it would stay in its pristine state for only a very short period of time, changing profile and depth very rapidly. Ashbee suggests the intention to accelerate the rate of silting could have been driven by a desire to make the ditch look old and weathered, and hence archaic, early on. In this sense it would soon resemble the ditches of earlier enclosures such as that on Windmill Hill, which in certain ways the Avebury earthwork appears to mimic. Here there could also be a fundamental distinction between earthwork and stone components at Avebury: the former envisaged as a moving, changing, even living entity, and the latter as unchanging, static and enduring.

The process of constructing the earthwork was accompanied by the deliberate deposition of antler and bone tools, along with other selected items. As mentioned above, a number of antler picks and rakes used in digging the ditch were found on the base during Gray's excavations. These had obviously been disposed of with some formality, rather than being casually discarded. Instead of being randomly distributed along the base there were specific concentrations of picks and rakes in Gray's cuttings I (nine examples) and IX (13 examples). In the latter trench, which was sited to take in the east terminal flanking the southern entrance, Gray's records show that most of the antler had been carefully placed against the ditch butt. Two dog jaws were found in association (Gray 1935, 158) and these must be regarded as purely symbolic offerings since they could hardly represent implements used in digging. In cutting II a pick was placed alongside two ox scapula 'shovels', which were otherwise absent from the ditch base; and in cutting VIII a scored cattle rib bone and two rib spatulae were found. The latter are, on analogy with similar implements from later Beaker grave assemblages, best interpreted as leather-working tools (Smith & Simpson 1966, 134-5). Perhaps as tools belonging to specific individuals, their placing in the ditch represented personal offerings, and/or a way in which people incorporated something of themselves in the fabric of the monument.

There were further deposits built into the bank of the major second-phase earthwork. Other rib spatulae were found in Gray's cutting X, during Keiller's excavation of the bank in the south-western sector (Smith 1965, 226), and in Henry Meux's 1894 cutting through the south-eastern section (Gray 1935, 104). Several small sandstone and limestone slabs recovered from the north-west section of the bank excavated in 1982 (Evans et al. 1985, 305) also sound like placed deposits.

One particularly unusual deposit was recorded by Meux's site foreman, Thomas Leslie, during the 1894 excavation. Here a collection of antler picks was found within a 'cist' built of large chalk blocks constructed deep inside the body of the bank (Gray 1935, 104). At first sight the care afforded to the burial of antlers seems out of line with their status as used and worn digging tools. However, it is easy to imagine them becoming 'sanctified' through use, and their removal from the site prohibited. Furthermore, as Wainwright points out, their value as digging tools and the logistics involved in their acquisition made them an important commodity, and one probably 'derived from a variety of sources via ... trade networks' (Wainwright 1989, 160). Like stone axes (Bradley & Edmonds 1993), certain antlers may well have travelled far, accruing stories of the transactions needed to secure them, and embodying something of the distant places from which they came. They became more than mere 'goods', their use almost a form of ritual consumption. In another sense, these deposits participated in what Julian Thomas has described as an 'economy of substances': a dynamic exchange of materials between different domains – some dug out of the ground, others placed within it – creating a 'set of relations of reciprocity with the earth itself' (Thomas 1999b, 76).

Making megaliths

Although the earthworks are truly staggering in their scale and execution, it is the stones that first catch the attention of many people visiting Avebury, their sheer bulk leading to bewilderment as to how prehistoric people could move and erect them without mechanical aid. In fact, quite elementary techniques and sheer force of labour achieved much (cf. Richards & Whitby 1997). Given the size of the sarsens, a typical weight of between 20-30 tonnes is not an unreasonable guess, while at the top end of the scale the western stone of the Cove is now known to weigh in the order of 100 tonnes. Even if sarsens were relatively close to the site, the process of freeing them from the soil, constructing sleds of timber and rope, hauling them into position and packing them in place would have involved considerable effort; and the movement of giant blocks such as the Obelisk must have been important events involving several hundred people. Intrinsic to each act of stone selection, movement and erection are ideas of communal labour, co-operation and group effort. If particular groups were tasked with raising individual stones or constructing separate sections of each megalithic setting, then they would embody a similar expression of diverse identity and participation within a community project as was seen with the team-digging of ditch segments.

Much of our knowledge of the process of erecting the megaliths comes from the 1930s excavations of Keiller (Smith 1965, 218-222) and more

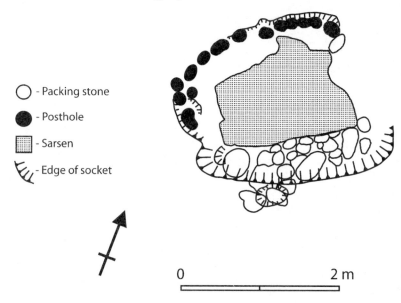

○ - Packing stone

● - Posthole

▦ - Sarsen

〰 - Edge of socket

0   2 m

7. Excavated socket of stone 46.

recent work undertaken by the authors at the Cove and on the Beckhampton Avenue. Once the sarsens had been selected and dragged into place they were carefully set into bespoke holes that had been dug to reflect basal irregularities in the sarsens. The sockets were often not deep, the majority of those excavated within Avebury being cut less than 0.6 m into the chalk. In general, the size of the stone is reflected in the depth of the socket, that belonging to the vast western stone of the Cove being the largest excavated to date at around 1.5 m deep and 5 m long. The sides of the sockets were steep to near vertical, usually with one side cut to form a sloping ramp to enable the stone to be gently slid in (Fig. 7). Occasionally, instead of a sloping cut, ramps of sarsen blocks or packed chalk were constructed against one of the inner faces of the socket.

In some cases lines of wooden stakes had been driven into the chalk against the back of the socket, opposite the ramp. These 'anti-friction stakes' served to guide and direct the position of the stone as it was erected. Where present, the number of stakes varied from as few as two to as many as 15. Other stakeholes within and around the sockets appear to have been related to wooden structures used to lever and support the stones as they were raised.

The stones themselves were placed directly on the base of the socket, although in the case of more irregular stones, blocks of sarsen and flint, along with packed chalk rubble were used to create a stable platform. Once erect, sarsen boulder packing stones, along with occasional blocks of lower chalk and flint and deposits of clean dark brown clay, were used to stabilise the stone and fix it in place (Plate VIII). As with the stakes, the number of packing stones depended upon the shape and stability of the erected sarsen, ranging from none to in excess of 50, with some stones requiring over 900 kg of boulders to fix them in place.

One peculiarity of the socket fill of the western Cove stone was the presence of vertical interfaces between discrete areas of clay and chalk rubble packing, implying the use of shuttering and a compartmentalised process of filling. Such 'staged' filling might have allowed the stone to be temporarily supported while still capable of being manipulated into its correct position. However, it would be premature to rule out a degree of symbolic expression in this process, which perhaps deliberately reflected the kind of compartmentalised construction common to earlier Neolithic long mounds (cf. local examples at South Street and Beckhampton Road: Ashbee et al. 1979).

It is important to acknowledge that the erection of any standing stone was more than a mere technology or means to an end. In many ways the very acts of stone selection, the dragging of the sarsen into position, the breaking of the ground, careful shaping of the socket, and ultimately the hauling up of the stone, may have been as important and rich in significance as the resultant megalith. The sense of stone erection as an event, accompanied by due ceremony and observance, can be seen in the choice of materials used to stabilise and support the stones in their new locations, and in attendant offerings placed in the sockets of the stones.

At first glance the deposits of clay, sarsen boulders and chalk used in the sockets appear to be wholly utilitarian. However, they result from a careful process of selection which was intended as much to 'presence' different materials within the megalithic settings as to provide appropriate packing material. There is no obvious local source for the clean, dark brown, chalk-free clay that was frequently employed. Although initially thought to be of riverine origin (Smith 1965, 221), recent analysis suggests a source in the beds of Kimmeridge Clay outcropping several kilometres to the west of Avebury. Likewise, the chalk blocks used to pack the stones included lower chalk that had to have been quarried from excavations far deeper than the sockets. This suggests that it had either been especially quarried for the purpose or carefully selected and brought to the site from existing monuments (Pitts & Whittle 1992).

Other stony materials were also incorporated in the sockets, a process that is particularly evident in the north-west quadrant of the outer circle. One interesting deposit occurred in the socket of stone 33, where a distinctive lozenge-shaped sarsen had been placed on top of the packing boulders supporting the stone (Pollard & Gillings 1998, 159). This was identical in shape to the lozenge sarsens that Keiller (among others) had claimed was an Avebury archetype (Smith 1965, 197). Alongside this miniature standing stone was a fragment struck from a polished mace-head of Palaeozoic sandstone and a collection of flint flakes, a core and a knife.

Other stones were treated in similar ways. Collections of flint flakes were placed in the sockets of stones 40 and 44; while in the former was another knife and a fragment of a Group VI axe from the Great Langdale region of Cumbria. Why were these different materials being gathered together and incorporated in stone sockets? A lead may come from Mary Helms' comments on how materials acquired from distant places 'are marked by the inalienable qualities associated with their ... sources of origin' (1993, 99). Perhaps we should read the process at Avebury as one in which the qualities or essences of different places were being brought into and incorporated within the monument. Elements of the wider land-scape – clay from the west, sarsen boulders from valleys and downland slopes, chalk from deep beneath the ground, and fragments of stone implements from exotic locations – were being gathered together and condensed within a symbolically-charged space to create something far greater than the sum of its constituent parts. This leads onto a considera-tion of Avebury as standing for, or being a representation of, the wider world, a point that we shall return to shortly.

Origins and inspirations

Any consideration of the creation of Avebury must beg the question of motivation and inspiration. Where did the idea for a monument like Avebury come from? Perhaps such a question is inappropriate, since we have already discussed how the final form of the monument should be seen as the culmination of many individual projects rather than a single planned vision. However, the earthwork, stone circles, avenues and struc-tures like the Cove do have parallels elsewhere, and it is not unreasonable to suppose that the communities responsible for creating these were, to some extent, drawing upon pre-existing traditions. Some of these could have been local, others more distant; a sense of the exotic perhaps adding to the wonder and sanctity of the monument. This is a point that has been raised by Julian Thomas and Alasdair Whittle in consideration of other monuments in the region such as Silbury Hill, inspiration for which may have come from the construction of large mounds in the Boyne Valley of Ireland, Brittany, or even further afield (Whittle 1997a, 150; Thomas 1999a, 216-17).

Prehistorians have long recognised that the earthwork at Avebury is one of many similar constructions, labelled 'henges', that are linked by morphological traits such as their circularity and the presence of an external bank and internal ditch (Kendrick & Hawkes 1932; Harding & Lee 1987; Harding 2003). These are widely distributed across Britain and Ireland, examples occurring as far north as the Orkneys. However, the term is extremely general, serving to lump together a fairly diverse range of monuments by focussing upon broad similarities at the expense of local contexts and variations. Indeed not all enclosures labelled as henges possess an arrangement of internal ditch and external bank (e.g. Stonehenge), and there is a great deal of variation in size (from *c.* 10 to 480 m in diameter), internal features, and the layout of entrances (Harding & Lee 1987, 27-9).

The scale of the Avebury earthwork frequently leads to it being referred to not as a classic 'henge' but a 'henge-enclosure' (e.g. ibid., 31), and it is placed alongside the sites of Durrington Walls, Marden, Mount Pleasant and Knowlton as one of a group of so-called Wessex 'super-henges' (Wainwright & Longworth 1971, 198-203; Wainwright 1989) (Fig. 8). These sites undoubtedly share features in common, including the size of the areas enclosed, the presence of circular settings within them and the existence of multiple entrances. However, caution should be exercised in viewing them as a unitary phenomenon, and therefore as an expression of similar belief systems or structures of power (e.g. MacKie 1977, Renfrew 1973b). These monuments are far from identical. Their landscape settings are markedly different: Avebury in an open basin; Durrington Walls enclosing a dry valley; Marden adjacent to the River Avon in an essentially open landscape; and Mount Pleasant situated on a hilltop. The sheer depth of the Avebury ditch and height of its bank are not matched by the earthworks of these other enclosures, nor do they contain the same range or scale of megalithic settings. Associated with large quantities of Grooved Ware, animal bone and worked flint, the activities performed within Durrington Walls, Marden and Mount Pleasant also seem to have been dramatically different to those enacted inside Avebury. Despite its obvious morphological dissimilarity, with its restricted range of deposits and complex stone settings, Stonehenge provides a closer counterpart.

There are clearly problems in attempting to understand the place of individual sites like Avebury within such broad classificatory schema. Avebury was part of a much longer, if fragmented, tradition of creating earthwork enclosures that extended back to the earlier Neolithic in Britain and continental Europe (Oswald et al. 2001). A local background is provided by the causewayed enclosure on Windmill Hill, perhaps half a millennium old by the time the primary earthwork at Avebury was created, but still visited and apparently respected during the late Neolithic (Whittle et al. 1999). Contemporary with the second phase earthwork was a small oval ditched enclosure at Beckhampton, which

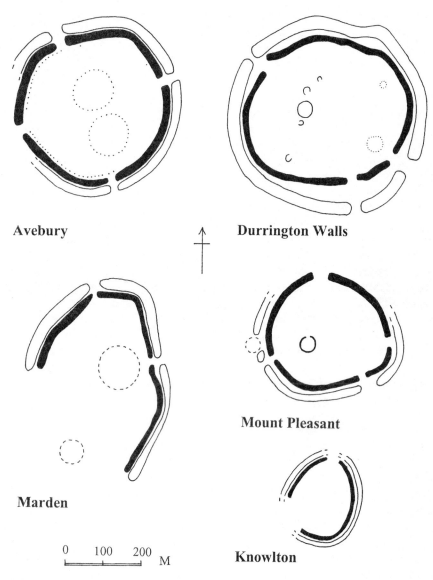

Avebury

Durrington Walls

Marden

Mount Pleasant

0   100   200   M

Knowlton

8. Wessex 'henge enclosures'.

would later be linked to Avebury, if in part through memory, by the construction of the Beckhampton Avenue (Gillings et al. 2002). Inter-visible, comparable in scale, and arguably serving similar 'functions' as a communal ceremonial centre, Avebury has often been viewed as the successor to Windmill Hill (Smith 1965, 251-3; Ashbee 2004). Indeed, it is not unreasonable to view the creation of the Avebury earthwork as an emulation of the substantial outer bank and ditch of the earlier enclosure, though it was different in its setting and in the permeability of the space that it defined. Caution has rightly been voiced over viewing henges as a simple 'evolution' from causewayed enclosures (Clare 1986, 1987), but here we appear to have a much more dynamic act of interpretation and creative reworking underpinning the connection between the two monuments.

An alternative to the model of exclusively local origins is to see the inspiration for Avebury coming from much further afield. Given the extensive lifetime movements of some Neolithic individuals (Montgomery et al. 2000) this is not beyond probability, and information could also be passed over considerable distances by stories travelling along exchange networks. If the first phase earthwork at Avebury belongs around 3000 BC, this would be contemporary with the circular enclosures of Stonehenge 1 (Cleal et al. 1995) and Flagstones, Dorset (Smith et al. 1997), though with overall diameters of *c*. 100 m these are much smaller constructions. Other late third- to early fourth-millennium BC enclosures are not hard to find. The forms of many of these are either eclectic or regionally specific, as with the recently excavated pit circle at Monkton Up Wimborne, on Cranborne Chase (Green 2000), and the complex embanked ring-ditches in the Thames Valley such as Linch Hill Corner, Stanton Harcourt (Grimes 1960), and Newnham Murren, Wallingford (Case & Whittle 1982).

As with the earthwork, the stone circles, Cove and Obelisk can likewise be fitted into broader traditions of later Neolithic monumental construction (Burl 1988, 2000), yet remain unique in terms of their particular format. In considering the 'origins' of the stone settings, Isobel Smith noted that 'the Avebury monuments seem to embody so many elements of the older practices and beliefs' (1965, 253). We have already mentioned Burl's view that the form of the Cove may copy that of earlier chambered tombs; while on a specific level Piggott saw the megalithic blocking of the West Kennet long barrow as a possible prototype for the Avebury Cove (Piggott 1962, 65). The linear setting within the southern inner circle has also evoked comparison with the stone kerbs surrounding megalithic long mounds in the region (Smith 1965, 251), though it may be more constructive to think of it as a stone façade, akin to those constructed in timber and belonging to the first phase of the southern and northern circles at Durrington Walls (Wainwright & Longworth 1971, 27, 43). Perhaps there was even deliberate ambiguity in terms of what these settings were meant to represent.

We would argue that Avebury's inspiration came from both near and far, the earthwork and stone settings resulting from a process of *bricolage*, drawing upon both local and distant sources of inspiration, and inventively weaving into their architecture specific foci of long-standing significance, such as the zones of earlier occupation. The picture is not one of local reference or broad tradition but an amalgam of the two, a complex inter-play between theme and diversity, tradition and invention. Avebury clearly drew themes from earlier monuments and monumental traditions but was not built simply to emulate them, albeit in its own idiosyncratic way. Its sheer scale displays a desire on the part of those who created it to surpass what had gone before, and in so doing perhaps lay claims to the symbolic pre-eminence of this place.

Structure and meanings: cosmology and content

Our frames of reference are so different to those of Neolithic communities that an encounter with the remains of the Avebury henge often leads to feelings of alienation and sheer puzzlement. These are sensations com-monly shared by visitors to the monument who long to know 'what it all might mean' and 'what went on here'? Guided by diverse archaeological and anthropological theory and analogy, and recognising the interpretive potential of material evidence, prehistorians are now more willing to engage with such questions than has perhaps been the case in the past.

Interrogating the structure of Avebury, the landscape setting of the monument and the kinds of deposits associated with its use, can do much to 'flesh out' the picture of its symbolism and associated meanings, and how its architecture guided encounter and experience. However, to reiter-ate an earlier point, we must resist the urge to search for an elusive single meaning. Multiple readings and understandings of Avebury must always have existed, even in the Neolithic and early Bronze Age. For those visiting the monument or engaged in its construction, any understanding of what Avebury stood for would surely have varied according to identity, age, gender and level of initiation (Brück 2001). Even though religious institutions can be very successful in preserving particular views of the world and projecting a sense of unchanging continuity (Bloch 1986), in the case of Avebury the resilience of any religious system needs to be set against the long period of time over which the monument was in active use, and the evidence for progressive alteration and elaboration of its structure. Like Chinese whispers, each alteration to the fabric, every ceremonial performance, and every transmission of the bodies of esoteric knowledge that were linked to Avebury, could have produced subtle and incremental shifts in how it was understood (cf. Barth 1987).

Before we explore the roles it may have played it is necessary to emphasise the ceremonial or 'non-domestic' character of Avebury. Burl has recently suggested that the henge was an occupation site, with an early settlement growing up around the Cove, and the putative pit/timber circle in the north-eastern quadrant being the remains of a large dwelling

Avebury

(Burl 2000, 319-22). In this view Avebury was a place of homesteads, cattle stalls, barns and ritual monuments. Although other later Neolithic enclosures are associated with occupation of sorts, even if by a restricted social group and only on a temporary basis, such an interpretation cannot be supported in the case of Avebury. The interior of Avebury is remarkably 'clean' of cultural material, and what does occur looks to have been brought from elsewhere explicitly for symbolically-motivated deposition within the ditch or against the stones (see below).

Architecture and power

If Avebury was not a settlement, what was it? As with many henges, the configuration of an internal ditch and external bank could not operate as a defensive feature. Rather than a measure designed to keep people out, it could have operated as a controlling mechanism to keep something in, and that something could be as much supernatural as corporeal. At another level, the creation of a bank and ditch introduced an element of closure and restriction to this space. A number of writers have commented on how the creation of earthworks such as those at Avebury formalised a distinction between inside and outside, restricting visibility into their interiors and controlling inward and outward movement (e.g. Bradley 1998, 126-8; Thomas 1999a, 54-60).

In understanding the architecture of these monuments patterns of physical movement, visibility and audibility are important, because they relate to the way in which participation and access to esoteric knowledge might be controlled. Such formalised architecture might provide a means by which the activities of a chosen few, be they elders, initiates or ritual specialists, were carefully secluded from onlookers. Control over ritual practice, exercised through manipulation of the very fabric of the monument, would help to maintain the secrecy and potency of esoteric knowledge and could therefore be utilised in the maintenance of asymmetric relations of social power – separating those who had such knowledge from those who did not (Thomas 1993).

Certainly the bank at Avebury is so massive that it hides much from view, effectively insulating the interior from the outside world and vice versa (Bradley 1998, 127). While there are external vantage points on Silbury Hill, Windmill Hill, Avebury Down and Waden Hill, all but the latter are quite distant and would not have afforded a clear view of activities taking place within the henge. Even if the bank itself was used as a viewpoint, like the tiers of an amphitheatre, viewers were kept physically separate from the goings-on within the enclosure by the presence of the ditch.

Within the interior, the progressive elaboration of the stone settings

62

generated further divisions and 'regionalisations' of space (Barrett 1994, 14-19). In its latest form, a clear spatial hierarchy was developed, comprising outside henge>inside henge>outer circle>inner circles>Cove and Obelisk (Thomas 1993, 43). For anyone coming into the henge from the northern and southern entrances the density of stone settings would have prevented clear views of activities taking place within the inner circles, while the façade-like linear setting adjacent to the Obelisk and the box-like structure of the Cove further restricted visual access to the deepest spaces of the henge.

Topography was subtly employed to enhance these spatial distinctions. The earthwork in fact encloses a shallow north-south ridge, with the innermost settings being placed along its length. The fall away in slope to either side of the ridge is sufficient to block direct lines of sight across the henge interior from east to west. It is within the inner circles that the greatest visual envelope occurs, allowing views across much of the interior and beyond. This zone is also the only part of the monument from which both Silbury Hill and Windmill Hill are simultaneously visible (Watson 2001, 306). Therefore, while the views afforded to those gathered around the periphery of the enclosure were limited and controlled, those of participants in the heart of the complex were extensive and encompassing.

It was not just visual access that was structured by the architecture of the henge. Recent work by Aaron Watson and David Keating has drawn attention to the acoustic properties of many megalithic monuments (Watson & Keating 1999). Experimental studies have demonstrated that sounds created through activities such as chanting or drumming are reflected off stones, and in enclosed spaces can become filtered, distorted or enhanced by echoes. Whether fortuitous or not, these effects were almost certainly exploited by those orchestrating and performing rituals within these spaces, perhaps to generate an 'otherworldly' environment that was thought to provide access to spiritual realms. Because of its closed format, the Cove is particularly interesting in this respect. Acting 'rather like a stage in a theatre' (Watson 2001, 308), the flat stones used in its construction had 'considerable potential to create unusual echoes' (Watson & Keating 1999, 335), as well as directing sound in a particular way. Again, the ability to hear clearly what was going on depended upon one's position in relation to the stone setting. For those privileged to be facing the open north-eastern side much would be clear and audible, but from other directions the sounds accompanying ceremonies and observances might become muted and distorted.

However, caution should be exercised in placing sole emphasis upon the control of access and movement. The sheer scale of a monument like Avebury provides the most immediate impression of power. Like the awe-inspiring architecture of a medieval cathedral, the magnitude of both the enclosure and the stone settings evokes a sense of the sublime. Here power *over* (Dovey 1999, 10) people is perhaps exercised through an exaggerated scale that dominates the human body and generates a perceptual awareness of the colossal labour necessary for its production. Such a scale of work could serve to legitimise the authority, whether worldly or supernatural, that lay behind the creation of Avebury. In discussing the Wessex henge enclosures, Wainwright comments that:

> Once built, the monuments ... had a massive physical presence which must have invested them with an important role in legitimating power structures, enhancing ceremonial activities and protecting traditional values from challenge by coming to epitomize past achievements.
>
> Wainwright (1989), 166

While we recognise that architecture provided conditions in which control, social division and power relations might be exercised, we do not subscribe to the view that power is *inherent* in a monument like Avebury. Power relations come about through social practices and not just physical conditions, though the latter may be drawn upon to achieve such ends (Dovey 1999). Furthermore, if Avebury was simply about restriction and control then a more effective architecture could be devised, such as the use of continuous timber walls to block even the most partial view of proceedings taking place inside. Rather than encapsulate, stone circles serve to define a permeable, open perimeter, with as many potential entrances as there are gaps between the stones (Bradley 1998, 126). The scale of the earthwork enclosure and the presence of multiple entrances also implies participation on a large scale – inclusion rather than exclusion – even if certain areas of the henge were 'off bounds' to certain people. Besides, the whole argument over controlled access can be turned on its head. Perhaps people were reluctant to enter the henge because of its potency and association with powerful and dangerous spiritual entities. In this sense, being inside and isolated from the familiar sights and routines of the surrounding landscape would be highly undesirable.

Cosmology, homology and materiality

If we acknowledge that there is more to the architecture of Avebury than a prop for power relations, then explanations of its structure must also be sought in the specifics of beliefs and worldviews that could have guided its conceptualisation. Central to this is an understanding of cosmology and concepts of homology and materiality. These terms require some introduction.

Cosmology refers to the symbolic ordering of the natural and human world that defines key cultural values. It often has a spatial dimension and finds expression in the association of different qualities with particular spatial forms and cardinal directions. For example, within Balinese cosmology south is associated with fire and the colour red, and north with water and black, while north and east are regarded as auspicious and south and west as inauspicious. This symbolic classification is reproduced through the spatial structuring of routine activities and guides the layout of houses, compounds and temples (Richards 1996a).

Homology refers to correspondence and sameness. It has been used within archaeology to refer to the way in which the form of a monument reflects and encapsulates the form and essence of the surrounding landscape: the world in miniature, as it were (Richards 1996b). This is evident not only in the location chosen for the monument, but also in the complex combination of elements brought together in its construction.

Materiality is a more slippery term, but here we use it to refer to how the material character of the world is comprehended, appropriated and involved in human projects. It is about understanding the nature and potential of the material world.

The cosmological structuring of Avebury embodied a concern with circularity, and also radial, binary and concentric division. The earthwork and stone settings share a common concern with circularity. Given that a setting of earth, timber or stone can effectively be of any shape, it is interesting to note that the question 'why adopt the circle?' has only recently been raised and considered by archaeologists (e.g. Gibson 1994, 192). Circles exist in nature in a bewildering array of forms, from the sun and moon to the ripples on a pond and the shape of the human eye (Parker Pearson & Ramilisonina 1998, 322). The form of the circle serves as a rich metaphor for the endless repetition of the seasons and mirrors the human cycles of birth, reproduction and death. Circles allow people to place themselves centrally within a world that recedes away to the horizon and reaches upwards to the sky. Such an interpretation is reinforced by the location of many later Neolithic and early Bronze Age circular monuments in areas of the landscape which themselves accentuated a sense of circularity. Avebury is no exception. It is located in a lowland bowl surrounded on all sides by higher downland. Building upon this theme, despite their constructional differences and specific choice of media, it is best to see stone and timber circles as different expressions and transformations of a similar cosmological order, rather than thinking of them as distinctive types of monument (Bradley 1998, 118).

The circle of the earthwork is broken by four more or less equidistantly spaced entrances, dividing it into quarters. In part, this format may have been worked with reference to existing networks of pathways coming in from the north, east, south and west, but if so the earthwork perhaps provided a nominal rather than literal representation of this arrangement. It also reproduced in material form a cosmological quartering. Cosmological schemes which sub-divide the world into four quarters are well attested, and can be seen to operate in the architecture of monuments and the ordering of deposits in later Neolithic Britain (Darvill 1997; Pollard & Ruggles 2001, 81-2). For example, the arrangement of posts within the timber circles of the Sanctuary on Overton Hill subdivides that structure into four quarters, each of which was treated in a distinctive manner through the formal deposition of artefacts (Pollard 1992).

At Avebury the apparent unity of the outer circle belies subtle differences in its architecture that reinforce this symbolic quartering. Different sizes and shapes of sarsen were employed in the north-west and south-west quadrants of the outer circle (where the settings are most complete). Those in the north-west are smaller and more geometric in shape than those making up the south-west quadrant, which include a series of particularly massive blocks running from stones 7 to 12 (Pollard & Gillings 1998, 156). This increase in the size of stones in the south-western part of the circuit fits a common pattern found in late Neolithic and early Bronze Age stone circles across the British Isles (Bradley 2000a, 217). Additional distinction was given by the placing of deposits of worked flint against selected stones of the north-west quadrant, while the south-west was apparently kept 'clean' (information from Alexander Keiller Museum). The implication is that some activities were deemed appropriate in certain parts of the monument but not others, and that these were guided by accepted cosmological schemata.

To circles and quarters, further layers or complexities of meaning were added through binary and concentric divisions. Once constructed, the two inner circles divided the interior of the henge into two halves – a northern and southern – each with its own distinctive central focus – the Cove, opening to the north-east, and the Obelisk. Concentric division was provided by the multiple circuits of bank, ditch and stone, marking progressive transition from the wider world to the deepest, and conceivably most sacred, space of the henge. The sarsens employed in the interior settings show a progressive increase in size, from the outer to the inner circles, then culminating in the massive settings of the Cove and Obelisk; the profiles of which would seem to rise above the bank and surrounding downland, connecting earth and sky. The effect is a more attenuated version of the stepped profile given by the settings at Stonehenge, and also seen in timber at constructions like the Sanctuary. In the context of Stonehenge, Whittle (1997c) suggests this deliberate grading may have symbolised a belief in a hierarchy of spirits and beings.

If it was guided by a particular conceptualisation of the world, the construction of the various components of the Avebury henge also sought to re-create a version of that world. Here we are dealing with processes of homology: the collapsing of the wider world into the physical presence of the monument. With the progressive clearance of the landscape there was a commensurate opening-up of the views possible from any given location. No longer confined by the edges of a clearing and the gloom of the forest canopy, views could extend to the very limits of the horizon. As a result, the earthwork may have acted to mediate between the extremes represented by the openness of a circular monument and the bounding horizon of the circular landscape that surrounded it. In so doing, it served to bring the very horizon itself into the fabric of the monument. Whether an intentional feature or fortuitous product of a particular construction style, there is a striking match between the profile of the bank and the surrounding downland horizon, such that the hills often seem to 'adopt the role of the bank' (Watson 2001, 302). It is also possible to envisage the stone circles as echoing the upright trunks of the trees that encircled the earliest ancestral clearings, or as providing a symbolic mapping of the sarsen spreads littered across surrounding valleys.

In effect, the henge appears to replicate the form of the landscape in which it was created. In this respect Avebury is not unique. Richards and Bradley have recently drawn attention to the manner in which henges seem to replicate in microcosm features of local landscapes (Richards 1996b; Bradley 1998, 116-31). Bradley suggests 'these constructions encapsulated the nature of ... places and reproduced them in architectural form' and that 'the finished monument ... provided a metaphor for the wider landscape' (Bradley 1998, 123).

Homology and cosmology can be conflated, and the gradual elaboration of Avebury can be read as a progressive condensation and distillation of significant elements of the known world into a single place: a physical recreation of both cosmic order and the physical world. If Avebury is anything it is a *microcosm* or *Imago Mundi*, a symbolic version of the world as it was encountered and understood by the late Neolithic communities who constructed it.

One very important question remains, and this brings us to a consideration of materiality. Why was stone chosen as the principal material for constructing the inner settings and avenues? The choice of stone is highly significant, in that other later Neolithic monuments in the region, such as the Sanctuary and the massive palisaded enclosures at West Kennet (Whittle 1997a), made extensive use of timber. Little, if any, use was made of timber at Avebury. We have already argued that the large post-hole adjacent to the southern entrance at Avebury could be considerably earlier than the earthwork and megaliths, while the interpretation of the geophysical anomaly in the north-east quadrant as a multiple timber circle remains open to doubt. We would argue that sarsen was a preferred material because of its physical qualities and associations. Because the stones are unmodified blocks of sarsen it is all to easy to dismiss them as merely a convenient building material. However, the fact that they are not dressed could equally reflect a desire to retain their original identity.

There seems little doubt that certain stones were chosen for incorporation within the henge because of their shape, colour, surface features or biographies (Pollard & Gillings 1998, Gillings & Pollard 1999). Some, for example stones 4, 24 and 31 of the outer circle, show evidence of axe polishing having taken place prior to their erection (Smith 1965, 223). Others have distinctive natural features that must have captured the attention of those choosing the stones: the perforated Ring-stone is one and the 'cup-and-ring' on stone 34 another. These natural cup-like hollows bear a remarkable similarity to motifs used on Neolithic rock-art (ibid.), and may have been mistaken by those selecting the stones for the handiwork of ancestral or mythic communities. One of the most striking natural features can be found in the distinctive small reddish sarsens making up the linear feature inside the southern inner circle, where fragments of fossilised root are visible running through the stone. Their appearance is not dissimilar to that of bone and could easily have led people to believe that the stones actually contained the remains of ancestors or mythic beings (see Boardman 2002 for a discussion of how the discovery of fossilised bones in classical Greece led to their being regarded as the remains of giants or monsters who lived before the age of heroes).

Another important quality of sarsen is its durability, and it is through an awareness of this that ethnographic analogies have been used to link Avebury not with the living but with the ancestral dead (Parker Pearson & Ramilisonina 1998). Parker Pearson and Ramilisonina have drawn attention to the linkage made in many cultures between stone as a solid, durable and resistant material, and immutable, eternal and unchanging sacred realms. In contrast, wood, which is seen to grow, mature and decay, is more closely associated metaphorically with the corporeal world of the living (e.g. Bloch 1995). In this scenario Avebury becomes a monument created for, and used exclusively by, the ancestors. This is an attractive model, though it might be criticised on several grounds.

First, there is its generalist stance, and the unsupported equation, in the case of Avebury, between sacred realms and concepts of ancestry (Barrett & Fewster 1998, Whitley 2002). Secondly, the evidence of deposits within the henge shows that people were visiting the site, if only occasionally. It also fails to deal adequately with the complex visual effects and choreographies that are embodied within the structure, from the contrasting colours and textures of the stones to the kinking avenues and exaggerated entrances (e.g. Whittle 1998, 853). Were these too for the sole benefit of the ancestors? And if aspects of the architecture of the complex were intended to control access and restrict evaluation of events taking place, does this imply the ancestors were being deliberately mystified?

In support of Parker Pearson and Ramilisonina's interpretation is a case of precedence, namely the use of sarsen in the chambers of the region's earlier Neolithic tombs. Here at least a metaphorical and physical link between stone and ancestry is reasonably solid, and could easily have provided a pre-text for later symbolic structures. We also know that Avebury became the focus for the deposition of large quantities of human bone and even burials during the latest Neolithic and early Bronze Age (see below), but this activity does come late in the monument's history. Perhaps such a strict distinction between domains of the living and those of the dead and/or ancestors is inappropriate. The monument may have been closely identified with generalised or specific ancestors, but the efficacy of these supernatural agents could only be maintained through the constant engagement of the living with their affairs.

If we accept that concepts of ancestry and ancestor worship are closely associated with Avebury, though perhaps more so late in the henge's history, then ethnographic analogy could be taken further. One aspect of the ethnography that has gained little discussion in the archaeological literature is a view of the efficacy and animate nature of stone held by some traditional societies (e.g. Kahn 1990; 1996). In certain parts of Melanesia stones are thought to have an agency of their own, or to be petrified ancestors, or even living entities capable of movement and pro-creation (Kahn 1990; Roe & Taki 1999). To such social groups stones can be regarded as much more than mere representations of ancestors, being seen instead as a physical embodiment of them (Taçon 1991). Such a perspective could be applied to Avebury.

Elsewhere we have argued that each sarsen was carefully chosen, and that each had its own biography and personality prior to being incorporated into the monument (Gillings & Pollard 1999). It is our suggestion that in the latter part of the period this relationship became more sedimented, with certain of the sarsens becoming the direct embodiment of ancestor spirits. In this perspective, rather than Avebury being *for* the ancestors, to an extent it was built *of* them. However, the term 'built' with its connotations of construction and alteration should perhaps be replaced with 'gathered'. Avebury would become not a *structure for* the ancestors but a carefully choreographed *gathering of* them.

In the light of such discussions, might we not interpret the careful process of stone selection and erection as a strategy for fixing the stones, as *living* entities, in their new place? Rather than an architectural configuration, the complex arrangement of sarsens set into their lines and rings could be regarded as a cosmological re-creation of the hierarchy of ancestor spirits (Whittle 1997c, 163), growing and developing with each carefully mediated act of stone selection, re-planting and incorporation. With their removal from the landscape and incorporation within the henge their power was appropriated and concentrated. In conjunction with the materials brought into the henge, the effect was to evoke the familiar undulating chalk downlands and river valleys for both the people engaged in activities within the henge, and the ancestors, insulating the latter from the realisation that their spatial context had in fact been altered. The creation of the bank and ditch may thus represent another strategy for fixing the stones in place, serving to make the ancestors feel 'at home', and thus less likely to want to return to their original locations in the sarsen fields, or acting as a barrier to prevent them from wandering.

These may be regarded as rather extreme interpretations, but they perhaps come closer to the kind of pre-modern, Neolithic logic that lay behind the creation of Avebury than many would like to acknowledge.

Activities

We know relatively little of what went on inside Avebury. The creation late in the Neolithic of stone avenues leading to (or from) the henge implies procession to the monument, and perhaps inside, as seems to be the case with contemporary timber circles (Thomas 1999a, 57-8). Through a process of gradual revelation, Bradley has suggested that orchestrated movement inside these monuments provided a mechanism for delivering narratives, perhaps even recounting origin myths (Bradley 2000b, 117-31). While architecture can provide us with some clues as to the nature of activities, the presence of deliberate deposits of artefacts, bone and other materials tells a little more.

Most Neolithic ceremonial sites are associated with formal depositions, with some of the most spectacular evidence coming from the Wessex henges of Durrington Walls (Richards & Thomas 1984), Woodhenge (Pollard 1995) and Mount Pleasant (Thomas 1996, 197-233). Massive quantities of ceramics, worked flint and animal bone were recovered from excavations within these monuments, and analysis of their spatial patterning and compositional relationships shows a high degree of purposeful, symbolic structuring to their placement. By comparison, Avebury is relatively 'clean'. Neither Gray's nor Keiller's excavations produced much artefactual material (Smith 1965, 224-9) and, as we have already seen, a good proportion of what was present relates to pre-enclosure activities. Nonetheless, people were gathering together objects and collections of material, bringing them into the henge and deliberately depositing them in the ditch or against stones (Fig. 9). This activity went on for a long period of time, beginning with the construction of the earthwork and continuing well into the early second millennium BC. Over time, the

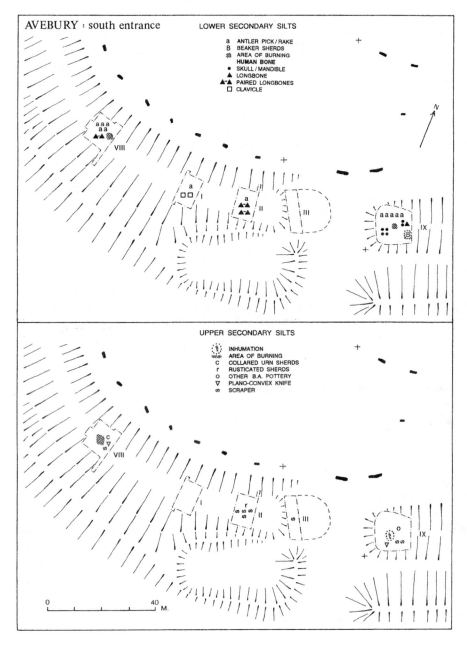

AVEBURY : south entrance   LOWER SECONDARY SILTS

a   ANTLER PICK / RAKE
B   BEAKER SHERDS
※   AREA OF BURNING
HUMAN BONE
●   SKULL / MANDIBLE
▲   LONGBONE
▲-▲ PAIRED LONGBONES
□   CLAVICLE

UPPER SECONDARY SILTS

INHUMATION
AREA OF BURNING
C   COLLARED URN SHERDS
r   RUSTICATED SHERDS
O   OTHER B.A. POTTERY
▽   PLANO-CONVEX KNIFE
s   SCRAPER

0   40
                      M.

9. Deposits in the secondary ditch silts adjacent to the southern entrance.

71

character of those deposits changed in such a way as to suggest that the monument's significance gradually altered.

Judging by the finds from Gray's excavations at the southern entrance, the ditch provided the focus for much of this depositional activity (Gray 1935). Antler continued to be deposited while the primary fills of chalk rubble were forming, particularly in the eastern terminal of the southern entrance where there was a concentration of 29 picks and rakes along with further placements of worked cattle ribs. Representing the first in a series of similar deposits, fragments of human skull and a longbone were placed further to the west, in the section of ditch adjacent to stones 5 and 6 of the outer circle (Gray's cutting I). Gray's report also records several cattle bones from a single animal in the upper primary fills of this cutting (ibid., 157). Principally comprising foot bones, the latter may represent the deposition of a hide, recalling comparable associations of human remains and cattle hides from an early Neolithic context at Fussell's Lodge in south Wiltshire (Ashbee 1966) and an early Bronze Age burial on nearby Hemp Knoll (Robertson-Mackay 1980).

During the early part of the Bronze Age (*c.* 2300-2000 BC) the scale of deposition of human remains increased markedly. Disarticulated human bone was present in the secondary fills of all of Gray's cuttings except III (the west terminal). Some indication of the scale of these deposits is given by Burl's estimate that if their distribution is uniform, up to 500 human bones may lie within the ditch (Burl 2000, 329). These are unlikely to represent the displaced remains of bodies left exposed on the side of the ditch (contra ibid., 329-30), since the only skeletal elements present are pieces of skull, mandibles, longbones and clavicles (shoulder-bones). They were therefore selected from mortuary deposits elsewhere, and may even have been quite ancient ancestral relics by the time they were deposited here.

Most striking are the separate distributions of mandibles, limb-bones and clavicles, with the exception of one collection of bones from the eastern terminal. In three instances, all from Gray's cuttings II and VIII, paired longbones were recovered, each pair consisting of an upper and lower limb-bone – perhaps a token representation of a nominal individual. The number of people represented is difficult to determine, but the bones of at least three adults were present in the eastern terminal (Gray 1935, 148). These deposits remain quite exceptional in an early Bronze Age context. Inhumation within flat graves or under round barrows is often regarded as the normative funerary rite for the period 2300-2000 BC, and the deposition of these collections of human remains may be seen to continue a well-established Neolithic practice (Thorpe 1984). If the bones were considered to hold the essence of a deceased individual, then their inclusion in the ditch at Avebury was a mechanism by which ancestral agencies were physically incorporated within the monument (cf. Watson 1982). Seemingly, it was the earthwork itself that was being emphasised in this way. Only two fragments of human skull have been recovered from the interior, both from stone-hole 41 of the outer circle (Smith 1965, 227).

Other human remains were deposited in the environs of the henge. Parts of two femurs and a pelvis were found in stone-hole 5b of the West Kennet Avenue, and a skull fragment from 25a (ibid., 210). By the early part of the Bronze Age burials were being interred against stones of the West Kennet Avenue, and at the Sanctuary and Longstones Cove (ibid., 209-10; Cunnington 1913, 1931). Dated to the second half of the third millennium BC, a human femur recovered from alluvial silts adjacent to the Winterbourne stream, 350 m to south-west of the henge, shows that the deposition of human bone was also taking place in the landscape close by (Evans et al. 1993, 146-7).

The deposits of human bone in the ditch at Avebury were accompanied by other materials. In the secondary silts of the eastern terminal flanking the southern entrance (Gray's cutting IX) were two areas of burning, either dumps of hearth debris or the residue of *in situ* fires (Gray 1935, 126, 147).

The first of these was sited centrally within the ditch c. 5 m from the upper lip of the terminal, at the same depth and close to three human mandibles. Gray recorded this deposit as being about a metre in diameter with a seam of silt and fine chalk dividing the burnt material in two, perhaps indicating two distinct episodes of deposition or burning (ibid., 147). A peculiar mix of material was recovered from this deposit, including flint debitage, burnt and unburnt animal bone, the points of four antler tines and a human incisor. The second deposit of burnt material was 5 m to the east, at a similar level in the silting (ibid., 126). It was associated with a flint flake and over 20 small sherds of Beaker, all apparently from a single comb-decorated vessel (Piggott, in Gray 1935, 138; Clarke 1970, no. 1053). Close by were fragments of a human cranium, mandible and longbone. A third area of burning was recognised in the secondary silts of Gray's cutting VIII to the west of the entrance. Like the first two, it contained a rather bizarre range of items: a dog mandible, a boar tusk, a piece of burnt bone, an antler fragment, and a complete antler beam with all tines except the trez (third tine) present (Gray 1935, 119).

At certain times people were evidently climbing into the ditch to undertake some highly specialised activities, often involving the lighting of fires (or depositing of ashes) and the handling of human bone. Finds of antler and an association with human bone provide connections between these deposits, the contents of which sound more like ritual paraphernalia than debris from routine activities. Could these have been attempts to commune with ancestors or other spirits? Whatever their intent, these could be events with complex meanings. Pieces of antler were perhaps symbolic of regeneration, but because of their modified state, also of transformation. Likewise, disarticulated human remains, debris from fires, a broken pot, butchered animal bone and flint debitage might be metaphors for change and transformation, while human and animal remains speak of powerful connections between people and other living beings.

Later deposits in the ditch include less human bone, though connections with mortuary and ancestor rites can still be detected. Belonging to the first quarter or so of the second millennium BC, they include sherds from Collared Urns and rusticated vessels, and also fine flint plano-convex knives that would not be out of place in early Bronze Age burials (Gray 1935). Fittingly, one of the latest acts actually involved a burial. Placed with due ceremony in the upper secondary silts of the eastern ditch terminal was an adult female inhumation; incorrectly identified at the time of excavation as the body of a dwarf (ibid., 145-7; Ucko et al. 1991, 254n2) (Plate XIX). This was placed directly above one of the areas of burning referred to above. The body lay with her head to the south, facing east, and was surrounded by a setting of small sarsen boulders, perhaps replicating in miniature the larger stone circles of the henge. Accompanying the burial were several worked flints, potsherds from two different vessels, a sheep/goat metacarpal and a carved chalk ball; items more likely to have been included for their explicit symbolic value than as personal grave goods. Burl sees the burial as a possible sacrifice, and draws attention to similar interments at the henges of Stonehenge, Gorsey Bigbury and Marden (Burl 2000, 330). Whatever the mode of death, this burial is clearly rather special and stood for more than the identity of the person concerned. Coming towards the end of a lengthy history of deposition, and perhaps even activity within the henge, it could be seen as a form of 'decommissioning', or at least as marking a critical transition in the significance of the site.

A striking feature of the sequence of deposits in the ditch at Avebury is its similarity to those at other Wessex sites, such as Maumbury Rings, Wyke Down and Stonehenge (Barrett et al. 1991, 96-106; Bradley 2000b, 124; Pollard & Ruggles 2001). At each monument the sequence begins with deposits of antler, then later retouched artefacts and more animal bone, followed finally by extensive deposits of human bone (including full burials and cremations). The sequence at Avebury is more lengthy than those at Maumbury Rings and Wyke Down, which Bradley sees as a way of establishing a narrative 'concerned with history, with origins and with the place of people in the world' (Bradley 2000b, 127). However, the progressive shift towards the incorporation of transformed human remains seen at both Avebury and Stonehenge could equally be read as reflecting the developing ancestral associations of these monuments as they gathered increasingly long histories and associations with a deep past. In this sense, the remains of the dead stood for that past.

There was correspondingly less deposition within the interior of the henge, and what did take place was different in kind. In the north-west and south-east sectors in particular, collections of worked flint were placed around the bases of selected stones; acts that again reinforce the distinctive identity of individual megaliths. The Obelisk was one, where quite dense concentrations of flint debitage and implements were recovered during the Keiller excavations (Smith 1965, 227). Included in this material are distinctive latest Neolithic and early Bronze Age pieces such as flakes with inverse retouch and a scale-flaked knife.

Another deposit, found next to stone 37 of the outer circle, seems to comprise a token selection of tools gathered from a midden or refuse spread. It includes a small number of flakes from different cores, along with a scraper, a knife, and notched, retouched and denticulated flakes (information from Alexander Keiller Museum). Similar deposits of worked flint, either gathered from elsewhere or representing *in situ* working, are known from other later Neolithic megalithic settings in the region. The most extensive is probably that associated with the Longstones Cove, where over 10,000 pieces of debitage generated through very rudimentary knapping were recovered during partial excavation of that feature in 2000 (Gillings et al. 2002). We are again forced to consider issues of materiality. While flint was placed against stone, pottery and fresh animal bone was placed next to the wooden posts of the contemporary West Kennet palisaded enclosures and the timber circles of the Sanctuary (Whittle 1997a, Pollard 1992). The nature of the deposits reflects the materials they were placed against. All sorts of metaphoric connections can be imagined, but perhaps the most attractive is that flint, like sarsen, was increasingly imbued with ancestral connections.

There is surprisingly little prehistoric pottery from Avebury, again reflecting the site's symbolic and conceptual distance from the routines of daily life taking place around it. Some of that from the ditch is almost certainly residual, derived from pre-enclosure episodes of occupation, while early Bronze Age sherds from the secondary silts are intimately linked to unusual deposits that may have more to do with mortuary and ancestor rites than acts of consumption by the living. There is a small amount of pottery from the interior, all of it Beaker. Much of this comes from the area of the northern entrance and amounts to no more than 20 sherds in total (Smith 1965, 226-7). However, one poorly-recorded pottery find is worth noting. In 1880, while digging a post-hole for the village maypole near the centre of the southern inner circle, residents discovered an urn containing animal or human bone (Smith 1885, 142). Unfortunately, it was rapidly carried away and the fragments lost, but the description of an urn 'containing bones' does sound like that of an earlier Bronze Age cremation.

Connections: the avenues

Towards the end of the Neolithic a dramatic attempt was made to physically draw disparate sites and landscape features together into a coherent whole through the construction of radiating stone avenues. Taking the form of regularly spaced pairs of carefully set sarsens, the avenues stretched for distances up to 2.5 km from Avebury, serving to physically connect the henge with a widespread and diverse set of pre-existing sites and monuments.

Two avenues are known: the West Kennet Avenue, leading from the southern entrance of Avebury and terminating at the Sanctuary on Overton Hill, 2.4 km to the south-east; and the Beckhampton Avenue, which runs from the western entrance and terminates at the Longstones Cove 1.3 km to the south-west. Both remain poorly dated, but on the basis of their physical relationships to an earlier enclosure at Beckhampton, a midden at the foot of Waden Hill and the stone circles at the Sanctuary, they most likely belong in the period 2600-2300 BC. Evidence to support this assumption is provided by a large sherd of Grooved Ware from the packing of stone-hole 15b of the West Kennet Avenue (Smith 1965, 232). This acknowledged, their construction may have been undertaken in stages, spanning a reasonable period of time. This is certainly suggested by the evidence of phasing from the terminal of the Beckhampton Avenue, changes in the format of the West Kennet Avenue along its middle section, and the sheer scale of the undertaking involved. However, whether we are looking at construction over a generation, or over two or three centuries, remains uncertain.

The stones employed in the avenues are, in general, much smaller than those utilised for the inner settings at Avebury. However, the same techniques were adopted to erect them. The sockets include settings of stakeholes for guiding the stone in, and sarsen packing material to stabilise the stones once erected. Once again, there is strong evidence for the careful and deliberate selection of the sarsens incorporated into the fabric of the avenues. This is clear from the zones of axe polishing seen on stones in both the West Kennet and Beckhampton Avenues (ibid., 223; Gillings et al. 2000, 5), which implies that these stones were already known to people long before their incorporation. Deliberate selection is also evident in the shape of the stones. One of the surviving sarsens of the Beckhampton Avenue had a peculiar, folded, organic form, complete with a natural perforation wide enough to push an arm through (Gillings et al. 2000, 5). Along certain stretches of the West Kennet Avenue there appears to be a deliberate choice of stone shape, consisting of long thin stones (Keiller's type A) and squat lozenge-shaped stones (type B) deliberately set in opposition. Although much has been made of this apparent patterning, too little either survives or has been investigated to determine whether it persisted along the entire length of the monument.

Given that Avebury has four entrances, why do archaeologists at present acknowledge the existence of only two avenues? Could there originally have been four? This is highly likely. Until recently, our knowledge of the Beckhampton Avenue derived only from the fortuitous observations made by William Stukeley during the 1720s, a time when many of Avebury's megaliths were in the process of being destroyed. Had Stukeley visited Avebury ten years later it is doubtful whether he would have recognised the Beckhampton Avenue, and it is just as likely that any evidence for avenues to the north and east had long been dismantled before Avebury's 'discovery' by the antiquaries. There is also the possibility that other avenues may have been marked not by stone settings but by wooden posts or shallow earthworks, as at Stonehenge. A geophysical survey outside the eastern entrance certainly indicates the existence of an earlier trackway or other linear feature running up towards the Ridgeway (Ucko et al. 1991, 186; Loveday 1998, 27). However, in the absence of any detailed excavation around the northern and eastern entrances it is difficult to arrive at a definitive answer to this question.

Where do the avenues go?

In discussing the routes taken by the avenues we have adopted the convention of describing Avebury as the starting point. It is important to stress that this is merely a convention – we do not currently know whether the avenues began or ended at Avebury, or out in the landscape at monuments such as the Sanctuary. With this caveat in mind, of the routes taken by the two avenues that of the West Kennet Avenue is best known. The first feature to note is the marked dogleg in its course as it leaves (or arrives at) the southern entrance of the henge (Fig. 6). This apparent change in course has been noted by a number of commentators and used to argue for the presence of distinct phasing in its construction (e.g. Burl 1993, 45-7). Central to such arguments is the assumption that the dogleg reflects an accidental misalignment between two stretches of avenue, one constructed in the direction of Avebury and the other radiating out from it. In essence the kink is a result of shoddy workmanship. Others have argued that it is deliberate, serving to dramatise the view into the henge through the southern entrance through a subtle visual game. Here the viewer's gaze is directed away from the monument (teasing) until the last moment when the avenue swings around (e.g. Burl 1979, 198; Barrett

1994; Thomas 1993). Stimulating though such interpretations are, the excavation records for this portion of the avenue are far from conclusive, and even the excavator doubted the interpretation tendered (Smith 1965, 208). There is undoubtedly a kink or dogleg, but it is likely to be far less pronounced than published records would suggest. This casts serious doubt over interpretations of phasing and misalignment based upon it.

Upon leaving the southern entrance of Avebury, the West Kennet Avenue headed south-east, running along the western slope of the valley between Waden Hill to the west and Hackpen Hill to the east. Approximately 300 m from the southern entrance it approached the crest of a gentle rise running perpendicular to the valley floor. At this point the size of the stones increased markedly, falling again as the avenue crossed the crest and followed the topography down the slope to the south. It is almost as if the rise in the land was matched by a commensurate increase in the height of the avenue stones, accentuating the crest and perhaps the false horizon it created as an observer looked along the avenue's length. This could be viewed as another deliberate visual game (Pollard & Gillings 1998).

Approximately 630 m to the south of Avebury the avenue passed through an area of earlier occupation, marked by a dense surface spread of artefactual material (effectively a midden) and a series of pits and post settings (Smith 1965, 210-16). It is interesting to note that while the course of the avenue deliberately bisected this area it left it largely undisturbed. A gap even exists in the western side where it crossed the centre of the midden spread. To the west of the avenue at this point, and in clear view, were the stones of the Falkner's Circle.

The avenue then continued south, though with a short gap in its length as it entered the bottom of the dry valley leading towards the Kennet. It came to within 100 m of the river and the massive palisaded enclosure complex before curving eastwards to rise up the side of Overton Hill. On the end of the hill, overlooking the river, the avenue terminated at the site of the Sanctuary, its stones keyed into the outer stone circle of this monument (Fig. 10).

The Sanctuary acquired its rather suggestive title from the imagination of the antiquary William Stukeley, despite his claims that it was a local name (Cunnington 1931, 301). It began its life as a circle of six concentric settings of upright timber posts, constructed sometime around the middle of the third millennium BC (Cunnington 1931; Pollard 1992). Like so many other monuments in the Avebury landscape, it was located in a spot that had witnessed activity during the early and middle Neolithic – it was a known and frequented locale. The timber rings were far from being a static, fixed setting. There appears to have been frequent replacement of some of the larger posts, possibly on an interval of only a few years (Pitts

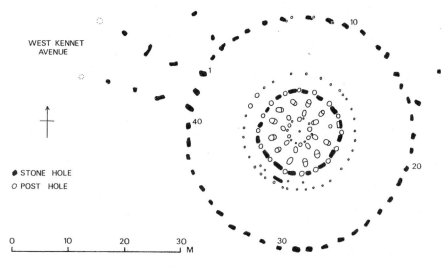

WEST KENNET
AVENUE

● STONE HOLE
○ POST HOLE

0   10   20   30   M

10. The Sanctuary, Overton Hill.

2001, 20-1). This was not a response to the posts rotting away or collapsing since none remained *in situ* sufficiently long for post-pipes to form.

The Sanctuary seems to have been a uniquely dynamic structure, continually being remade through a process of repetition and renewal. Pitts has argued that rather than the monument itself, it was the very act of bringing timber to the site, removing an existing post and replacing it with the new timber that was significant (Pitts 2000, 244-7). This is not to say that the final form of the circles was unimportant. One of the remarkable things about this continual process of renewal was the careful way in which the original plan, with cruciform 'passages', was respected.

The arrival of the avenue at the Sanctuary was marked by a decrease in the lateral spacing between the stone pairs, and there are tantalising hints from early excavation records that the original double row was elaborated into a triple row of stones (Cunnington 1931, 306). The arrival also marked the addition of two circles of sarsen into the timber structure. The first was inserted between the posts of an existing wooden ring, serving to enclose the two timber rings that had witnessed the most concerted episodes of renewal and replacement. The second stone circle formed a perimeter to the overall structure and was carefully bonded into the terminal of the avenue, suggesting that both were constructed at the same time (Pollard 1992, 217). This served to effectively loop or 'lasso' the Sanctuary – the ever renewing and changing circles of wood harnessed by enduring, timeless rings of stone.

The course of the Beckhampton Avenue has only recently been eluci-dated through excavation (Gillings et al. 2000, 2002). Leaving the western

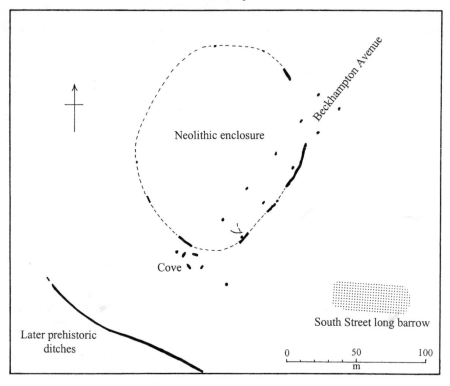

Neolithic enclosure

Beckhampton Avenue

Cove

South Street long barrow

Later prehistoric
ditches

0   50   100

m

11. Excavated features of the Beckhampton Avenue, Cove and Enclosure, also
showing position of South Street long mound and later prehistoric ditch system.

entrance of the henge, it took a course along the line of the present day
High Street, crossing the Winterbourne within full view of Silbury Hill to
the south. Along the second half of its length it then ran within clear site
of Windmill Hill, 2 km to the north. Its ultimate destination was the site
of an earlier earthwork enclosure in Longstones Field, near Beckhampton
(Fig. 11).

Constructed adjacent to the mid-fourth millennium BC South Street
long mound, the style of this enclosure, with a segmented ditch and
internal bank, was reminiscent of earlier constructions such as Windmill
Hill. It may even have been built as an anachronism – a deliberate
reference to much earlier traditions. The enclosure was oval, *c.* 140 by 110
m, with a wide principal entrance on the east. It displayed no geometric
regularity and was curiously flattened along its south-eastern side. Radiocarbon dates on bone from the base of the ditch show that it was
constructed around 2700 BC, slightly earlier than the main earthwork
phase at Avebury.

3. Rings of Earth and Stone

The creation of the avenue marked the deliberate eradication of the enclosure, with the material from its bank being used to level the ditch. The avenue passed directly through its original eastern entrance, and at this point its course was marked by a remarkable pair of stones: the surface of one was covered by extensive areas of axe polishing, while its partner was a perforated and distinctly folded stone. The avenue terminated immediately to the west of the former enclosure, where a line of three large sarsens was set perpendicular to its course, effectively blocking its passage. After a relatively short period of time the outer stones of this 'T-shaped' terminal were removed and a large cove constructed in their place; the middle stone of the original terminal becoming the south-eastern side of the cove. Comprising a four-sided setting of enormous sarsens (over 60 tonnes each in weight), this setting appears to have been rather more open than the Avebury Cove.

What were the avenues for?

At one level the avenues served to prescribe pathways, enforcing certain approved ways of moving through an increasingly open landscape and into specific types of monument – circles – that could effectively be approached from any direction (Thomas 1993, 41; Bradley 1998, 126). There is reason to suppose that they represent a 'monumentalisation' of existing, and perhaps in some instances quite ancient, trackways. Further support for such an interpretation comes from the Beckhampton enclosure and the way the flattened side of the circuit respected the path taken by the later avenue. While the general routes themselves may have been ancient, there is evidence that some degree of flexibility was exercised when the time came to fix them permanently within the landscape. For example, there are hints in the alignments of the avenues, their kinks and meanders, that the local topography was being subtly utilised so as to maximise the visual impact of a journey through the open landscape (Pollard & Gillings 1998; Watson 2001). This is most evident at the southern entrance, where on the final approach the West Kennet Avenue seems to lead the viewer not into Avebury but past it, before a final kink brings the site into view. It is also suggested by the way in which stone size increases towards intermediate horizons, creating a sense of urgency in the viewer to reach the crest to see what mysteries lay beyond.

As well as fossilising pathways, the avenues also served to link and reference a series of other sites in the landscape, ordering them into a sequence to be encountered and experienced. Some of these monuments and occupation areas had been a presence in the landscape for over a millennium, while others appear to have been constructed alongside the avenues themselves. The process of incorporating sites into the physical

81

fabric of Avebury was complex and selective. Like an itinerary map incised in stone, every inclusion was matched by a number of exclusions. There was also considerable variation in the ways in which this process of incorporation was effected. Some sites were referenced in a purely visual way, for example the Falkner's Circle and South Street long mound. In these cases the avenues passed close enough by to ensure that these features could be seen. Other sites were referenced in a much more physical way. Some, like the West Kennet occupation site, were directly incorporated yet wholly respected, the avenue passing through, yet apparently not disturbing, the earlier traces of activity. At other sites, for example the Beckhampton enclosure, the act of incorporation was also an act of negation, the avenue acknowledging the feature and even going as far as respecting its original entrance, but ultimately leading to its eradication from the landscape. At the Sanctuary another form of incorporation is evident, the arrival of the avenue perhaps coinciding with the structural enhancement and elaboration of an existing monument. A complex process of negotiation and careful selection was clearly taking place.

As intimated earlier, rather than wholly new routes through the landscape, defined by the locations of the monuments and features they sought to link and incorporate, the avenues followed paths whose origins may have lain in the thick forests of the earlier Neolithic. These ancestral trackways had linked clearings, selected nodes within the web of paths that criss-crossed the forest. In time certain of these clearings became the focus of monument construction, and knowledge of the specific pathways linking them became an important aspect of social and ritual life. With the gradual opening up of the landscape their utilitarian importance would have diminished. After all, a cleared landscape is a world of potentially infinite ways of getting from A to B. On the other hand, the ritual importance of these paths may have remained wholly unaffected. Knowledge of these routes remained critical and the most effective way of preserving and communicating this knowledge would be through ceremony. Ceremonies are highly effective mechanisms for preserving versions of the past, and it is through prescribed bodily behaviour within ceremony (for example, formalised patterns of movement) that memory is sedimented (Connerton 1989). The avenues served to formalise these patterns of procession, functioning as what might be termed a technology of bodily remembrance. Taking the aspects of pathway and linkage together, we can see the avenues as serving to create a narrative experience by which myths and histories relating to particular places could be retold or brought into memory through the orchestrated movement of participants during ceremonies.

Though unique in their own particular format, the Avebury avenues are part of a much broader tradition of monumental linear constructions extending back to the mid-fourth millennium BC. Many are united by similar roles: the orchestration of movement through the landscape and the physical linking of significant places. The earthworks of earlier cursus monuments were often laid out in such a way as to incorporate existing features in the landscape and perhaps monumentalise long-standing pathways (Barrett et al. 1991, 47-51; Last 1999; Barclay et al. 2003, 237). The same is true of stone rows. The famous multiple stone alignments at Carnac in Brittany incorporated earlier monuments along their routes, that of Kermanio taking its alignment from the earlier long mound of Le Manio. Ironically, in the latter case, these earlier structures were obscured by the sheer scale of the later alignments meant to commemorate them (Bradley 2002, 102-9).

Summary

The third millennium BC was a very busy time at Avebury, and this chapter has been by necessity complex. During the course of the discussion we have reviewed the chronology of the monument and have not only looked at the technology of construction but sought to explore the reasons why Avebury took the form it did and the activities that took place within it.

The late David Clarke talked of two different perceptions of archaeological knowledge. The first was a traditional model which, like an Emmenthal cheese, was seen to consist of a body of information with holes in it. The second he described as akin to 'a sparse suspension of information particles of varying size, not even randomly distributed in archaeological space and time' (Clarke 1973, 10). As the detail in this chapter has illustrated, our knowledge of later Neolithic and early Bronze Age Avebury is more a 'suspension of information particles' than it is a Swiss cheese. Much remains uncertain, even at quite a basic level. The chronology of the earthwork and stone settings requires considerable resolution, and the status of several suspected components, such as the putative pit or post circle in the north-western sector, remains unresolved. This does not prevent interpretation – and we hope to have offered much here – but it considerably restricts the limits of our current understanding.

We must also recognise that a monument as complex as Avebury, which came together through a protracted process of piecemeal and inventive working of earthen and stone architecture, cannot be contained within a single narrative. Any interpretations of Avebury are going to be varied and sometimes conflicting because the monument as we see it today does not represent a single construction, with a single purpose and meaning, used during one occasion by a group of people united through common goals. It embodies changing structures of esoteric knowledge and views about the world, mediated through available resources and relations of social power.

This acknowledged, the final stages of Avebury's coming into being are perhaps more intelligible and more susceptible to an over-arching narrative than its beginnings. During the mid to late third millennium BC a deliberate attempt was made to concentrate and condense significant places, materials and objects into a single locus, most dramatically through the construction of megalithic avenues. So at one level the surrounding world was drawn into the fabric of Avebury. On another, an explicit connection with a generalised or mythologised past was seemingly being created through the increased deposition of human remains and the use of a material – sarsen – that held close metaphoric associations with ancestral realms.

4. Avebury's Dark Age

There are some notable disjunctures in the history of Avebury. The punctuated acts of digging, moving and erecting stones, and depositing materials, that began around 3000 BC and spanned over a thousand years, are followed by a lengthy period of silence. Avebury's history during the 1600 or so years between the early Bronze Age and the Roman occupation remains stubbornly elusive. None of the excavations that have taken place within the henge since the beginning of the twentieth century have revealed any later Bronze Age or Iron Age features, or produced material culture of that date. We can assume that the site was little visited, perhaps even abandoned and vegetation left to grow. In consequence, Avebury at 1000 BC was a very different place to Avebury at 2000 BC. We can envisage stone settings and the earthwork partially obscured by the growth of scrub and trees, some stones fallen, and the henge inhabited by birds and deer rather than people engaged in making observances or participating in set-piece ceremonies.

The context for the apparent abandonment of Avebury must be sought in the major social, economic and ideological changes that took place during the second half of the second millennium BC (Barrett 1994). For the first time in the prehistory of southern Britain we see the formation of agrarian landscapes. Occupation throughout the Neolithic and early Bronze Age had been characterised by varying degrees of mobility. It was generally not accompanied by solid domestic architecture, and what little cultivation took place occurred in fixed plots worked as part of a long-fallow system rather than in established fields. Ontological stability was provided by reference to the timeless and immutable domains of spirits and ancestors, made material by constructions such as Avebury. It was also through the creation of monuments that dispersed and fragmented social groups gained a broader sense of community.

In the centuries around 1500 BC a fundamental reorientation of basic values took place. The establishment of formal field systems and their working through a system of short-fallow agriculture meant that people became more closely identified with particular areas of land (Barrett 1994, 143-5). More sedentary modes of settlement became commonplace, and the locus of ritual activity shifted to the domestic domain. Enclosed settlements consisting of small numbers of roundhouses may suggest a desire on the part of family or immediate kin groups to project a sense of bounded identity and autonomy, rather than collective endeavour and community cohesion.

The Avebury landscape sees the establishment of extensive field systems and enclosed settlements in the centuries following 1500 BC, many of these on the highdown to the east and south (Gingell 1992). By the latest Bronze Age and early Iron Age a substantial number of these field systems may have reverted to pasture, and the focus for activity shifted to the edges of the region (Pollard & Reynolds 2002, 141-7), particularly the Vale of Pewsey to the south where there are a number of very substantial settlements spanning the transition (e.g. All Cannings Cross: Cunnington 1923). New communal foci were created during the second quarter of the first millennium BC in the guise of hillforts, whose massive ditches and ramparts represent the creation of monumental earthworks on a scale not seen since the late Neolithic. These appear to ring the edge of the region and include the sites of Oldbury to the west, Rybury and Martinsell to the south, and Barbury Castle to the north.

The beliefs and values that drove the creation of Avebury, Silbury Hill and other Neolithic monuments were long gone by the Iron Age, but the henge and avenues still retained a very real physical presence in the landscape. If nothing else, they were far too large to ignore. The routine movement of people through the landscape of the Upper Kennet Valley, whether going from settlements to fields, visiting neighbours or herding animals, would have led to encounters with these earlier remains. Their presence would have to be accounted for in stories, histories or myths and as a result they would have been worked into contemporary accounts of the landscape (Barrett 1999; Gosden & Lock 1998). Avebury did not lose meaning; it merely changed significance.

There is good reason to believe that the henge and associated stone settings still held a considerable potency, and may even have become a 'taboo' space, perhaps considered to be the domain of ghosts or other dangerous supernatural agencies. This is implied by the total absence of later Bronze Age and Iron Age settlement and agriculture in the immediate vicinity of these monuments. Here though, we should be careful to distinguish between later prehistoric attitudes towards earlier earthworks on the one hand and megalithic settings on the other. It seems as though it was the stones themselves that were being deliberately avoided. The Neolithic enclosure at Rybury, to the south, was re-worked as a hillfort during the Iron Age (Oswald et al. 2001, 141), while a field system encroached upon the earthworks on Windmill Hill (Whittle et al. 1999, 16). Earthen long barrows in the west of the region were also readily incorporated into agricultural landscapes from the middle Bronze Age onwards. Other Wessex henges without megalithic settings were treated quite differently to Avebury. Excavation and geophysical survey has revealed Iron Age settlement inside the henge enclosures of Durrington Walls (Wainwright & Longworth 1971; David & Payne 1997) and Mount Pleasant (Wainwright 1979). Perhaps to communities now familiar with creating enclosed spaces for settlement these sites were not so alien. In fact, as 'ancestral hillforts' they provided a useful link to mythical pasts and legitimated rights of access to local resources.

Megaliths, however, were treated in a much more circumspect manner. Stonehenge again provides a useful parallel to the situation at Avebury. Although activity of sorts may have continued here longer than at Avebury, as indicated by a low-level scatter of later second millennium BC ceramics, the monument was little visited thereafter (Cleal et al. 1995, 366-7, 491). A respectful distance was maintained in placing a human burial in an earlier palisade trench next to, but outside, the monument during the Iron Age. Furthermore, although this became a very busy landscape during later prehistory, field systems and settlements barely encroached upon the visual envelope of the stones (Richards 1990, fig. 160). It remained a place 'of some veneration and mystery' (Cleal et al. 1995, 491), while 'the stark abandonment' perhaps spoke of 'an unofficial, unofficiated, power' (Bender 1998, 66).

In the Upper Kennet Valley stone was in the process of being recontextualised. Throughout the Neolithic and earliest Bronze Age there was a close identification between sarsen and sacred realms, regardless of whether stones were part of natural spreads or components of monumental constructions. Now a distinction was being made between standing stones as a potent artifice of a remote, even mythical, past, and the unaltered spreads of sarsen on the sides and bottoms of valleys. Many of the trails of sarsen lying on the Marlborough Downs, previously respected and venerated, were incorporated into field boundaries, broken up for hearthstone, burnt or used as the foundations for timber buildings (Gingell 1992). The contextual link between the unmodified sarsens on the high downlands and the stones at Avebury became severed. The identity of individual megaliths also became eroded, and instead it was now the collective nature of the stones making up the circles, avenues and coves that became significant. Rather than providing the security of a link to ancestral domains, megalithic settings were instead attributed with agency of a deeply ambiguous or unpredictable kind, which required distant respect or avoidance.

The conceptual distance that these later prehistoric communities wished to maintain between the stones and areas of contemporary habitation and cultivation is seen in the form of a recently investigated boundary feature immediately to the south-west of the end of the Beckhampton Avenue (Fig. 11). Dating to the later Bronze Age or Iron Age, this may have begun as an alignment of pits. It was then repeatedly re-defined through the digging of a series of shallow ditches, each of which had been immediately backfilled with chalk rubble. It could in no sense have acted as a physical barrier, and the impression is of a largely symbolic boundary, maintained through periodic reinstatement, that distanced the stones from the rest of the landscape.

Whether venerated or treated with cautious superstition, can we identify any activity at Avebury during the late second and first millennia BC? The only evidence, albeit indirect, consists of two Iron Age radiocarbon dates and a luminescence determination, all associated with the stone settings. The radiocarbon dates are on ash and charcoal from stone-holes 8 and 44 of the outer circle, the first giving a date range of 770-390 BC and the second a span of 400 BC-AD 150 (Pitts & Whittle 1992). Preliminary results from optically stimulated luminescence dating of one of the Cove stone sockets shows a secondary, post-erection, peak for the early/mid-first millennium BC. All are broadly consistent in suggesting one or more burning events during the Iron Age.

Quite what these dates mean in terms of human activity remains uncertain. Do they imply people were lighting fires inside the henge, and if so was this undertaken as part of ritual observances – and by whom – or was it carried out by casual visitors to the monument? Alternatively, they could reflect attempts at clearing areas of scrub or trees around the stones; but again, what would the motivation for this be? Finally, there is the possibility of natural conflagration created through lightning strikes. Human agency need not be evoked. The evidence is tantalising, but natural fires are perhaps a greater possibility than the sacrificial fires of the druids of popular imagination.

5. Avebury Bypassed

Avebury slumbers

For much of the first millennium BC Avebury appears to have been
neglected, if not deliberately shunned. As we have discussed, the absence
of any recognisable Iron Age artefacts has been a noticeable feature of the
major excavation campaigns that have taken place within the henge. This
situation was to change, albeit slightly, with the coming of the legions and
the absorption of Britain into the Roman Empire. After centuries of
conscious avoidance, people once again began to enter the Avebury circles,
and carefully place deposits within the silted up circuit of the ditch.
Something had clearly changed – the question is what? Did the renewed
acts of deposition reflect a dramatic change in the perceived role Avebury
played, or were they symptoms of a set of wider changes in the social
landscape, as Avebury and the people dwelling around it were brought into
the Roman world?

AD 43 and all that (on becoming Roman)

The conquest of Britain has been thoroughly documented and it is not our
intention to follow in the footsteps of the legions here. Looking to Avebury,
of much more interest is what happened in the period following the
invasion. The conquest began in AD 43, with the army reaching Wales
around AD 60 (Millet 1995, 14). In the Avebury area this invasion period
appears to have been effectively over by AD 45 (Griffiths 2001, 41). What
followed was a gradual process of 'becoming Roman' that was to have a
powerful impact upon the way in which Avebury was understood and
interpreted.

This process of Romanisation is both interesting and complex. As
Millett has argued, the conquest of Britain is perhaps best viewed not as
an exercise measured solely in terms of military achievement and territorial gain. Indeed in the case of Avebury less martial factors seem to have
prevailed and the 'invasion' appears to have been more an act of persua-

sion and gentle coercion than military conquest. There is certainly no suggestion of any conflict or destruction of native sites taking place, nor any substantial military garrisoning. What we do have is the rather circumstantial evidence of a fort, constructed at the junction of two major roadways some 10 km east of Avebury (Griffiths 2001, 44; Corney 1997a). Located close to an existing Iron Age enclosure, it appears to have been built shortly after the conquest and then deliberately abandoned in the early AD 60s, the site developing into the prosperous civilian town of Cunetio (modern Mildenhall) (Burnham & Wacher 1990, 148-52). The suggestion is of a structure that served more as a staging post for the advancing army than a permanent frontier installation.

Of more lasting and direct relevance to Avebury itself was the construction in this early period of a road (Margary 53), cutting east-west through the heart of the Avebury landscape (Plate XI). A principal branch of the Foss Way, this comprised the main western road of Roman Britain (Margary 1967, 135), passing through the site of Cunetio, to link the major centres of Bath (Aquae Sulis) and Silchester (ibid., 84-5). As we will discuss, this road, more than merely a communications corridor, was to have a profound impact upon Avebury's perceived place in the landscape.

To return to Millett's point, the invasion should instead be judged in terms of the success with which indigenous communities were persuaded to become part of the empire rather than on purely military grounds. In other words, it was first and foremost about people. Depending upon the characteristics and belligerence of a given tribal group a number of courses of action were available to the invading army: direct military action, intimidation, forceful persuasion or peaceful collaboration leading to gradual assimilation (e.g. Millett 1990, 44; Laurence 2001, 68-9). Whether or not these options were embedded in a deliberate policy of Romanisation working at the level of native elites is at present unclear. There may have been a clear strategy at work whereby existing native hierarchies would have been maintained, with existing tribal elites being effectively 'mapped' onto a Roman model. However, rather than dressing up an existing social hierarchy in sandals and toga, it could equally have been achieved through more pragmatic means, such as daily personal contact and a series of more immediate social negotiations which over time served to engender a recognisably Roman population (e.g. Grahame 1998, 6-7).

Whatever the precise mechanism (policy or pragmatism), what is clear is that in the decade or so following the invasion in AD 43, the Avebury landscape became what we might term 'Romanised'. The native community was rapidly and peacefully assimilated into the Roman world, coming under Roman administrative rule and with distinctively Roman styles and material culture rapidly becoming the norm throughout the Upper Kennet Valley (Griffiths 2001, 41).

5. Avebury Bypassed

The puzzling factor is that the people dwelling in the Avebury landscape after the conquest were much the same as those who were living there before. We are not dealing with an influx of new occupants. Nor, as discussed earlier, is there any evidence for any major military action or garrison. Indeed it is easy to overestimate the impact of the invasion army. Although the early fort at Mildenhall would undoubtedly have generated a local demand for grain and other foodstuffs, this would have been relatively short-lived (Millet 1990, 56-7). Likewise the building of the road, with the construction gangs and engineers moving through the area rather than remaining static within it.

So what then was happening? The presence of Roman artefacts and building styles need not necessarily indicate dramatic change. It could, for example, merely reflect changes in fashion among the ruling factions of the social hierarchy. However, in the case of Avebury this process of Romanisation does not appear to have been exclusive to the elite, nor simply a thin veneer of Roman culture spread across the surface of a largely unchanged native population. The invasion engendered dramatic changes right the way across the economic and ideological landscape of the region.

For example, detailed survey of the downland to the immediate east of the Avebury henge has revealed that a large-scale reorganisation of the landscape took place in the Roman period. Earlier fields were refurbished, and wholly new field systems were laid out around a network of trackways (Fowler 2000, fig. 4.3, 55). Along with these new field systems came a concomitant restructuring of rural settlement patterns, with the creation of a series of small farms along with a number of suggested villa sites that have been tentatively interpreted as estate centres (ibid., 54-6, 226-7).

What we appear to be witnessing is real social change. So how did this come about? It is tempting to look to the army and attribute this to externally imposed factors leading to involuntary change. Indeed, the rural restructuring has been interpreted in precisely this way – a direct result of the system of taxation the army left imposed in its wake, the wholesale reorganisation of the landscape explained as a productivity measure in response to the burden of taxation (ibid., 227).

However, we would argue that the key to understanding this process may lie with the way in which aspects of Roman culture were actively used by people in their everyday lives – change, if you like, from the bottom up. The later Iron Age communities of southern England had been in contact with the Roman world for a considerable time before the invasion (Millet 1990, 40). The difference following the conquest was that Roman artefact styles and fashions became accessible to a wider proportion of the population than ever before. As Grahame has argued, the widespread availability of Roman artefacts and 'ways of doing things' would inevitably lead to change and transformation. This is because material things are never passive reflections of an existing social order. Instead, they are actively drawn upon by people in the creation and maintenance of their own personal identities. By employing the newly available types and styles of artefact and behaviour, personal and group identities would be modified, leading inevitably to changes in the broader social structure (Grahame 1998, 4-8). The key point is that rather than being merely indicators that such a process has taken place, Roman objects were active in the very process of becoming Roman. We will develop this point shortly in the context of the Roman road.

It may be that in ascribing such transformations to unequivocal 'impacts' we are overly simplifying the situation. As intimated above, rather than a single act of conquest involving the wholesale transplantation of new people, ways of life and understandings of the world, the invasion may be better thought of as resulting in a number of impacts and influences operating at a range of different levels and scales. Some would have been highly visible, others much more subtle. Working together they would have led inexorably to the widespread social changes we see in the landscape.

This can be illustrated by a careful consideration of what we would argue was the most significant impact of the invasion, an impact that underpinned both the reorganisation of the landscape and the rapid acceptance of Roman ways of life. This is an event that has more in common with the processes of change engendered by the active use of material culture, and with everyday life, experience and memory in the Avebury landscape than the cold logic of modern day economics – the construction of the road.

The Roman road

> The road was a mechanism of Roman power that physically reshaped the landscape after Roman control had initially been asserted through military intervention.
>
> Laurence (1999), 197

Traditional archaeological accounts of Roman roads have tended to focus upon their more functional aspects. Roads are seen as strands in a complex web of communication routes, facilitating military and strategic movements and linking together various economic hubs and centres (Witcher 1998, 60). When individual roads are the topic of study, it is the techniques used in their construction and the surveying challenges and triumphs of engineering they physically embody that dominate (e.g. Margary 1967, 17).

5. Avebury Bypassed

The road cutting across the Avebury landscape is no exception. To date discussion has tended to focus upon factors such as how it was surveyed and constructed, its role as a relative dating tool and its function as an 'attractor' for later settlements and burials. For example, many researchers have noted how the road appears to have been deliberately aligned upon Silbury Hill. This has been interpreted as reflecting the use of the hill as a surveying station by the Roman engineers charged with the laying out of the road line (e.g. Margary 1967, 136; Corney 2001, 27). Likewise, the fact that the road detours around the base of Silbury and cuts through a number of earlier round barrows has been used to affirm the antiquity of these features (Stukeley 1743, 26; Wilkinson 1869, 113-18).

While undoubtedly interesting, such studies have failed to consider fully why the road goes exactly where it does, nor the psychological impact the construction of the road would have had upon the people dwelling in the landscape. What is more, in much the same way as material culture and distinctly Roman 'ways of doing things', roads should be seen not so much as symbols of 'having become Roman' but active catalysts in that very process – to do otherwise is to confuse cause with effect. Roads must be seen as active agents of change (Witcher 1998; Laurence 1999).

We have argued that the Avebury landscape was already criss-crossed with routeways. Some, such as droveways and paths were in everyday usage. Others, fossilised and fixed by lines of sarsen, were mythical and ancestral. Whatever else the Avebury landscape was, it was first and foremost a landscape of long-established trackways. And then along came the road. This was a new axis not only of movement, but also of the very landscape itself; an axis from which later developments sprang, whether field systems (Fowler 2000, 26, fig. 2.5) or settlements (Corney 1997b). The building of the road imposed a new and wholly Roman spatial order upon the ground, what might be thought of as a symbolic conquest of the very landscape itself, a physical reshaping which served to affirm Roman control (Witcher 1998, 64; Laurence 1999, 198). In much the same way as with material culture, by adopting and using the road the local population would have given legitimacy to this new spatial order. That they did so is evident from the axial role the line of the road played in the reorganisation and layout of field systems (Fowler 2000, 227). It is also clear in the way in which later burial mounds clustered close to the road's line (Smith & Simpson 1966).

Critical for this notion of symbolic conquest (and for the ultimate fate of Avebury in the Roman period) is the issue of exactly where the road went, and, by implication, where it did not go. We have traditionally tended to think of Roman roads as models of efficiency, linking various important hubs together using the most direct path possible. However, between these important nodes, a given road passed through a host of other sites, locales and places. If we accept that the road was a powerful and active tool in the negotiation of Roman authority then it follows that the precise route taken is crucially important. In the laying out of any road, important ideological decisions are taken as to which of the intermediate places on its approximate route are to be included, and thus embraced by the new spatial order, and which excluded and effectively bypassed.

So what of Avebury?

At this point the reader may well be wondering what all of this talk of roads has to do with Avebury, an entity that has been curiously absent from discussions so far. We have looked at how the conquest led to a large-scale reorganisation of the surrounding downland through the establishment and elaboration of field systems and the construction of farms. It also saw the building of villas, major administrative centres and the driving of a road through the heart of the Avebury landscape. Yet at Avebury itself we see essentially nothing. There was no settlement or concerted structural activity of any other kind within the henge – no additions, alterations or evidence of destruction. It seems clear that the process of forgetting that had begun in the later Bronze Age continued. This is perhaps most clearly evident in the line taken by the road. While passing close to both the Sanctuary and Silbury Hill it completely bypasses the circles at Avebury, writing it out of the new spatial narrative.

However, the shunning of the circles does not seem to have been quite as complete as in the pre-Roman Iron Age, for we do find Roman material within the henge. For example, Stukeley speaks of 'several' Roman coins being found in and around Avebury (Stukeley 1743, 26). Looking to the excavations carried out by Keiller, although quantities were small – less than 50 Romano-British potsherds along with fewer than 12 coins – Roman material was found within the interior of the henge (Smith 1965, 243). Likewise, in Gray's cuttings through the ditch, sherds of coarse and fine Romano-British pottery were found in the upper 2.5 m or so of silting. Although the precise number of sherds was not consistently recorded, we know that these densities were relatively small – of the order of 10-20 sherds (Gray 1935, 112, 115, 118-19, 125-6).

Of perhaps more interest were the finds of bronze objects. These included two rings and a twisted wire bracelet found in the eastern ditch terminal of the southern entrance, and an inscribed bronze brooch (fibula) found in a ditch section dug 90 m to the west of the southern entrance (ibid., 119, 125-6, 156-7) (Plate XI). The clustering of these finds raises the distinct possibility that these acts of deposition were deliberately concentrated around the entrances and the southern entrance in particular, though it should be remembered that Gray's cuttings were themselves concentrated in this area. However, the presence of the brooch in the cutting furthest from this point suggests that deposition may have been taking place more generally around the perimeter of the monument, and although of low density, the presence of Roman material in the majority of Gray's cuttings suggests that an appreciable quantity of material was deposited in the ditch as a whole.

The bronze brooch is particularly interesting. The deliberate deposition of brooches appears to have been an Iron Age practice that continued into the Roman period. Of particular relevance is the fact that they are frequently found at many pre- and post-conquest shrines and temple sites (Jundi & Hill 1998, 129; Haselgrove 1997, 65). Like coins, brooches appear to have been items which were deemed to have been particularly appropriate for ritual or special deposition. The presence of the brooch in the Avebury ditch is therefore important as it suggests that what we are seeing is evidence for some form of ritual activity rather than chance loss. The question is whether this reflects an act of gradual rehabilitation, after centuries marked by an absence of such behaviour at the monument, or perhaps an act of covert defiance in the face of the new spatial order; a traditional act carried out in an old place?

The first thing to note is that the circles were not unique in acting as a focus for renewed acts of deposition. Roman artefacts are frequent finds in and around the prehistoric monuments of the Avebury landscape. For example, six late Roman coins were found in the topsoil around the façade of the West Kennet chambered tomb (Piggott 1962, 55-6). At Avebury itself it was not only the circles that witnessed acts of deposition. Excavations along the line of the West Kennet Avenue produced a scattering of coins and potsherds. Likewise the eighteenth-century stone destruction pits and disturbed sockets at the site of the Longstones Cove produced quantities of Roman material mixed in amongst the backfill. This included sherds of Samian Ware and animal bone (dated by radiocarbon to the second-third centuries AD). As no other Roman artefacts had been found in excavations along the line of the Beckhampton Avenue, the suggestion is of material that had been deliberately deposited at the foot of the stones.

One of the most curious finds made at the Cove was of an iron spearhead along with fragments of a distinctive type of scaled Roman armour (Gillings & Pollard 2002) (Plate XI). This appears to have been deliberately deposited within the box defined by the sarsen settings. Owing to later disturbance it is not clear whether these items were deposited with or without an accompanying burial. Although no human remains were discovered while excavating the stone destruction pit, Stukeley rather teasingly noted that bones had been removed from the site following the digging of the burning pit (Gillings et al. 2002).

As well as acts of deposition taking place at monuments already millennia old, we also see contemporary Roman structures, such as tombs, being constructed in among existing barrow cemeteries. A good example can be found where the Roman road crosses Seven Barrows Hill, a kilometre or so to the north of the Sanctuary. Here a cluster of peculiar Roman burial mounds were discovered nestling within the barrow group (Smith & Simpson 1966). It is quite likely that many more Roman funerary structures lie along the line of the road as it passes to the west of Silbury Hill, lurking as yet unrecognised amongst the dense groups of Bronze Age round barrows (e.g. Smith 1885, 101-6).

The activity at Avebury was thus not unusual. It seems that throughout the Roman period people were drawn to earlier monuments, either as foci for their own constructions or as places to visit and make deposits. This phenomenon has been termed 're-use' and is interesting on a number of levels; not least the implication that these people themselves had an explicit concern with the monuments of their own deep past. It is important to realise that the term 're-use' masks considerable variation in how earlier monuments were appropriated and utilised (Williams 1998a, 77). Indeed the term itself may be rather misleading, implying as it does that monuments had somehow fallen out of everyday life or been forgotten, only to be rediscovered and appropriated for entirely new ends. Are monuments ever really forgotten?

One of the underlying themes of this book is the notion that Avebury has never 'gone away' – every generation has had to confront and interpret it. As we have stressed throughout this chapter, the Roman conquest did not result in the replacement of an existing population with a wholly new one; the landscape was populated by pretty much the same people who had always lived there. Avebury have may not have witnessed significant acts of deposition in the pre-Roman Iron Age but that is not to say that it had slipped out of popular consciousness. In a landscape riddled with pathways and full of people how could it? It has to be remembered that even the apparent shunning of a site takes effort and in the final analysis is as conscious an act as veneration and ritual deposition.

While it is tempting to interpret these acts as part of a concerted drive to appropriate past religious or ritual foci by a new social order, or as acts of resistance in the face of social change and transformation, they could have served a variety of purposes; individual acts driven by largely pragmatic considerations. Taking place at a time when new identities were being negotiated and expressed, the old monuments may have been drawn upon as a powerful symbolic resource to legitimise identity. Likewise, as the very landscape itself was being re-organised, deliberate acts of deposition, or the decision to place the dead in close proximity to the sepulchres of the past, may have served to reaffirm ancestral links between individuals and land. At the same time some of the older monuments may also have been seen as places of supernatural importance, the shrines and temples of local deities and ancestor figures, or gateways to otherworldly places (Dark 1993, 141-3; Williams 1998a, 77). They may even have been regarded in purely superstitious terms as places of efficacious good luck, in much the same way as wishing-wells are today.

Whatever the precise reason, people had returned to Avebury and were depositing objects in its silted-up ditch. Perhaps it was the very bypassing of Avebury by the road that enabled people to visit the site once more. As it was excluded from the new landscape that was forming around the axis provided by the road, any influence the earthwork and stones exerted would slowly be diluted – its power, and any taboos or restrictions emanating from that power, effectively fading. The acts of deposition may then have taken place more out of superstition than active respect. The Avebury circles were no longer seen as an *active* part of the ideological landscape but a place instead whose special status was embedded firmly in the realms of myth and folklore.

At the Longstones Cove something different appears to have been happening. One aspect of the process of 'becoming Roman' that we have yet to discuss concerns the way in which Classical and indigenous religious beliefs were negotiated and merged. A central aspect of this process of syncretism was the direct linking of deities from the Classical Roman pantheon to local analogues – a strategy termed the *interpretatio Romana* (Frere 1974, 326). This pairing of deities is as much about cultural imperialism as it is about any perceived similarities between the attributed roles of a given set of deities. In much the same way as the construction of the road imposed a new spatial order on the Avebury landscape, the name pairing of native deities with the Classical Gods was also a powerful tool of control and transformation (Webster 1995, 155-7).

At the Longstones Cove we find the boxlike structure of enormous sarsens being treated more like a shrine or sacred place. Building upon our discussion of *interpretatio*, the finds of animal bone and Roman military equipment are particularly interesting. In the absence of any evidence of a burial this suggests that they were deposited as a votive offering, perhaps even a deliberate sacrifice. Webster has noted the high proportion of name-pairings that involve the Roman God of war, Mars, reflecting the strong influence of the military upon the process of *interpretatio* (Webster 1995, 157; Jones & Mattingly 1990, 280-2). It may be no coincidence that a rare inscription found to a paired native-Roman deity on the nearby Marlborough downs linked a local God to Mars (Robinson 2001, 152). The implication is that the Cove may have functioned as a shrine for some time prior to the conquest and continued to do so, albeit with a slight adjustment of its divine focus, into the first millennium AD.

If not Avebury, then where?

As Avebury's influence waned, a powerful new cultic centre arose only 1.2 km to the south, where the road passed between Silbury Hill and the Swallowhead Springs that, along with the Winterbourne stream, comprise the source of the River Kennet (Plate XII). During the course of a pioneering series of excavations carried out in the 1860s to determine the precise relationship between Silbury and the Roman road, excavators chanced upon a large pit that they described as being filled with Roman kitchen refuse. The finds included late Roman coins (fourth century AD), pottery, iron tools, animal bone and, rather unusually, a chunk of human palate with one molar still attached (Wilkinson 1869, 117-18). It was obviously a very odd type of kitchen.

Further excavations carried out in the late nineteenth and early twentieth centuries uncovered a series of what appeared to be wells and so-called 'kitchen middens' clustered around the base of Silbury Hill and the area extending south to the springs. All of these features were packed full of Roman material including coins, jewellery, pottery, animal bones and fragments of building masonry and tile. Interestingly, the wells also included deposits of large sarsen stones, some weighing as much as half a ton and requiring special pulleys to enable them to be removed from the shafts (Brooke & Cunnington 1896, 168-9).

More recently, limited excavations and aerial photography to the east of Silbury have identified a Roman burial and a large complex of substantial, stone-built structures extending northwards along the Winterbourne Valley. Covering 22 ha, the suggestion is of a substantial Roman settlement, equivalent in size to many of the small towns of Roman Britain (Corney 1997b; 2001, 29). Finds from the excavations suggest activity was taking place at the site throughout the Roman period (Powell et al. 1996).

Taken together with the wells, we are dealing with a remarkable burst of activity in an area of the landscape that appears to be lacking in evidence for any substantial Iron Age presence (Corney 2001, 27). Hampered by the limited scale of modern excavation in the area, the proximity of the complex to the road has encouraged a number of rather functional and prosaic interpretations of this group of features. For example, it has been suggested that the site may have grown out of either a *mutatio* (a changing place for horses) or *mansio* (posting house) linked to road maintenance (Corney 1997b, 141). Another suggestion, based upon excavated evidence for grain processing, has been to postulate a large agglomeration of farm buildings (Powell et al. 1996).

The key question has to be what came first, the road or the settlement? Interpretations to date have relied upon the assumption that the road provided the stimulus for the developments around Silbury. That it provided the axis around which the settlement was subsequently laid out does not appear to be in doubt. However, following our earlier discussion of the role of the road as an active component of the Romanising process, could it be that the decision to direct the road to Silbury was not made on the chance whim of a surveyor, but instead because there was something significant already there worth incorporating into the route; something that at the time had more relevance and significance than the Avebury circles?

Excavations of the Silbury ditch revealed a deposit described as a 'Roman midden' that produced substantial amounts of pottery, a bronze bracelet and over 100 coins (Whittle 1997a, 24). This suggests that votive deposition was taking place on and around the hill during the Roman period. In addition, springs, along with other watery places, constituted a powerful foci for Iron Age shrines and artefact deposits (Bradley 1990, 179). Indeed a major Roman shrine has been suggested at the nearby spring site of Mother Anthony's Well (Corney & Walters 2001, 24). This raises the distinct possibility that rather than a service industry function related to the road, the settlement grew out of a pre-existing cult complex related to a shrine or *temenos* centred upon Silbury and the Swallowhead Springs.

The so-called 'wells' and 'kitchen middens' are integral to this interpretation. From the published account of the excavation of one of the former, it is clear that the 8 m deep shaft functioned as a well for a very short time prior to being deliberately filled up (Brooke & Cunnington 1896, 170). What is of particular interest is not so much the features themselves, but the ways in which they were filled. The original excavators interpreted the fills as a mass of undifferentiated rubbish and destruction debris originating from middening activity and the subsequent demolition of nearby buildings. It is difficult from the published accounts to reconstruct the precise contexts of many of the finds. To quote Brooke, 'from this point downwards relics came up in every bucket' (1910, 374). However, where details are given the suggestion is that far from being an undifferentiated mass, there was a clear structure to the deposits. For example, Brooke and Cunnington appear to have encountered discrete groups of objects at different depths in the fill of the particular well they excavated. These included a cluster of bronze objects, a group of antler tools and frequent layers of often large sarsen blocks. Similar structures have been noted on other Roman sites, perhaps most spectacularly the fort of Newstead in the Scottish borders (Clarke 1997). Here we have examples of functioning wells, or at least shafts that penetrated down to the water table, that were subsequently filled through a series of deliberate acts of ritual deposition taking place over an appreciable period of time (ibid., 75; Clarke 2000). Taken together, the finds from the so-called 'wells' and pits, and their distribution around the base of Silbury Hill and the Swallowhead, suggests that they may be better thought of as ritual shafts rather than decommissioned domestic structures.

Avebury bypassed

As the stone circles and earthworks slipped into the background, a thriving cult complex grew up around the base of Silbury Hill. Avebury had been effectively bypassed. It had little role to play in the changing social landscapes that were taking shape around it. No longer active, Avebury became a place of superstition and mystery, linked to a mythical or supernatural world whose everyday efficacy had waned. Neither forgotten nor shunned, people began to once again visit Avebury, making small votive deposits but perhaps more in the hope of soliciting good luck than the direct intervention of powerful ancestral or mythical entities.

6. *Avreberie juxta Waledich*

Avebury was quite literally bypassed during the Roman period, but, supported by bodies of myth and tradition, it still exerted some potency as a place of superstition and reverence. Things were about to change. Set within a complex series of cultural, political, economic and religious changes, the six hundred or so years between the 'official' end of Roman Britain in AD 410 and the Norman invasion witnessed a gradual but fundamental transformation in attitudes to the prehistoric monument complex. In broad terms, this might be styled as a secularisation of Avebury.

For over three thousand years the henge and its attendant megalithic components were regarded variously as sacred, special or potent places. From the earlier Bronze Age onwards, occupation of the surrounding landscape was organised in such a way that settlement and agriculture were kept largely away from the henge, only slowly encroaching during the Roman period, and then kept behind the visual cover provided by Waden Hill (Powell et al. 1996). We have argued that such respect may have been engendered by attitudes towards the megaliths themselves, rather than the henge as a totality, simply because other prehistoric earthworks in the Avebury environs were not afforded the same degree of 'distance'.

However, by the tenth century a thriving settlement, perhaps even a small urban centre, had developed immediately outside the western entrance of the henge (Reynolds 2001a, 28-30). The bank and ditch had acquired a new identity as *waledich* – the 'ditch of the Britons' – a name that while implying a connection with the 'past' or 'ancestors', need not evoke any sense of great antiquity or an association with the sacred (Pollard & Reynolds 2002, 203). The stones themselves may have been disregarded, their presence perhaps ascribed to 'natural' rather than human agency.

Early Anglo-Saxon Avebury: history or prehistory?

It is important to begin with a consideration of the background to this process. Traditionally accounts have talked of a collapse of Roman lifestyles after the withdrawal of the legions in AD 410, followed by numerous barbarian attacks and the settlement by Saxon invaders of what would eventually become England. These narratives often place great reliance on the veracity of events recorded in the *Anglo-Saxon Chronicle*. In the context of the broader Avebury region, the *Chronicle* describes the energetic activities of two warlords, Ceawlin and Cynric, who led battles against the British at *Beranbyrg* (Barbury) in 556 and Woden's Barrow (Adam's Grave) in 592, when Ceawlin was driven out. Avebury lies in between: the hillfort of Barbury is 7 km north-east, and Adam's Grave 6 km to the south. Such events might be taken at face-value as part of the expansion of Anglo-Saxon kingdoms in southern Wessex and the Thames Valley (Eagles 1994, 27), but can they be treated as reliable historical 'facts'?

Yorke has recently outlined the problems with the *Chronicle* as an historical source (1995, 32-4). Its compilation began in the later ninth century, some three hundred years after the events described here. She notes that it is based on oral accounts that often follow a mythic formula, and were susceptible to embellishment or even a degree of invention by later elites as part of a process of creating a 'suitable' past. They are in effect pseudo-historical records, or 'faction': a mix of fact and fiction (ibid.). There is also an important material dimension to these stories. The association of the two battles of Ceawlin and Cynric with prehistoric monuments, whether reflecting reality or not, is perhaps telling of a process by which features in the landscape were continually re-appropriated, historicised and brought into the contemporary political domain (Gosden & Lock 1998; Bradley 2002) – a theme that we return to repeatedly within this book.

It is perhaps best to acknowledge the limitations of these supposedly historical sources, and realise that for the early Anglo-Saxon period (*c*. AD 400-650) we are still dealing with a kind of prehistory, or at best a watered-down 'proto-history' (Arnold 1997). Only during the middle (AD 650-850) and late (AD 850-1100) Anglo-Saxon periods might developments at Avebury be broadly linked to historical events, and then with a degree of caution. In fact, the earliest documentary reference to Avebury comes at the very end of the period with the Domesday Book record of the church:

> Rainbald the priest holds the church of AVREBERIE to which belongs 2 hides. It is worth 40s.

This in itself tells us comparatively little, and makes no reference to the settlement associated with the church. It is for this reason that so much of our knowledge of Anglo-Saxon Avebury, and the place of the henge within this, must derive from archaeological evidence alone (Pollard & Reynolds 2002, ch. 6).

'Romans' and 'Saxons': events and ethnicities

So what does archaeology tell us of events during the fifth and sixth centuries? Across much of southern Britain urban life underwent a dramatic decline after AD 410, if not before, precipitated by processes of economic collapse and political fragmentation. In the broader Avebury region this process may have been slower than elsewhere, since a number of rural settlements and perhaps even the small town of Cunetio show signs of continuing to function well into the fifth century. Among the local rural sites with evidence of such late Roman activity are the Silbury settlement (Powell et al. 1996: 57) and that on Overton Down to the east (Fowler 2000). Fifth-century Saxon settlements, cemeteries and artefacts are absent from the region, being largely confined to the south and east of Wiltshire (Eagles 1994); leading to a suggestion that a distinct Romano-British identity may have been retained by communities in the wider Avebury region during this time. Further evidence may come from the concentration of British place-names in the region (Eagles 2001) and finds of 'late Celtic' metalwork from sites such as Oldbury Castle and the River Kennet near Waden Hill (Pollard & Reynolds 2002, 186-7).

It is only during the sixth century that an extension of Anglo-Saxon settlement across the north of the county might be charted from archaeological evidence. Such expansion could have been accompanied by conflict, or at least the threat of it. The remarkable linear earthwork known as Wansdyke, which runs along the crest of the downland ridge bordering the Vale of Pewsey several kilometres to the south of Avebury, may have acted as a temporary boundary between expanding nascent Anglo-Saxon communities and British groups to the north. However, the dating and political context of Wansdyke remain poorly understood: Eagles (1994) and Fowler (2001) opt for a sub-Roman context, while Reynolds considers a late date somewhere in the late seventh to early ninth centuries, when the area was border land between Wessex and Mercia (Pollard & Reynolds 2002, 187).

But what does talk of 'Romans', 'Britons' and 'Saxons' really mean? Here we are entering difficult territory. There are problems in the ascription of ethnic identities to post-Roman communities, not least because of the circular logic in which distinct styles of material culture are given ethnic labels and these in turn are used as identity markers for their makers and users. This is a legacy of an earlier culture-historical approach in which styles of artefact, settlement and burial were seen as essential components in the constitution of particular cultural identities (Jones 1997). Put simply, distinct styles of object were seen to equate with distinct groups of people. Thus fifth-century Jutish material culture from along the south coast around the Solent became evidence for the arrival and settlement of Jutish communities (Cunliffe 1993, 278). This may be a correct interpretation, but it is just one of a range of possibilities. It is vital to remember that while material culture can be employed to express an identity, possession of 'Anglo-Saxon' objects no more made someone 'Anglo-Saxon' than possession of 'Roman' things made someone 'Roman'. People have the inventive capacity to adopt alien and exotic elements of material culture and recontextualise them in terms of their own cultural systems of value.

In fact we are dealing with a highly complex period of cultural change and re-styling, in which varied local or context-specific identities may have existed which do not correspond neatly with commonly used labels such as 'British' or 'Anglo-Saxon'. And it must be realised that while identities may have changed, populations need not. There is certainly no need to see the arrival of new groups of people into the region supplanting those already resident. With these observations in mind, we should point out that here 'Anglo-Saxon' is used in much the same way as 'Neolithic' or 'Roman' – largely denoting a particular chronological horizon, and not carrying any presumptions about certain kinds of ethnic identity.

The beginnings of Avebury village

In the centuries following AD 500 occupation slowly shifted northwards along the edge of the Winterbourne towards the henge, and what may originally have begun as an off-shoot from the Roman settlement around Silbury Hill eventually became the village of Avebury. Perhaps the area of the Silbury settlement had become tainted by association with ways considered old and unsavoury, or the ruins of buildings thought of as the abodes of ghosts. Whatever the case, values ascribed to places were changing, and it is conceivable the Roman settlement was now regarded with more superstition than were the remains of the henge (Fig. 12A).

The evidence for early Anglo-Saxon settlement in this area is good, but it is frustratingly under-explored and what has been recovered remains largely unpublished. Much of what is known derives from a series of rescue excavations undertaken between 1976 and 1988 in the Glebe Field car park, two hundred metres to the south-west of the henge (Pollard & Reynolds 2002, 192-8; Last 2002). The first of these, at the southern end of the car park, was directed by the husband and wife team of Faith and Lance Vatcher, then curators of the Alexander Keiller Museum. Within a relatively small area, they revealed the remains of at least one building (termed 'Hut A'), a possible second structure ('Hut B') and a kidney-shaped pit. A further building was excavated immediately to the east of these during 1988, and a fourth during work by Wessex Archaeology, 90 m to the north, in 1985 (ibid.).

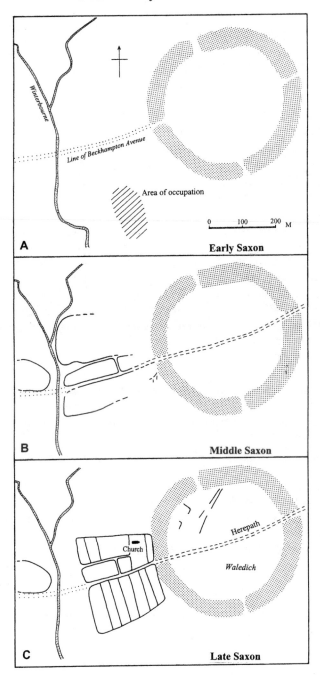

12. Saxon Avebury (A – Early Saxon; B – Middle Saxon; C – Late Saxon).

Variously termed Grubenhäuser, sunken-floored or sunken-featured buildings (SFBs), these structures are highly distinctive, comprising shallow rectangular pits, usually with post settings at either end of their long axes. There is debate over how such structures should be reconstructed, and particularly the question of whether or not they had suspended wooden floors (e.g. West 1985; Hamerow 1993). Lines of stake-holes marking internal fittings or partitions in the base of 'Hut A' show that the pit base of this structure at least acted as a floor surface. It is not uncommon to find evidence of SFBs being used as receptacles for the deposition of refuse once they had gone out of use (Tipper 2000). Conforming to pattern, the pit fills of three of the Avebury SFBs included rich deposits of refuse which included metalwork, organic-tempered pottery and animal bone (mostly sheep and cattle).

Despite the results of the Glebe Field excavations, we know little about the extent and status of the early Anglo-Saxon settlement at Avebury. Did it comprise a collection of small farmsteads, or might it have been a village? Did it consist solely of SFBs, or were there associated timber halls?

Educated guesses at the answers to these questions might be made on the basis of analogy and the density of features. So, for example, a recently excavated settlement at Collingbourne Ducis in the east of Wiltshire included at least ten SFBs and one possible post-built hall extending across a similar sized area (Pine 2001). Here though, the buildings were quite dispersed, whereas the success rate in locating SFBs through small excavations at the Glebe Field site implies a high density. If their distribution is even, there might be a many as 20 or 30 SFBs within this area.

In response to the second question, associated post-built timber halls could exist, in which case we might see the SFBs as ancillary structures and the halls as residences. Their absence to date could reflect the limited extent of excavation, spatial zonation within the settlement or, simply, their non-existence. We do not know where the limits of the settlement lie, but sherds of organic-tempered pottery from meadows adjacent to the Winterbourne, almost 200 m to the north-east, are possibly of early Anglo-Saxon date (Evans et al. 1993, 154). Overall, the indications are of an extensive and sizeable settlement running north-south along the terrace fronting the stream. It is worth noting that at the time, water management of the Winterbourne floodplain would have readily permitted settlement and agriculture along the valley floor (Powell et al. 1996, 59).

However, before images of a thriving and bustling early Anglo-Saxon settlement are conjured up, it should be stressed that not all these structures will have been in contemporary use. The active use-life of any individual building was likely to have been in the order of two or three decades at most, with structures going through regular cycles of construction, use and abandonment. SFBs were rarely re-built on the same spot, so over an extended period of time the cumulative pattern is one of numerous structures – the size of a settlement is as much a product of longevity as it is of scale. It is this process of building abandonment and rebuilding on adjacent areas that results in the kind of settlement drift seen at Mucking in Essex (Hamerow 1993), and which is perhaps applicable at Avebury.

Middle and late Saxon *Avreberie*

Not all early Anglo-Saxon settlements were successful, but at Avebury life apparently continued uninterrupted. During the middle and late Anglo-Saxon period (*c.* 650-1000) there was a steady consolidation of the village to the west of the henge, leading to the establishment of a pattern of streets and land divisions that, in places, continues to the present day. These relatively quiet developments are set against some momentous events in the wider region – the emergence and consolidation of the kingdom of Wessex, the conversion to Christianity, the re-establishment of urban centres and centralised systems of political authority, and the Viking raids of the ninth century (Cunliffe 1993, 297-306; Yorke 1995, 107-12). All had some impact on Avebury and the surrounding landscape. There are failed attempts at developing the settlement as a small town; a church is built adjacent to the bank of the henge; and a late Anglo-Saxon fortification is created on the summit of Silbury Hill. All contribute to the unique quality of Avebury's Anglo-Saxon archaeology, constituting the only location in Wiltshire with both excavated and up-standing structural remains of an Anglo-Saxon settlement (Pollard & Reynolds 2002: 185).

Through a detailed study of the extant earthworks and excavated evidence, Reynolds has been able to postulate a complex developmental sequence for middle and late Saxon Avebury (ibid., 198-210). From the beginning this was a large settlement, formed of a series of curvilinear enclosures around an elliptical street plan (Fig. 12B). In this respect it was similar to other large middle Anglo-Saxon settlements in the region, such as Tilshead and Ramsbury (ibid., 201). The enclosures extended east-west over a distance of *c.* 400 m, from the western entrance of the henge to the Winterbourne. Another oval enclosure on the west bank of the stream, within which Truslow Manor now sits, could very well be an extension of this complex. What remains unclear is the density of occupation within these enclosures, though one large-scale excavation by the Vatchers in the grounds of Avebury School, immediately to the south-west of the western henge entrance, revealed a dense pattern of boundary ditches, fencelines, pits and three rectangular timber structures (ibid., 198-202). Of post-trench construction, two of the buildings were substantial affairs, around

9 m long with internal sub-dividing walls. One of the pits contained a large deposit of charred grain (mostly wheat, with some barley and weed seeds) that produced a calibrated radiocarbon date of AD 660-1020 (ibid., 199). An almost identical date was obtained from cattle bone in association with sherds of Anglo-Saxon pottery from excavations adjacent to the Winterbourne (Evans et al. 1993, 154), and demonstrates the spread of occupation traces close to the stream.

Avebury prospered, and by the late Anglo-Saxon period the settlement may even have achieved the status of a small defended town or *burh* (Reynolds 2001b) (Fig. 12C). Based upon surviving earthwork detail and the fossilised layout of individual property boundaries, Reynolds has argued that the settlement was now contained within a substantial sub-rectangular enclosure, *c.* 300 by 270 m in extent, abutting the western side of the henge and having as its axis the line of the current High Street (ibid.). There are some problems with Reynolds' projected eastern edge of the *burh* – that portion which abuts the western edge of the henge – in that it extends across sections of the henge bank that were only levelled in the later seventeenth century (Ucko et al. 1991, 170-1). This, however, is a matter of a detail, and does not affect the overall validity of his interpretation.

The identification of Avebury as a *burh* is given further support both by the place-name itself, which may be translated as the 'fortified place by the Avon (water or stream)' (Reynolds 2001b, 30), and by the substantial nature of the church located in its north-east corner. To date, the best evidence comes from the School Site, where late Saxon ditched boundaries were observed to run perpendicular to the present High Street, a kind of planning that is not normally associated with rural settlements (Pollard & Reynolds 2002, 206). The *burh* was perhaps created in the late ninth or early tenth century, partly in response to the threat of Viking attack, but Avebury ultimately failed as an urban centre with the rise of the nearby towns of Calne and Marlborough (Reynolds 2001a, 29). Again, the relative absence of archaeological investigation within this area makes it difficult to understand what was going on within the settlement.

The conversion of Wessex to Christianity during the mid-seventh century resulted in a new religious order, and the creation at Avebury of a church to serve the growing settlement. In much the same way as the henge three thousand years before it, the church acted as a medium through which communal religious practice was institutionalised and fixed within a certain locale. Whether a timber church was constructed at Avebury in the decades immediately following the conversion is uncertain. An early church is nonetheless indicated by elements of ninth-century sculpture, including part of a cross shaft or coffin lid, re-used within the fabric of the later stone church of St James (Pollard & Reynolds 2002, 235).

The nave of the latter is of late Anglo-Saxon date, probably tenth-century, and clearly of 'some pretensions' (Jope 1999, 61). With a nave over 12 m long and nearly 7 m wide this was a substantial building, and one probably of minster status (ibid.).

Waledich

By the late Anglo-Saxon period there are two distinct elements to the settlement: the cluster of houses, property boundaries and the church within the *burh*, known as *Avreberie*; and the earthworks of the henge, referred to as *waledich*, or the ditch of the Britons (Pollard & Reynolds 2002, 203-4). So far we have concentrated on developments between the western entrance of the henge and the Winterbourne, but are there any indications of Anglo-Saxon activity within the henge itself, and if so what do these tell us of contemporary understandings of and attitudes to the remains of the prehistoric monument?

The extensive excavations conducted by Keiller inside the henge produced a small assemblage of late Anglo-Saxon pottery (Jope 1999, 67), added to which are a few sherds of organic- or chaff-tempered pottery from the upper fills of the ditch (Gray 1935). While not necessarily an indication of settlement itself (i.e. the presence of dwellings), this still demonstrates activity of sorts. The bulk of the pottery came from the south-west and north-west sectors, and it might therefore indicate a late Saxon 'spill' into the western part of the interior.

While Keiller's excavations did not reveal any Anglo-Saxon features in this area, a network of ditches discovered through recent geophysical survey in the north-western quadrant may be of this date (Bewley et al. 1996). At least two of these, running diagonally from the edge of the putative oval barrow described in Chapter 2 and into the north-eastern quadrant, pre-date the Swindon road and the laying-out of property boundaries during the medieval period. The Swindon road itself is likely to be later than a putative late Saxon drove road running from Berwick Bassett north of Avebury (Pollard & Reynolds 2002, 226), though was probably well established by the high middle ages. In the same area of the interior, four lengths of angled ditch, apparently forming the sides of small enclosures (Bewley et al. 1996, fig. 3), also fit uneasily into the medieval and later sub-division of the henge interior, and so might be accommodated in the context of late Anglo-Saxon extra-mural settlement.

There is one further feature of critical importance in the context of both the late Anglo-Saxon settlement and the medieval and post-medieval development of Avebury village. This is the course of the present High Street and Green Street, running from the Marlborough Downs, into the henge via the eastern entrance and exiting through the western. By the seventeenth century a coach road on the route from London to Bath, it has its origins during the Anglo-Saxon period as a *herepath* or army road, running from Marlborough, through the *burh* at Avebury and on to Yatesbury (Pollard & Reynolds 2002, 207).

Taken together, the presence of a major route-way, pottery finds and a network of possible boundary ditches, produce a picture of activity within the henge very different to that seen throughout the previous two millennia. The Avebury henge was beginning to look like a busy and well frequented place, and we must ask whether it had finally lost its potency as a place of superstition and awe.

Anglo-Saxon attitudes

How did the late Anglo-Saxon community of Avebury perceive the remains of the prehistoric monument complex? In his discussion of Avebury church, Burl argues that 'it was put up just outside the west entrance [of the henge] as if recognising that Christianity was as yet too feeble to destroy the alien and evil strength of the stone circles inside' (Burl 1979, 33). The juxtaposition of church and henge is certainly an interesting one – proximate but retaining a certain distance – and might be read as reflecting the pitting of a new faith against old and powerful beliefs. Viewed as the 'Christianisation' of a pagan site, analogy might be drawn with the siting of a Norman church inside a henge monument at Knowlton, Dorset, and the construction of another adjacent to a massive menhir at Rudston in East Yorkshire.

Burl's interpretation ascribes a lingering potency to the megaliths, but we must remember that there is nothing inherent within the stones themselves that leads to such a view of their continuing 'power' or significance. They are, after all, just stones; and it is the attitudes towards and practices associated with them that are important, and these readily changed from one cultural context to the next. In fact, we have already hinted that there is good reason to take a counter-view, and argue that the prehistoric megalithic settings were not intimately linked in the minds of the Anglo-Saxon inhabitants of Avebury to any religious, sacred or otherworldly dimension. The sarsens might instead have been perceived as an entirely 'natural' phenomenon (Pollard & Reynolds 2002, 192).

Semple (1998, 115) has made the pertinent observation that prehistoric stone monuments evoked little response from Anglo-Saxon communities, in terms of renewed ritual or 'special' activity. There are, as ever, exceptions to this pattern, seen in the creation of a cemetery around a small stone circle at Yeavering, Northumberland (Hope-Taylor 1977), and the choice of Stonehenge for the burial of a man subject to judicial execution by decapitation (Pitts et al. 2002). However, in the latter case the appropriation of the prehistoric monument for such a burial was probably driven by its position on or close to a territorial boundary, rather than any particular associations held by the stones (ibid., 143). In contrast to megalithic settings, earlier earthworks were commonly subject to re-use and given mythic associations (Semple 1998). Prehistoric barrows in particular were frequently re-used for burial during the early Anglo-Saxon period, a process 'important for construction and negotiation of origin myths, identities and social structures' (Williams 1998b). In the immediate Avebury region pagan Saxon burials have been found inserted in Bronze Age barrows on Overton Hill to the south-east of the henge (Eagles 1986).

Attitudes changed markedly in the post-Conversion world of the middle and late Anglo-Saxon periods, when barrows took on associations with varied supernatural entities, some rather unpleasant (Semple 1998). This was perhaps more a response to their immediate pre-Conversion employment for pagan burials than any sense of their belonging to a 'deep time' or alien cultural context. In other situations earlier monuments served as material props in the establishment of myths and histories used to legitimate emerging elites, the complex at Yeavering again providing an example, where a royal centre was established during the seventh century (Bradley 1993, 117-19).

Turning again to the Avebury landscape, we can see that the presence of earlier monuments evoked varied responses during the late Anglo-Saxon period, most of which appear pragmatic to our understanding at least. The parish boundary utilised many prehistoric features as key landmarks, including the barrow cemeteries on Windmill Hill and Overton Hill, part of the West Kennet palisaded enclosures, and a section of the Roman road (Pollard & Reynolds 2002, 220-3). Late Anglo-Saxon fortification of Silbury Hill was perhaps undertaken in response to Viking threats (Whittle 1997a, 22). There are traces of a palisade around the summit, late Saxon sherds, nails and a farthing of Ethelred II (ibid.). Stukeley records the discovery during tree planting in 1723 of human bones, antlers, an iron knife and an elaborate horse-bit on the top of Silbury (Stukeley 1743, 41-2). One interpretation is of a high-status Viking burial, although Reynolds suggests caution and argues that the horse-bit might equally relate to the late Saxon fortification (Pollard & Reynolds 2002, 227).

By this stage the *herepath* bisected the Avebury henge, and extra-mural settlement may well have developed immediately inside the western entrance. No attempt was made at removing or concealing the stones, and apart from the occasional fallen sarsen, the megalithic settings must have appeared more or less intact. Most striking and telling of all is the relationship between the eastern end of the Beckhampton Avenue and the settlement within the *burh*. Here the stones of the avenue delineated the

main road through the settlement, with both standing and fallen megaliths being incorporated into individual property boundaries – the
settlement took the remains of the avenue as its axis, as it still does today.
In the face of such an intimate relationship between stones and settlement, it is difficult to sustain the notion that great superstition was still
attached to the megalithic settings, or that they were imbued in the minds
of the late Anglo-Saxon residents of Avebury with a lingering 'alien and
evil strength'. As for the church, its position probably has more to do with
proximity to the settlement and the *burh* enclosure than it does to the
earthworks and stones of the henge.

By the eve of the Norman conquest a stable and reasonably substantial
settlement had developed at Avebury. While not a dramatic and unusual
development in its own right, it does nonetheless mark a significant
alteration in attitudes to the remains of the henge. The earthwork was
ascribed an historical significance, as the 'ditch of the Britons', and may
well have been accommodated into local understandings of the landscape
through stories and myths relating to those perceived to have created it.
However, with no sense of a deep history, or for that matter a 'prehistory',
Avebury was by this stage regarded as no different from the remains of,
say, an Iron Age hillfort, albeit one containing stones. Later Anglo-Saxon
communities, observing stones elsewhere in the landscape, particularly as
trails in the valley bottoms, need have made no distinction between the
megaliths of the henge and other, naturally occurring, sarsens. All in all,
it is difficult to perceive any lingering 'sanctity' attached to the henge,
instead just a sense of it belonging to the past, albeit not necessarily a very
remote one.

7. Priests and Peasants

By the time of the Norman Conquest Avebury was a substantial settlement covering an extensive area from the Winterbourne to the western edge of the henge. Yet the stones and earthworks of the latter remained relatively unmolested save the subtle, inexorable ravages of time and the elements. Much was to change during the following centuries as the village expanded further eastwards, along the former *herepath* road and into the very heart of the henge. By the thirteenth century, garden plots and fields were being laid out within the earthwork and selected areas were brought under cultivation. More interestingly, from the point of view of our account, the stones once again became a focus for activity, albeit of a kind that was very different to that which had gone before. Rather than providing the focus for worship or artefact deposition, or being simply ignored, they were progressively removed from the landscape as, one by one, they were toppled and buried.

The village of Avebury

Discussions of medieval Avebury have tended to dwell upon what we might think of as the more traditional concerns of history. In so doing, they have followed a well-trodden path from Domesday to the first antiquarian note of the site – an observation by John Leland in 1540 concerning 'camps and sepultures of men of warre' (Leland 1907-10, v, 81) – charting significant changes of estate and land ownership along the way.

For example, our first reference to Avebury comes with the Domesday Survey of 1086, where the church is listed as being held by Rainbald the priest, a man who is recorded as holding some 16 churches and numerous other properties at this time. The church held by Rainbald was extensively modified (Freeman 1983, 101), building upon and expanding the existing Saxon structure.

Although our first mention of Avebury is concerned explicitly with the church, documents from the twelfth century suggest that Avebury was at this time part of a considerable royal estate (Jope 1999, 61). This included a manor, which in 1114 was granted by Henry I's chamberlain to an alien priory, the Benedictine Abbey of St. George-de-Boscherville, near Rouen (ibid.). The cell that was established at Avebury was small and appears to have been largely administrative in nature, overseeing and managing the profits generated by the estates held by the Norman Abbey in England. The number of alien monks in Avebury was never large, records suggesting that it fluctuated between one and four. Although this Benedictine cell was granted a chapel sometime during, or after, 1162, no parishioner was allowed to attend the services, the religious needs of the village (and tithes extracted from the parishioners) continuing to be administered by the parish church (Freeman 1983, 102). The church itself had remained in the hands of Rainbald until his death, when it passed to Roger, Bishop of Salisbury, reverting upon his death in 1139 to Cirencester Abbey.

From the early fourteenth century the abbot of Cirencester had a manor house near the circle (ibid., 93) and a further manor, controlling a second Cirencester estate, also existed at Avebury Truslow. The alien house remained in Avebury until 1378 when such houses were suppressed and the monks expelled. In 1411 the manor was granted to a college of chantry priests at Fotheringay in Northamptonshire before being conveyed to the Crown following the dissolution in 1538 (Jope 1999, 64).

Although the respective roles of the two abbeys in the spiritual and economic affairs of the inhabitants of Avebury seem to have been clearly prescribed, tensions appear to have run high in the village. For a group whose sole luxury was listed in 1324 as a chess set, the small group of Benedictine monks ensconced in Avebury Manor appear to have spent an eventful 260 or so years in the village, pawns in a much bigger game, no doubt linked to the fluctuating relations that existed between France and England during the course of the thirteenth and fourteenth centuries. Evidence for this comes from the high number of disputes between the two abbeys listed in the documentary records. These ranged from charges being levelled regarding the collection of tithes and the role of the Benedictine chapel in the spiritual life of the parish, to the apparent jailing of the first Benedictine Prior of Avebury in 1249 on a charge of murder (Kirby 1956, 392-3).

Documentary sources also provide us with a series of colourful, if rather tantalising, glimpses of the social organisation of the village. For example, we know that any lawbreakers could expect robust punishment as records from 1235 list a tumbrel and gallows present in the village, and in 1281 we know that the abbot of Cirencester, sometimes resident of the village, claimed the right to a view of frankpledge at Avebury, a system by which each member of a tithing was responsible for the good behaviour of every other. In 1360 these viewings were held twice a year at Michaelmas and Hocktide (Freeman 1983, 101).

However, historical records provide at best a partial account of medieval Avebury, and so extra detail must also be sought in existing archaeological evidence. This said, while traces of medieval settlement in

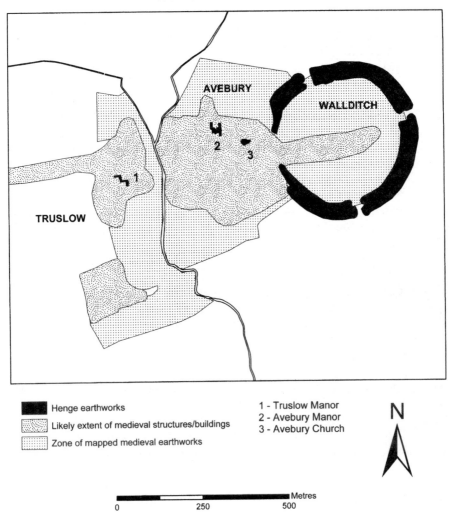

AVEBURY

WALLDITCH

TRUSLOW

Henge earthworks

Likely extent of medieval structures/buildings

Zone of mapped medieval earthworks

1 - Truslow Manor
2 - Avebury Manor
3 - Avebury Church

N

Metres

0   250   500

13. Medieval Avebury.

and around the henge are certainly extensive, they remain frustratingly under-explored.

An earthwork survey by the former Royal Commission on Historical Monuments (England) provides the clearest record of the extent of medieval and early post-medieval settlement, with the earthworks of house platforms, tracks and boundary ditches being seen to extend over a considerable area on either side of the Winterbourne, effectively covering the area between present-day Avebury and Avebury Truslow (Fig. 13). The indications are of a sprawling settlement with several foci, each perhaps linked to different manorial estates. This is certainly more than the 'ordinary' village of some 30 families and a total population of around 100 suggested by Jope (1999, 65).

Excavations outside the henge, at the Vatcher's School site and in the southern car park, have produced later medieval material (Pollard & Reynolds 2002, 247) and further evidence of settlement has come from test pits and a sewer pipe trench in Butler's Field, adjacent to the Winter-bourne. These revealed pits, trenches, ditches and building foundations, along with substantial amounts of pottery and animal bone – the normal debris of settlement (Evans et al. 1993, 153-4; Powell et al. 1996, 59-65). Dated by the pottery to the mid-twelfth to late thirteenth centuries, these features indicate a short-lived expansion of settlement on to the dry valley floor during this period. Further evidence of medieval activity undoubt-edly lies under the present village both inside and outside the henge.

Cultivating Avebury

One of the key issues that this raises concerns the relationship between the medieval village and the remains of the henge and its associated megalithic settings. Historical records are stubbornly silent on this, and again we must turn to the archaeology, particularly the fieldwork under-taken by Gray and Keiller in the first half of the twentieth century, which comprise the only major excavations to have taken place within the henge (Gray 1935, Smith 1965). The medieval material recovered from their work sheds fascinating light upon the relationship between henge and village during the eleventh to fourteenth centuries.

Medieval pottery was everywhere. Although it gets little more than a passing mention in Gray's account of his excavations through the earth-work, it is at least noted, appearing in a number of his sections through the ditch. For example, in cutting I, to the west of the southern entrance, the upper 1.4 m of the ditch silts were found to contain Norman and medieval pottery. In his only excavation within the interior of the monument, diggings around one of the prostrate stones of the southern inner circle produced sufficient amounts of pottery for Gray to speculate as to whether a medieval dwelling had once been built against the stone (Gray 1935, 132).

We have more information from the extensive campaign of excavations undertaken by Keiller, who found considerable quantities of medieval pottery spread across the western sector of the monument. To his credit, and reflecting unusual practice for the time, Keiller retained selected finds of medieval pottery and commissioned a detailed report on them. The picture provided by this material, spanning the eleventh to early four-teenth centuries, is of an 'entirely appropriate' assemblage for a peasant rural community: bowls, dishes, cooking pots, pans and pitchers in mainly

I. Avebury from the air looking north-east.

II. Excavations at the end of the Beckhampton Avenue in 2000.

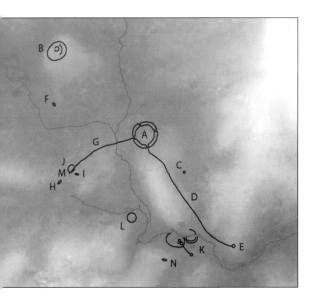

A - Avebury
B - Windmill Hill
C - Falkner's Circle
D - West Kennet Avenue
E - The Sanctuary
F - Horslip Long Mound
G - Beckhampton Avenue
H - Longstones Long Mound
I - South Street Long Mound
J - Beckhampton Enclosure
K - West Kennet Palisade Enclosures
L - Silbury Hill
M - Longstones Cove
N - West Kennet Long Mound

0   2 km

III. Components of the prehistoric monument complex around Avebury.

IV. Natural sarsen field at Lockeridge, to the south-east of Avebury.

V. The primary bank of the henge as exposed in the 1969 excavations at the Avebury School site. The figures in the photograph are Faith and Lance Vatcher, then curators of the Alexander Keiller Museum.

VI. (*left*) The eastern terminal of the ditch at the southern entrance under excavation.

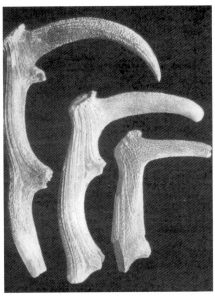

VII. (*above*) Antler picks from the base and primary fills of the ditch recovered during the Gray excavations.

VIII. In situ sarsen packing.

IX. The Avebury Cove from the east.

X. Stones of the outer circle flanking the southern entrance. The stump of the Ring Stone is visible in the foreground.

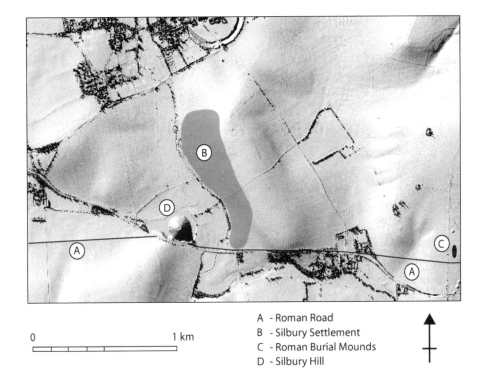

XI. Roman Avebury (above: features to the south of the henge; below: a bronze brooch from the henge ditch and a Roman spearhead from the Longstones Cove).

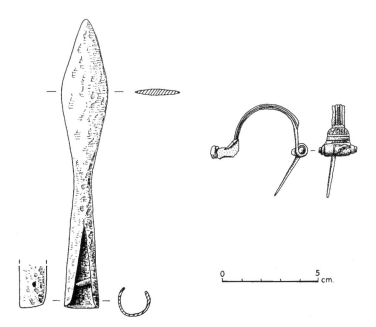

0   5
                      cm.

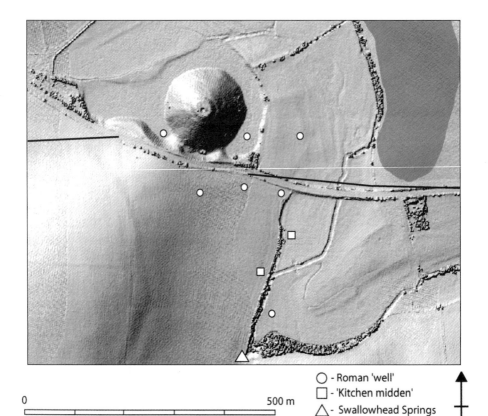

O - Roman 'well'
□ - 'Kitchen midden'
△ - Swallowhead Springs

0   500 m

XII. Roman complex around Silbury.

XIII. Excavation of the possible medieval building and Obelisk destruction features from the north-west.

XIV. Buried megalith on the line of the Beckhampton Avenue.

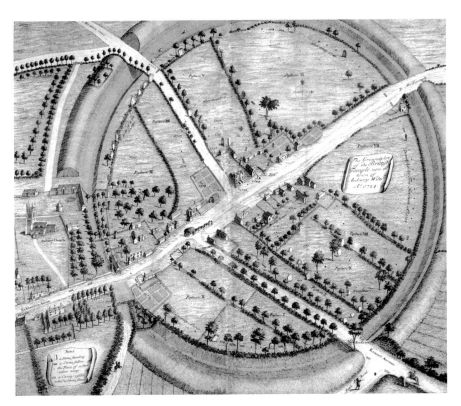

XV. Stukeley's 'Groundplot of the Brittish Temple' at Avebury.

XVI. Early post-medieval stone destruction pit under excavation on the line of the Beckhampton Avenue. Note the spread of fractured sarsen and charcoal lining the base.

XVII. The massive stone destruction pit of the north-western stone of the Longstones Cove.

XVIII. Mrs and Master Gray at Avebury.

XIX. Gray's unexpected discovery. The sarsen-ringed burial of an adult female (thought erroneously by Gray to be a dwarf) – see also Fig. 15.

XX. General view of Gray's excavation of the ditch near the southern entrance.

XXI. The West Kennet Avenue (above: prior to Keiller's 1934-5 excavations; below: the restored section of the Avenue today).

XXII. Alexander Keiller's excavations at Avebury (above: a buried stone under excavation; below: re-erecting a megalith).

XXIII. The early non-conformist chapel at Avebury, with stones of the linear setting within the southern circle visible in the foreground.

XXIV. Reconstructing Avebury. The demolition of a cottage during Keiller's campaign of work within the henge.

local wares, the majority coming from within a 32 km radius around the village, interspersed with vessels from as far afield as Buckinghamshire and Gloucester. The occurrence of fragments of fineware jugs with French parallels may be due to the presence of the small alien priory, and perhaps even derived from the prior's table (Jope 1999).

Much of the medieval pottery came from the topsoil. The presence of sherds from the same vessel at a variety of dispersed locations across the interior of the site suggests that rather than being accidentally dropped or deliberately buried, pottery was entering the topsoil through a much more haphazard process (Jope 1999, 68-9). The most likely explanation is that it results from manuring, whereby organic rubbish held in household midden heaps was spread across cultivated areas to increase soil fertility. Any non-organic rubbish (such as broken pottery) also present in the midden would be carried along and spread with the fertiliser. As manuring is reserved for field and garden plots, the conclusion that can be drawn from this observed spread of material is that much of the interior of the monument was cultivated in some way during the eleventh to fourteenth centuries. The area may even have been in part ploughed, but the presence of very large pieces of pottery suggest that it had not witnessed repeated episodes of ploughing as this would have quickly broken up these larger fragments. We have deliberately said *partly* ploughed as this pottery spread is far from uniform across the interior of the monument and differs in its precise composition. The pottery recovered from the areas excavated by Keiller contained some large, fresh sherds suggesting non-intensive or rare episodes of ploughing or cultivation. This can be contrasted with the worn and abraded sherds found in a small excavation undertaken in 1982 in the south-west of the interior, some 40 m east of the western entrance. Here cultivation may have been more intensive or prolonged (Harrington & Denham 1986, 221). In complete contrast, limited excavations in the north-eastern quadrant of the henge during the 1960s failed to recover any evidence of medieval manuring (Piggott 1964); and very few medieval sherds came from the 2003 excavations at the Cove, within the same quadrant. What the distribution and character of the topsoil pottery finds suggests is a pattern of small cultivated plots interspersed with areas of pasture – in effect a patchwork.

We know that by the eighteenth century the interior of the henge comprised a complex pattern of hedgelines and fences defining a series of pastures and orchards. Evidence for this comes from a 1794 Inclosure map, the detailed drawings and plans of the site produced in the 1720s by William Stukeley (Ucko et al. 1991, pls 34-44, 47), and from archaeological evidence. Stukeley's drawings provide an incredibly detailed view of the village and henge at this time. An excellent example is his 1722 drawing of the stones of the southern entrance, that also shows long, and from the

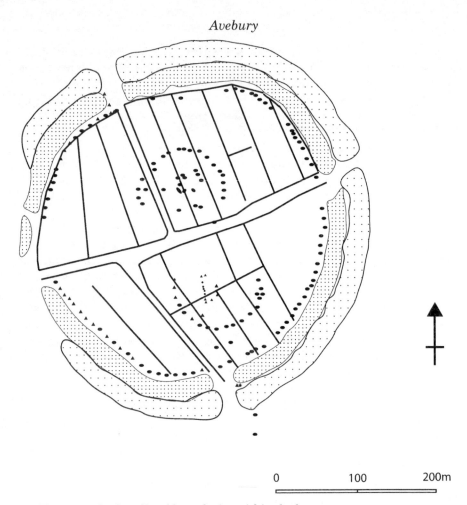

14. The network of medieval boundaries within the henge.

evidence of the trees growing against them, well-established fencelines crossing the interior of the henge (Stukeley 1743, pl. XII; Ucko et al. 1991, pl. 44). Many of the boundary lines recorded by Stukeley are still visible today as a series of low earthworks, attesting to the veracity of his record.

The fencelines and boundaries recorded by Stukeley seem to have fossilised an earlier, medieval, pattern of landholdings that can be reconstructed from excavated, earthwork, cropmark and geophysical evidence (Bewley et al. 1996; Ucko et al. 1991, 167-70) (Fig. 14). These partition much of the interior of the henge into a regular series of narrow rectangular units, *c.* 30-40 m wide and running perpendicular to the line of the High Street – Green Street road. The whole has the appearance of being a planned in-take.

That these boundaries are medieval in date was demonstrated by the results of Keiller's campaign of excavation in the south-eastern quadrant. This work included cuttings across a section of the boundary recorded by Stukeley as separating his pastures IX and X, a ditch that had earlier sub-divided pasture IX, and others running at right-angles across the north of these plots (Fig. 15). The pasture IX-X ditch showed evidence of re-cutting, the earlier ditch being deeper and narrower. The later cut followed the line of the earlier closely, only deviating when it encountered the position of the fallen stone 102 of the southern inner circle. Here the line of the earlier, deeper ditch respected the location of the socket of the stone (i.e. its standing position), while the later cut deviated to respect the *fallen* position of the sarsen. At the base of the earlier ditch were sherds of fourteenth-century pottery.

Other trenches revealed a similar story; for example, in cuttings to the south-west of the Obelisk, the ditch and bank defining the top of Stukeley's pasture IX was seen to run alongside an earlier ditch which had been covered by the bank of the later boundary. Further dating evidence comes from sherds of thirteenth-century pottery found in the fill of the V-shaped ditch that sub-divided pastures IX and X. Another substantial ditch, up to 1.8 m wide and 1 m deep, that ran across the north of pastures IX and X, had a very distinctive profile with one side sloping and the other almost vertical. The form of this ditch and the pottery found within it suggested a fourteenth-century date to Keiller. The pattern of fills suggests that it was in use for a considerable period of time before its abandonment, showing evidence for a gradual sequence of silting and stabilisation (information from Alexander Keiller Museum).

All of this suggests that the boundary divisions recorded by Stukeley followed the lines of a much earlier system, and one that relied upon ditches and banks rather than fences to delineate the various plots. At some point, possibly at the end of the fourteenth century when the evidence for manuring disappears, this system was effectively abandoned in its original form. Over time, some ditches were retained, while other boundaries were deliberately levelled, allowing parcels of land to be lumped together to form the well-established pattern of pastures recorded in the eighteenth century. This alteration may have involved a single remodelling or, more likely, reflected a gradual and piecemeal process of rationalisation and change.

Living within the henge

While the evidence for boundaries and land divisions is unambiguous, that for medieval buildings within the interior of the henge is far less clear. Gray found no structural evidence during the course of his limited excava-

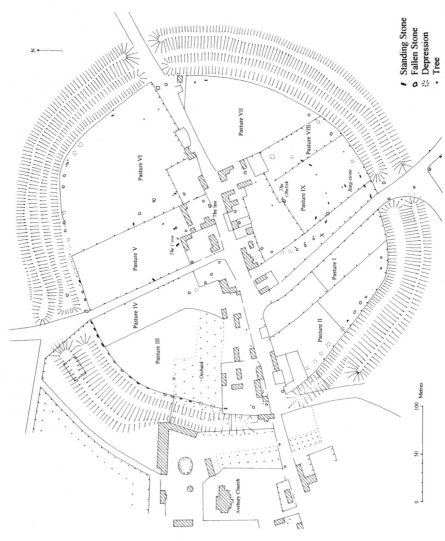

15. Early eighteenth-century Avebury. Tentative reconstruction based on Stukeley's 1743 frontispiece, Smith's 1965 plan, and various other archaeological sources.

- ▮ Standing Stone
- ◗ Fallen Stone
- ✳ Depression
- · Tree

N ←

Pasture VII

Pasture VI

Pasture VIII

The Obelisk

Pasture IX

Ring-stone

The Inn

The Cove

Pasture V

Pasture I

Pasture IV

Pasture II

Pasture III

Orchard

Avebury Church

Metres

0   50   100

tions in the interior, his putative dwelling being argued from pottery densities alone. Jope (1999, 68) considered that the interior of the henge was used largely for gardens, with houses perhaps clustered outside the earthwork around the church. However, the most likely location for medieval dwellings is against the road, where the presence of more recent buildings has prevented excavation from taking place. In fact, it is not impossible that one or two of the older houses within the village incorporate elements of late medieval fabric (Pollard & Reynolds 2002, 247).

Despite Jope's statement that Keiller's excavations failed to produce evidence of medieval buildings within the earthwork (Jope 1999, 68), one group of features within the centre of the southern inner circle is suggestive. These were clustered in the area to the immediate north of the Obelisk (Smith 1965, fig. 69), and comprise a number of pits, trenches and post-holes (Fig. 16). Most striking were a series of large, shallow pits cut into the chalk subsoil, the most fully excavated of these being 2.7 m long by 1.8 m wide, reaching a depth of 0.7 m below the level of the turf. Keiller interpreted these features as pits for the extraction of marl, a calcium-rich soil used as a fertiliser. These pits were far from haphazard affairs; indeed at the southern corner of the central pit a flat platform of solid chalk had been left projecting from the base to act as a hearth, the purpose of which 'had probably been the cooking of soup or some such meal by the marl diggers' (unpublished site notebook, Alexander Keiller Museum). Finds of conjoining sherds of twelfth- to thirteenth-century date in the lower fills of these features suggested that they had been dug in the medieval period. Adjacent to these so-called marl-pits were a series of more shapeless, irregular depressions associated with lines of stake-holes. Although one of the depressions clearly cut into the side of one of the marl-pits, similarities in the fills of the two classes of feature led Keiller and his foreman, W.E.V. Young, to interpret them as broadly contemporary, the depressions either trial diggings or marl mixing areas.

Located in among the marl-pits and depressions was the best evidence for a medieval structure so far recovered from excavations in the interior of the henge. This comprised a pair of parallel trenches, spaced 6.3 m apart, running north-northwest from the location of the fallen Obelisk into the area of the marl-pits (Plate XIII). Each trench was around 4 m long and relatively shallow, cutting less than 0.3 m into the chalk. Scattered within and around the area were a series of post- and stake-holes. The suggestion is of a pair of wall-foundation slots for a structure that had been built up against the bulk of the fallen Obelisk, the stone forming one of the walls. On the basis of the shallow nature of the slots, Keiller argued that this would have been a flimsy, insubstantial structure, though he conceded that a single post-hole placed centrally between the two slots *may* have supported a simple roof. The lack of any evidence for a fourth wall, parallel

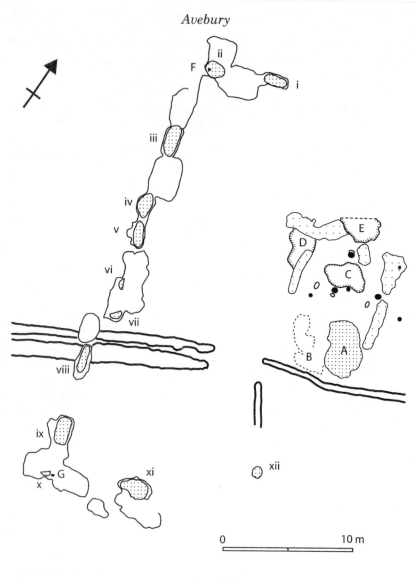

A - Obelisk
B - 1865 excavations
C - E - Medieval marl extraction pits
F - G - Prehistoric stakeholes

↗ - Medieval/post-medieval boundary ditches
⬠ - Stone sockets (i-xii)
⬡ - Possible medieval structural features
⬡ - Stone burial and destruction pits
● - Possible medieval postholes
○ - Prehistoric pits

16. Excavated features within the centre of the southern inner circle.

to that provided by the Obelisk, led the excavators to interpret the remains as a cart-shed (ibid.). However, it may be that Keiller was placing too many demands upon the evidence in front of him. Even quite shallow beam slots are capable of supporting substantial roofed structures. In addition, while there appears to be no third slot 'closing' the structure, there were several reasonably substantial post-holes at this end of the structure, as well as the irregular depressions and stake-holes associated by the excavators with the marl-pits, despite the clear evidence that at least one was later in date.

Ascribing an unambiguous medieval date to this structure is difficult. It appears to have utilised the prostrate bulk of the Obelisk, which we know had fallen or been toppled prior to the laying out of the first phase of boundary ditches, an event we have dated to the medieval period. In addition, the westernmost of the slots cuts into, and is thus later, than one of the marl-pits (interestingly the same pit cut into by one of the irregular depressions). This suggests strongly that the shallow depressions and beam slots may be contemporary and both are later than the marl-pits dated on the basis of pottery to the twelfth/thirteenth century. One factor that strongly implies a medieval date for this structure is the way the orientation of its long axis mirrors exactly that of the linear setting of stones around the Obelisk which were known to have been buried in the medieval period and thus removed from sight.

Finally, it is worth noting that the structure, whatever it was, made direct use of a prostrate stone. This makes Gray's suggestion, based upon the high density of pottery, that some form of structure may have stood against stone 102 in the medieval period all the more intriguing. However, despite the fact that we have only limited evidence for buildings being raised within the henge, enormous structural changes were taking place within Avebury during the medieval period. However, these were not concerned with putting structures up, but instead with taking things down.

The strange case of the missing stones

For the first time since the early Bronze Age, people were beginning to alter the fabric of the henge in a very significant way. In addition to parcelling up the land within the earthwork, cultivation and the construction of buildings, they were also dismantling the standing stones of the circles and avenues. This was achieved by deliberately toppling and burying the sarsens (Smith 1965, 176-8). Of the 98 or so stones of the outer circle, as many as 32 appear to have been deliberately buried along with 11 stones of the internal setting of the southern inner circle. Likewise, in the excavated portions of the West Kennet Avenue 14 of the 74 settings

123

investigated showed evidence for stone burial, and on the line of the Beckhampton Avenue five out of 15 (Smith 1965; Smith 1885; Gillings et al. 2000). It has also been suggested that alongside the sarsen burials, a number of stones of the southern inner circle, including the Obelisk, were deliberately toppled at this time, their enormous size precluding any subsequent burial (Smith 1965, 198).

The basic procedure for stone burial appears relatively straightforward (Smith 1965, 176-7). The first stage was to topple the selected stone by levering or hauling it out of its socket. This is evinced by the clear marks left by narrow metal spades and crowbars that were found in and around some of the original sockets (ibid., 176). The burial pit was cut, oversize but otherwise closely mirroring the shape of the stone. It was cut gener-ously enough to ensure a comfortable fit and deep enough to ensure that when buried the stone was well below the level of the subsoil (Plate XIV). The final stage was to lever the stone into the pit and then fill it in. This backfilling was far from haphazard: loose chalk rubble was used to fill the voids around the stone and then a compacted cap of chalk was added to level it off, leaving no trace on the surface that a stone had ever stood. This resulted in a characteristic plan with the burial pit adjacent to, but clearly separated from, the original prehistoric socket (e.g. Keiller and Piggott 1936, fig. 10).

There is in fact evidence for several different techniques being employed in the process of burial. Keiller noted a second form of stone burial which he referred to as the 'falling-leaf' method (unpublished site notebook, Alexander Keiller Museum). Here the toppled stone was left where it fell and the burial pit dug around it. Alternate sides would be dug out, the stone slowly working its way down into the ground, tilting from left to right. Recognised by the characteristic pattern of ledges this technique leaves on the sides of the burial pit, this was thought by Keiller to be the earliest mode of burial. Along the line of the Beckhampton Avenue, recent excavations have revealed another approach to the task. Here the various stages described above were concatenated. Involving a degree of physical risk on the part of those undertaking the operation, the stone was propped upright while the burial pit was dug directly adjacent, and right up to, its base. This served to effectively dig away one half of the socket, allowing the stone to fall forward into the pit as the restraints were let loose. The result was undeniably effective, if rather unpredictable. It could work perfectly, as was the case with one of the Beckhampton Avenue burials. However, there was always the possibility that the stone would twist or fall at an angle when the bracing was released. This appears to have happened with another Beckhampton Avenue stone, where despite the fact that the pit had been carefully cut to reflect the shape of the stone it was destined to receive, the sarsen sits at an awkward angle within it, its top projecting above the level of the subsoil. Scoring along the sides of the pit suggests that the stone became misaligned as it fell, wedging askew rather than falling neatly into the hole.

In the case of the stones of the linear setting within the southern inner circle, a wide variety of burial techniques appear to have been practised (Figs 4 (below) and 16). For example, the burial of stone *iii* followed the 'typical' sequence described by Smith. The stone was toppled, destroying much of its original socket as it fell. A burial pit was then dug 0.7 m away from the fallen stone and bars and levers were used to manoeuvre it across the intervening space and into the pit. This not only left a mass of pockmarks in the chalk subsoil but caused the edge of the burial pit to collapse as the stone was pushed in. In contrast, in the case of stone *iv* the pit was dug up to the base of the stone which was then toppled over straight into it, in the manner of the Beckhampton Avenue burials.

The treatment afforded to the other stones of this setting suggests a high degree of contingency and pragmatism. For example, stones *v*, *vi* and *vii* had all been buried in a single, long burial pit, implying that they were buried at the same time. Stone *vi* had been levered awkwardly into its burial pit and as a result had dragged against one of the sides. Those responsible for the burial then took the time to carefully trim the edge of the pit back to ensure a neater fit. In contrast, in the area of the pit reserved for stone *v* the digging was very rough and irregular. Not only that, the order of the stones had been transposed during the act of burial, with stone *v* relegated to a position between *vi* and *vii* (Smith 1965, 199). Perhaps the most obvious example of pragmatism involved the burial of stone *i*. Here the burial made direct use of an existing pit, interpreted by the excavator as a marl pit, similar to those found immediately north of the Obelisk (unpublished site notebook, Alexander Keiller Museum).

A very odd piece of stone packing

Dating evidence for these burials is provided by twelfth- to fourteenth-century pottery found in the backfill of a number of stone burial pits, as well as in the topsoil that had fallen into the voids left in the original sockets of the stones after they had been toppled (Smith 1965, 177; Jope 1999). In addition, a worn, halved Short Cross penny of Henry III was found at the base of the original socket of one of the buried West Kennet Avenue stones. This is a coin that could not have been lost before the second quarter of the thirteenth century. However, it is important to acknowledge that neither of these sources of evidence alone can be used to date the stone burials reliably to the medieval period. As we have discussed above, the presence of residual midden material in the ploughsoil means that the pottery could have been incorporated into the fills of the burial pits and sockets long after it was initially deposited. Likewise, the coin was found in a feature that had been badly disturbed by rabbit burrows (Smith 1965, 177; Jope 1999, 69).

All this evidence proves is that the stone burials began sometime after the pottery entered the topsoil as manure and before the site was visited by the antiquaries of the seventeenth and eighteenth centuries. However, one less equivocal piece of dating evidence exists that firmly places at least one act of stone burial in the medieval period: this is the unusual find made by Keiller in the burial pit of stone 9 of the outer circle.

Stone 9 was unusual in that its burial seemed to be incomplete. Rather than nestling neatly within its carefully prepared pit, part of the stone was found to be resting against the side of the cut, as if it had fallen awkwardly. Wedged between the stone and the edge of the pit was the body of a man (Smith 1965, 177-8). The excavators were in no doubt as to what had happened. The man had been engaged in digging the pit when the stone, which had been propped alongside ready to be lowered in, unexpectedly slipped. As it tumbled into the pit the man had no chance of getting out of its way. His body was crushed against the edge, fracturing his pelvis and trapping his foot beneath its bulk. Alongside the body were the remains of a leather pouch containing three pennies, a pair of hinged iron scissors, a small iron implement and an iron buckle. Hinged scissors are rare in rural contexts and their presence suggests that the man was a professional of some sort, perhaps a tradesman such as a hatter or tailor (Jope 1999, 66). Although these possibilities were considered at the time of excavation, the favoured interpretation, and one that has persisted down to the present day, was that the man was an itinerant barber-surgeon, based upon the identification of the iron implement as a probe or lancet (Smith 1965, 177-8).

Long thought destroyed during the Second World War bombing of the Royal College of Surgeons in London, the skeleton of the barber-surgeon was recently re-discovered and re-analysed (Pitts 2000, 129) shedding some intriguing light on his rather colourful life prior to his encounter with stone 9. Barber-surgeon or not, he had clearly survived a substantial sword wound to the head some time before his death. The re-examination also served to question the excavator's original interpretation that he had been crushed to death by the falling stone as the oft-cited damage to the pelvis appeared to be due to natural post-depositional breakage rather than deliberate crushing. The implication is that the man was either already dead when placed in the burial pit, or had been suffocated under the weight of the stone (Denison 1999).

Despite the fact that pottery of the twelfth and thirteenth centuries was recovered from the fill of the pit, our most reliable evidence for the date of this particular stone burial comes from the coins found in the man's leather pouch. These can be closely dated, and place the death of the man between 1320 and 1350, and most likely around 1320 (Ucko et al. 1991, 178). Whether the unfortunate victim of an accident, or the rather pragmatic disposal of a corpse, the remains serve to date at least one stone burial to the medieval period. Indeed, some researchers have gone on to suggest that this unfortunate event may have marked the end of this type of activity. The death of an individual engaged in the act of burying a stone by the very stone itself may have acted as an omen powerful enough to signal the end of this episode, the toppled stones representing 'works in progress', abandoned before burial could take place (Smith 1959, 21).

Why were stones buried?

Although the existence of buried stones was known long before the excavations of the 1930s, the Avebury burials were thought to be a relatively recent phenomenon, dating to the period immediately prior to Stukeley's visits in the 1720s. This was based upon comments he made which implied that memory of the practice had survived into the early eighteenth century (Stukeley 1743, 29-30). On the reasons why they were buried Stukeley was unambiguous – the stones were removed to free up the small areas of land they occupied for cultivation. Burial was motivated exclusively by greed and monetary gain. The fact that he was able to recount the relative cost of burial as compared to the value of the land liberated, suggests that these events took place within the living memory of his informants (Stukeley 1743, 15).

The discovery of the barber-surgeon and the dating of burial episodes to the medieval period served to question the veracity of this interpretation. As discussed above, although cultivation took place within the centre of the monument during the medieval period, the pottery evidence suggests that these episodes were neither concentrated nor sustained. If the interior was not being intensively cultivated then it is difficult to equate acts of burial with the need to free up the small patches of land occupied by the footprints of the stones. Furthermore, stone burial was a large-scale undertaking. Even Stukeley acknowledged that 'the expense of digging the grave, was more than 30 years purchase of the spot they possessed, when standing' (ibid.). If the motivation was simply to clear stones out of the way of the plough, then dragging off or breaking them up would have served the purpose better. Indeed, if not sufficiently deep, buried stones had the potential to cause far more mischief to the plough than standing examples that could easily be avoided (Young, cited in Ucko et al. 1991, 179).

This objection becomes particularly relevant when we look to the sarsens of the smaller setting immediately west of the Obelisk. With such small stones burial makes little practical sense, as it would have been far easier to drag them away (Smith 1965, 179). Nor are the deliberately toppled stones easily explained by such a rationale; indeed a toppled sarsen would *decrease* the amount of land available compared to when it was standing.

A further objection derives from the spatial distribution of stone burials. This is odd insofar as the burials seem to follow no discernable pattern. For example, recent excavations on the line of the Beckhampton Avenue have revealed a sequence where the alternate stones of two adjacent pairs had been buried, at the time leaving the other stones standing, followed by a pair of buried stones, and then the following pair left untouched. The same situation is found along the line of the West Kennet Avenue and within the henge itself, where once again the decision as to which stones were to be buried seems rather erratic. If the motivation was purely a desire to free up as much land as possible, then, following the same functional logic that gave rise to the regular pattern of boundary ditches and banks, a more structured and organised pattern of burial is to be expected. Indeed, during his excavations of the inner southern circle settings, Keiller found that while the burial of stone *viii* had been sealed by the bank of the later boundary feature, the burial pit itself had been cut through the line of an earlier medieval ditch. This not only suggests that the burial took place sometime after the laying out of the boundaries, but if the purpose of burial was to facilitate agriculture, then it seems counter-intuitive to destroy elements of the very boundary system that was implemented to facilitate and structure such activity.

It should also be noted that if manure pottery (that was later to find its way into the burial pits) had time to accumulate around the stones prior to their burial, then the onset of cultivation was not linked to clearance of the sarsens. Indeed, there are hints that the practice of stone burial may have begun after cultivation had ceased (Smith 1965, 179)

The idea that the stone burials had been motivated by economic gain had been based upon the assumption of their being of seventeenth-century date, when stone destruction for clearance and building material was very much in evidence. With the discovery that the burials were much earlier a new explanation had to be sought and one was quickly found, an explanation that continues to dominate discussions of medieval Avebury today. Rather than seeing the acts of burial as being fuelled by the requirements of agriculture or individual greed, they were instead attributed to the machinations of the Church.

The rationale is as follows. It was assumed that the monument would have acted as a powerful focus for pagan worship, centred not so much upon the complex as a whole but instead on individual stones. To support this assumption, an injunction issued by a Council of Nantes in the late ninth century was cited that specifically condemned the pagan worship of stones (Smith 1965, 179-80). The stone burials could therefore be seen as the Church's practical response to the need to free the village from any relic pagan practices centred upon the stones. In an effort to curb these ungodly acts, the simplest strategy would have been to remove the immediate focus, in this way 'the devils handiwork was to be destroyed' (Burl 1979, 37). This may have taken place as a concerted drive, or have been a more drawn-out process, the acts of burial being permitted only at specially sanctioned times in the calendar (Smith 1965, 180; Burl 1979, 37).

The fact that the stones were buried and not broken up or dragged away certainly seems to suggest that some powerful superstitions were attached to them. It was almost as if the sarsens were simultaneously feared and respected, being taken out of sight and hidden rather than being destroyed. As Burl rather elegantly puts it, 'doing God's work without upsetting the Devil' (1979, 37).

Interrogating the religious orthodoxy

It is easy to visualise the villagers, perhaps at the time of the yearly fair, apprehensively overthrowing the monstrous stones, encouraged by the priest, other onlookers, the peasant's wives, shepherds from the hills, watching, doubting, even scared of this interference.   Burl (1979), 37

This portrayal of an episode of large-scale, church-sponsored burial has become such a central aspect of conventional 'histories' of Avebury as to generate its own sense of authority and legitimacy (e.g. Burl 1979; Malone 1989). However, the evidence upon which it has been constructed is far from conclusive, and some writers have suggested that such an all-encompassing interpretation may misrepresent and simplify the processes at work in Avebury during the medieval period (Ucko et al. 1991, 179-81). Arguments can be made both for and against the notion that the stones were associated with superstition and pagan practices, and that the Church was involved with their removal. Ultimately, much ambiguity surrounds the motivation for this peculiar practice.

That the acts of stone burial were initiated by the Church receives some support from local events at the time. As we have discussed, there was considerable ecclesiastical activity taking place at Avebury in the medieval period and, as a result of the mistrust that existed between Cirencester Abbey and the alien priory, religious tensions and disputes were never far away. At first glance then the village seems an ideal context for such activities. This explanation might also account for why an individual such as the itinerant barber-surgeon would come to be involved in acts of stone burial. Unlikely to become engaged in routine agricultural clearance, he may have been more than willing to participate in such a divine undertaking.

A religious motive might also account for the decision to bury rather than destroy the stones, and may also shed light on the piecemeal pattern of burial. If the aim of the exercise was to defuse or decommission symbolically 'dangerous' stones, then the burials would focus primarily upon those sarsens that had attracted superstitious attention. But is there any evidence for unusual or pagan practices focussed upon the stones? The names given to some of these settings, such as the 'Devil's Chair' and 'Devil's Quoits' might imply a direct association with darker forces, although such appellations were probably given to the stones much later, in the early post-medieval period (Hutton, in Bender 1998, 137).

Evidence for certain stones acting as foci for unusual acts during the medieval period comes from one curious find made during the recent excavation of a pair of buried sarsens along the line of the Beckhampton Avenue (Gillings et al. 2000, 5). This particular stone was highly distinctive: squat and of a very folded, organic form. Passing completely through the stone was a natural perforation, large enough to push an arm through, and carefully inserted into this hole was a split cattle long bone. The latter was radiocarbon dated to between AD 1170 and 1280, the period just before stone burials began. Was this obviously deliberate deposit the result of idle 'play' or something more respectful and meaningful? Whatever the explanation, similar deposits have not been encountered elsewhere, implying that this was a one-off act.

Arguments against a religious motive are more numerous and substantial than those for. First, it should be noted that the oft-cited injunction issued by the Council of Nantes was several centuries old by the time the process of stone burial began, and that there is no direct link between this statement and Avebury. In addition, though it is tempting to see the presence of the alien priory and the documented tensions as a catalyst, we have already noted how few monks were actually present to coordinate any burial programme and how such cells were more concerned with investments and profits than missionary activity (Jope 1999, 67). At this time the Church was far from being a repressive, patrolling body, actively engaged in a battle against 'pagan' practices; if anything it tolerated a degree of polytheism (Hutton, in Bender 1998, 133-8).

Furthermore, to envisage the stones as a focus for pagan worship would be to acknowledge a fundamental change in their status around the late thirteenth or early fourteenth century, though, of course, this is a possibility. We have already seen that the megalithic settings had not maintained an unbroken sanctity from the Neolithic onwards. From the evidence of settlement and cultivation, it would appear that the Saxon and early medieval inhabitants of Avebury lived quite happily alongside the stones, perhaps even regarding them as entirely natural features.

It has also been assumed that because stone 9 was buried in the early decades of the fourteenth century all stone burials are medieval, and part of a concerted campaign of removal. However, although a considerable number of buried stones have now been excavated, convincing dating evidence linking these to the medieval period can only be produced for two. The same chronological ambiguity applies to many of those stones known to have been toppled. The assumption is that toppling and burial were part of the same process, the toppled stones simply being too big to bury.

Although there is talk of 'indications' of a medieval date for this alternative strategy, this appears to refer to sherds of medieval pottery found lying beneath disturbed packing stones in the original stone sockets (1965, 191n1; 199). As we have already discussed, pottery derived from manuring was present in areas of the interior and could have been incorporated into exposed sockets and burial pits as residual material (Jope 1999, 69). Such material simply places the event in the period following the deposition of the pottery (i.e. the twelfth and thirteenth centuries) and before the records of Stukeley and Aubrey (Smith 1965; Smith 1885).

The variations observed in the technology of stone burial outlined above could imply that we are dealing with several episodes of removal, rather than one distinct campaign. Dating evidence recently recovered from one of the Beckhampton Avenue burials firmly suggests we are looking at a protracted process that continued well into the post-medieval period. Here a cattle rib found in the loose rubble backfill of one of the burial pits gave a calibrated radiocarbon date in the sixteenth and seventeenth centuries. This is important as it appears to verify Stukeley's claim that burials occurred during the lifetime of those inhabitants of Avebury he spoke to (Stukeley 1743, 15). Rather than having to resort to claims of vestigial folk-memory, the evidence from Beckhampton suggests that not only may Stukeley's informants have remembered stone burial episodes, they may have actually taken part in them. This would mean that the practice of stone burial ran across all the ecclesiastical turmoil and changes of the Reformation.

As for the barber-surgeon, while the Church-sponsored explanation offers a satisfactory justification as to why such an individual would become involved in the burial process in the first place, it fails comprehensively to explain why his body was not dug out and given a proper interment in consecrated ground (Jope 1999, 67). Compared to the effort that went into digging the burial pit, it would have been a relatively trivial task to cut the side of the pit back to facilitate the removal of his body. Indeed, we already have evidence from the burial of stone *vi* that pits could be re-modelled following the addition of the stone.

Priests and peasants

Our understandings of medieval Avebury are dominated by received orthodoxies and stories that have gained authority largely through repetition. While the Abbeys of Cirencester and St. Georges jostled over tithes and parochial responsibilities (Kirby 1956, 393), the villagers began to leave their mark upon the interior of the henge.

Continuing a process begun in the late Saxon period, the layout of the monument was substantially altered for the first time in millennia. Cultivation took place within the henge, property boundaries were laid out, buildings constructed, and the sarsens began to gradually disappear, still in position but now buried beneath the surface of the ground. Whether obstacles to the plough, an awkward presence, or – as the traditional account would have it – an affront to the church, in the medieval period the stones once again began to play an active role in the everyday lives of the inhabitants of Avebury.

Rather than a concerted plan of eradication, the stone burials looked to have comprised a series of acts carried out as and when needed over a 300-year period, each being driven by a contingent and specific set of concerns. What links the burials is not a motive, but a common technology of riddance – a desire to remove the stones from sight by burying them deep underground. However, while explaining why stones were buried remains a difficult task, it is perhaps easier to understand why such a burial technology was adopted in the first place. The answer may well lie in local understandings of the origin of these stones. Rather than removing the stones from sight, the real reason may have been a concern with putting them back into the ground. In the mid-nineteenth century the local inhabitants of Avebury firmly believed that sarsens grew out of the ground, a view 'to which they adhere most perniciously' (Long 1859, 29). Although we have no evidence that such views were active half a millennium earlier, they do raise the tantalising suggestion that rather than burial what we are seeing enacted within the Avebury monuments is a re-planting, a returning of the sarsens to their place of origin. Thus, burying stones was an appropriate, commonly understood and accepted way of doing things. Whether driven by a need to clear an area of obstacles or religious zeal, the correct way of removing a standing stone was always to plant it back in the ground.

What happened to the Avebury megaliths during the fourteenth to seventeenth centuries appears unique, and therefore needs to be comprehended in the context of local developments. The eradication of megalithic monuments through the burial of stones is hardly attested anywhere else in medieval Britain, the exception being the burial of two stones at the Devil's Quoits, Stanton Harcourt, in Oxfordshire (Barclay et al. 1995,

42-3). Elsewhere, such structures were either dismantled and the stones dragged away, or they were left in place and worked around. The stone circles at Stanton Drew, Somerset, also adjacent to a village, were left unmolested; while at Long Meg and Her Daughters in Cumbria medieval ridge-and-furrow cultivation ran through the stone circle in a manner that seems oblivious to the presence of the megaliths (Soffe & Clare 1988). The process of stone burial at Avebury is both curious and still far from being properly understood.

8. Kings and Scholars

The mighty carcase of Stonehenge draws great numbers of people, out of their way every day, as to see a fight: and it has exercis'd the pens of the learned to account for it. But Abury a much greater work and more extensive design, by I know not what unkind fate, was altogether over-looked, and in the utmost danger of perishing, thro' the humor of country people, but of late taken up of demolishing the stones.   Stukeley (1743), 15

During the mid-seventeenth century two highly significant events took place that would prove to have a lasting and dramatic impact upon Avebury. The first was the academic discovery of the site by early antiquaries, bringing it to the attention of the wider world for the very first time. The second was a concerted campaign of stone destruction and reworking of the henge earthworks, linked to an expansion of the village in this area. Areas of the bank were slighted, portions of the ditch re-filled and, rather than simply buried, many of the remaining megalithic settings were broken up. Although this activity appears to have peaked in the two decades either side of 1700, stone destruction continued until the early nineteenth century, the last recorded act taking place around 1829 when gunpowder was used to remove a stone deemed to be stubbornly blocking the entrance to a rick-yard (Smith 1965, 202; Burl 1979, 54).

Either of these processes alone would have been significant, but the fact they occurred simultaneously, largely within an intense 80-year period between *c.* 1650 and 1730, resulted in one of the most active and vivid episodes in Avebury's long history. They also served to generate two unique sources of information for students of the site. The first is a remarkable set of field records, as antiquaries such as John Aubrey and William Stukeley recorded the prehistoric fabric of the monument as it was slowly being dismantled around them. The second is the archaeological evidence for stone destruction, and the vivid contemporary accounts of this dismantling, the latter describing the process, monitoring its pace and progression, and shedding light upon the motivations of those responsible.

The result is that the early post-medieval period appears to be one of the better understood phases of Avebury's history. However, as with Avebury's medieval history, a sense of familiarity surrounding these events has developed largely through repetition, and intricacies and ambiguities in the story are sometimes glossed over. For instance, our understanding of the episode of stone destruction derives almost exclusively from the records of a single antiquary, William Stukeley, these being based largely upon oral testimonies. As Ucko et al. have convincingly and elegantly illustrated, Stukeley's records of the stone destruction cannot be regarded as wholly authoritative, being riddled with internal contradictions and inconsistencies (Ucko et al. 1991, 182).

In addition, although a number of stone destruction features have been excavated over the years, the results of these investigations have made little impact on our received understandings. These features have tended to be treated as an unfortunate disturbance: the residue of a series of acts of vandalism that serve as little more than an hindrance to a pure understanding of the prehistoric fabric of the monument. Such an attitude has failed to consider the destruction features as important evidence in their own right, the crucial remains of a key episode in the ongoing life of the monument. As a result, many key questions relating to the phase of stone destruction remain relatively under-explored, such as when it began, its social and political context, and the motivations behind its enactment. Situated within the context of early antiquarian encounter and local developments, these are issues that we will seek to explore in this chapter.

A thriving village

For several centuries before the seventeenth century the ancient monument had not been seen as a particularly special place: the land encompassed by the earthwork had long been used for farming, while the living village had grown first towards then into it.   Ucko et al. (1991), 165

Beginning in the medieval period, there was a gradual trend towards erecting houses and farm buildings within the earthwork of the henge. By the early eighteenth century around 30 structures can be claimed fronting the roads that crossed the interior, possibly the result of the widespread building boom that was seen across southern England from the later sixteenth century onwards. Earlier buildings in Avebury were timber-framed with thatched roofs, following an established vernacular tradition, but by the second half of the seventeenth century increasing numbers of more substantial houses and barns were being built in brick and local sarsen stone. As well as the houses, the roads were important components, one of the two contemporary coach roads that served to link Marlborough (and hence London) to Bath passing directly through the henge, entering the eastern entrance and departing through the southern (ibid., 166-72). By the mid-seventeenth century the interior of the monument consisted of a confusing patchwork of roads, houses, outbuildings, hedgerows, closes and orchards. Rather than an adjunct to the village, the circles were now thoroughly embedded within it, part of a flourishing community sitting astride a major coach road (Plate XV).

Dis-empestring the Cathedral

The first antiquarian note regarding Avebury appears to be the brief mention by Leland around 1540, noting the presence of 'camps and sepultures of men of warre' at a site he refers to as *Aibyri* (Leland 1907-10, v, 81). A fuller, though still tantalisingly brief, description appeared in Philemon Holland's 1610 translation of Camden's *Britannia*, where an earthwork with four entrances and the presence of rude stone jambs is mentioned (Long 1858, 2). These circumspect notes did little to bring the site to any wider academic attention and it was not until January 1649 that Avebury can be said to have truly impacted upon the fledgling antiquarian consciousness.

While out hunting with Royalist friends in early 1649, the young John Aubrey followed a pack of hunting hounds into the village. An Oxford graduate and early member of the Royal Society, Aubrey was a passionate and committed scholar with a strong interest in antiquities; in his own words a man 'mightily susceptible of Fascination' (Tylden-Wright 1991, 16-22). He not only recognised immediately the human origin of the earthwork and standing stones, but also discerned that the megaliths appeared to define 'rude' circles. What is interesting is that his shock at the discovery of the site was matched by incredulity that Avebury had not been recognised and noted in detail before. This was particularly the case given the steady stream of coach passengers travelling to and from London passing directly through the monument.

Following his chance discovery, during the 1650s Aubrey spent a number of autumns in Wiltshire, in the company of his good friend Colonel James Long. During these rural sojourns he made further records of the Avebury complex, noting additional features such as the West Kennet Avenue and the Sanctuary (Ucko et al. 1991, 14) (Fig. 17).

In the early 1660s Avebury piqued the interest of another keen antiquary, Walter Charleton. Charleton was not only the Royal Physician to King Charles II, but a close friend of Aubrey's; indeed it was Charleton who had proposed Aubrey for membership of the fledgling Royal Society. In 1663 Charleton published his *Chorea Gigantum*, a work on Stonehenge that made mention of similar natural sarsens that could be seen on the journey from Bath to London. He presented a copy to his friend and fellow antiquary and it seems likely that not only did Aubrey recognise this brief reference as relating to Avebury, but also pointed out to Charleton that far from being natural these stones comprised part of another

136

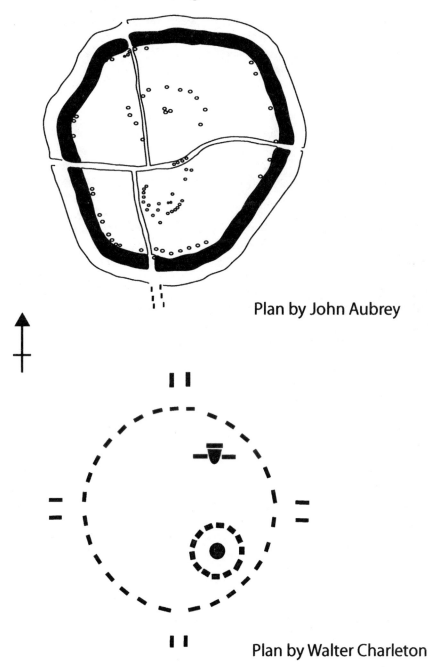

Plan by John Aubrey

Plan by Walter Charleton

17. Schematic copies of the early antiquarian plans of Avebury by John Aubrey and Walter Charleton.

major monument. The result was a joint presentation to the Royal Society in July 1663, the first antiquarian contribution to this learned gathering, where each of the two men presented a plan of the Avebury monument for discussion (ibid., 17-24) (Fig. 17). As the plans differed in as many places as they agreed, this discussion is likely to have been both spirited and lively!

That this meeting provoked learned interest in Avebury is attested by the fact that in August of the same year word of its importance reached King Charles II through the president of the Royal Society and Charleton, who recounted Aubrey's claim that Avebury 'did as much exceed Stoneheng as a Cathedral does a Parish Church'. Following a discussion with Aubrey and Charleton, the king arranged to visit the site, and in late August 1663 made a diversion while on route from Marlborough to Bath, in the company of Aubrey, Charleton, the Duke of York and Sir Robert Moray, a fellow of the Royal Society and court scientist (ibid., 25). While this visit marked the end of Charleton's interest and involvement with Avebury, in the month following the king's visit Aubrey undertook a measured survey and detailed description of the circles at his behest (Long 1858, 5). It was during this programme of fieldwork that Aubrey began to understand better the reason why the site had escaped the detailed attention of earlier antiquaries and chorographers, noting that:

> By reason of the crosse streates, houses, gardens, orchards and several small closes, and the fractures made in this antiquity for the building of these houses, it was no very easy taske for me to trace out the Vestigia and to make this survey. Wherefore I have dis-empestred the Scheme from the enclosures, and houses, &c.: wch are altogether foreigne to this Antiquity, and would but have clowded and darkned the reall Designe.
>
> Aubrey, quoted in Long (1858), 8

The work of Aubrey and Charleton provoked an initial burst of interest in Avebury as a unique monument of antiquity. Indeed the famous diarist Samuel Pepys explored Avebury in 1668, noting that the majority of people of learning passing through the village took time to visit (ibid., 11). However, this interest does not seem to have been long-lived or to have made a lasting impact upon the developing field of antiquarianism, leaving the importance of the site to be effectively 'rediscovered' by Stukeley during the first quarter of the eighteenth century. This is no doubt in part due to the failure of Aubrey to publish his research. It was destined to form part of his planned *Monumenta Britannica*, the draft of the book being revised repeatedly up until his death in 1697; the notes and plans eventually being purchased by the Bodleian Library in 1836. The manuscript finally saw publication in 1980 (Fowles & Legge 1980).

Where Aubrey's work on Avebury did have an impact was in the 1695 edition of Camden's *Britannia*, whose editor, Edmund Gibson, appears to have drawn upon Aubrey's unpublished manuscripts to offer a description of the site. While this should have served to arouse broader antiquarian interest, the entry was not only brief but poorly transcribed, giving the impression that Avebury was in no way unique or out of the ordinary (Ucko et al. 1991, 10-36).

Avebury under the microscope

This situation was to change dramatically when the site was once again 'discovered', this time by one of the most important figures in Avebury's long history, William Stukeley. Later ordained within the Church of England, Stukeley was a classic polymath, researching in fields as diverse as anatomy, theology, music and astronomy. However, although a qualified medical doctor, member of the Royal Society and at times a close acquaintance of the leading Newtonian scholars of the day, his interests lay more with natural history and antiquities than the more mathematical physical sciences. Indeed, he was a pivotal figure in the re-founding of the Society of Antiquaries in 1717 and was elected its first Secretary (Piggott 1985; Haycock 2002).

Stukeley's interest in antiquities had begun around 1710, when he initiated a series of annual summer journeys around the country visiting and recording sites of interest (Haycock 2002, 46). Although these journeys were originally undertaken for relaxation and leisure (and in later years to alleviate the effects of gout), Stukeley was soon reading widely, drawing upon his interests in history, natural history, philosophy, and contemporary religious and scientific debate, in an attempt to explain the antiquities he encountered (ibid., 5-9). His chorographic exercises resulted in the publication in 1724 of his *Itinerarium Curiosum*, whose subtitle *Or, An Account of the Antiquitys and Remarkable Curiousitys in Nature or Art, Observ'd in Travels thro' Great Brittan* gives an excellent idea as to its focus and content.

His first visit to Avebury took place in May 1719, in the company of his close friends Roger and Samuel Gale, fellow founder members of the reformed Society of Antiquaries. It is clear that Avebury had an immediate impact. Stukeley produced his first sketch plan of the monument on 19 May 1719, and this was followed by a series of annual visits between 1719 and 1724 (Piggott 1985, 165-6; Ucko et al. 1991, 42). During this time he gradually pieced together the remains of the site, recognising 'the entire work by degrees. The second time I was here, an avenue was a new amusement. The third year another' (Stukeley 1743, 18). Basing himself at the very centre of the henge, in the Catherine Wheel Inn, Stukeley spent

periods of typically a fortnight at a time, initiating an ambitious programme of measured recording of the henge and the monuments that
surrounded it, reporting his findings to the Royal Society and Society of
Antiquaries (Burl 1979, 47; Haycock 2002, 127) (Plate XV).

At this point it is useful to consider the relationship between Stukeley's
'discovery' and that made by Aubrey some 70 years earlier. The role
Aubrey's records played in guiding Stukeley to Avebury has been much
debated. Explicit acknowledgements to Aubrey are conspicuous by their
absence in Stukeley's published work on Avebury, yet it is known he had
seen some of Aubrey's written and drawn records prior to his first visit to
the site (Piggott 1985, 45-6; Ucko et al. 1991, 42-8; Haycock 2002, 129-30).
Indeed, in December 1718 Stukeley had made notes and redrawn plans
from a transcription of the unpublished manuscript of *Monumenta Britannica* made by Thomas Gale, himself a notable antiquary (Piggott 1985, 45).
This has led, understandably, to the suggestion that Stukeley deliberately
down-played the role played by Aubrey in the academic discovery of the
site in order to emphasise his own importance. While there seems to be
more than an ounce of truth in this accusation, recent research has
suggested that while Stukeley had indeed seen some of Aubrey's records,
he only had access to his more general notes and the rather misleading
account that appeared in the 1695 edition of Camden's *Britannia*. Without
access to Aubrey's detailed records and plans it would have been easy to
underestimate the value of the work the earlier antiquary had undertaken
(Ucko et al. 1991, 42-8). What is not in doubt is that in terms of volume
and detail, Stukeley's records of the Avebury landscape far outstripped
those of his predecessor. In addition, unlike Aubrey, Stukeley's work was
published, in the form of his 1743 tome *Abury, a temple of the British
druids*.

Stukeley, however, was not the first scholar to produce a publication on
Avebury. This honour went to a local vicar and keen antiquary, Thomas
Twining, who in 1723 published an essay entitled *Avebury in Wiltshire, the
remains of a Roman Work erected by Vespasian and Julius Agricola during
their several commands in Britanny*. Twining's study appears to have been
based on a single period of fieldwork, perhaps itself stimulated by
Stukeley's ongoing campaigns of detailed recording at the site (Long 1858,
12; Ucko et al. 1991, 38).

Twining's thesis was that Avebury was a Roman temple, and the overall
arrangement of the henge, avenues and Sanctuary corresponded to a
Roman map of Britain writ large upon the landscape. Although derided at
the time by Stukeley, and deemed to be of little more than novelty value
by the antiquaries and archaeologists of the nineteenth and twentieth
centuries (e.g. Long 1858, 12; Burl 1979, 51), it has recently been argued
that Twining's work was based upon a set of careful field observations

(Peterson 2003b). As a result, it provides a useful empirical adjunct to the pioneering records of Aubrey and Stukeley.

Aubrey found the clutter introduced by the presence of a working village in among the stones an impediment to their recording. During the 1720s Stukeley encountered the self-same problem as he sought to compile his carefully measured plans, perspective drawings and detailed textual descriptions of the site. Stukeley's task was made all the more difficult by the fact that he was recording a monument that was being systematically taken apart. This is reflected in the way Stukeley frequently annotated plans and notes to record stones recently destroyed. Indeed, he claimed that he had been so fastidious in recording such events that he could accurately recount the fate of the majority of missing stones (Ucko et al. 1991, 177-80; Stukeley 1743, 24).

This process of demolition, coupled with a tendency by Stukeley to rely rather uncritically upon oral testimony, let a number of inconsistencies and ambiguities creep into his records. These were in turn compounded by the delay of 20 years between his original recording and final publication, with numerous re-draftings and alterations introducing subtle changes into the plans and drawings (for a thorough and critical evaluation of both Stukeley and Aubrey's records see Ucko et al. 1991).

Inconsistencies notwithstanding, Stukeley's records, bolstered by the work of antiquaries such as Aubrey, and to a lesser extent Twining, still provide us with the most detailed and comprehensive record of the fabric and form of the monument we have, coming as they did at a time of great change. As we will see, they have been drawn upon extensively by subsequent scholars of Avebury, ourselves included, and still shape research agendas today. We will explore the impact of Stukeley's work on the fledgling discipline of archaeology in more detail in coming chapters.

Destructions and depredations – the earthwork slighted

The encroachment of the village into the henge interior came at a price. It is in the late seventeenth century that we witness the first major alterations to the earthworks of the henge, linked closely to the complex and fluid pattern of ownership of Avebury manor. Between 1685 and 1695 the then owner of the manor, Ralph Stawell, had an area of bank to the immediate north of the western entrance levelled and the ditch filled to facilitate the construction of a barn and tree-planting. A subsequent episode of levelling and planting took place to the south of the western entrance between 1721 and 1724, once again linked to changes in ownership of the manor (Ucko et al. 1991, 170-2). Other major interventions appear to have been concerned with Avebury's position astride the coach road. For example, in 1762 the bank to the west of the southern entrance was quarried to provide material for the raising of the road level as part of an improvement of the roadway (Smith 1965, 182; Burl 1979, 53).

Living with the stones

Both Aubrey and Stukeley commented on the diverse ways in which the inhabitants of Avebury made active use of the standing stones of the monument. For example, Aubrey claimed that one of the stones had been converted into a pigsty or cattle stall, while Stukeley records a fallen stone of the northern inner circle being regularly employed as a fishslab during market day (Ucko et al. 1991, 177). In addition, the excavations of Keiller in the south-eastern quadrant at Avebury and along the West Kennet Avenue showed how medieval and later field boundaries were aligned upon the sarsens, effectively using them as boundary markers (Keiller & Piggott 1936, 421, fig 2; unpublished notebooks, Alexander Keiller Museum).

There was also ad hoc destruction of stones as and when they fell down; what we might think of as an opportunistic form of monumental windfall. Aubrey records a stone at the start of the West Kennet Avenue falling in 1684 and breaking into two or three pieces (Fowles & Legg 1980, 37). Stukeley in turn records how a large stone in the northern entrance that fell within the lifetime of Reuben Horsall, the parish clerk, was subsequently broken up by the villagers through the use of wooden wedges (Stukeley 1743, 22-4). At other times stones were deliberately relocated. For example, in 1701 sarsens from the Beckhampton Avenue were used to create a bridge over the Winterbourne stream (Burl 1979, 46).

Stone burning and breaking

In each of the former cases we are dealing with largely pragmatic acts. Stones fall and then are broken, or are relocated but left intact. What sets the destruction episodes so vividly recorded by Stukeley apart from the above is *intent*. Here stones were not simply appropriated or relocated, they were deliberately and systematically destroyed. This was not restricted to recently fallen stones or those lying recumbent; standing stones were pulled down to facilitate destruction, and even stones that had previously been buried were dug up and shattered. Some of the latter were no doubt encountered during agricultural activity, the refurbishment of field boundaries and digging of ditches. Others, such as stone *xi*, appear to have been deliberately sought out by the stone-breakers (unpublished notebooks, Alexander Keiller Museum). So what was the nature of these acts of destruction?

8. Kings and Scholars

The antiquarian accounts of stone destruction

Stones were broken either through direct percussion or more commonly a combination of heat and percussion. The essence of the latter process was described by Aubrey, when it already appeared to have been an established technique:

> I have verbum Sacerdotis for it, that these mighty stones (as hard as marble) may be broken in what part of them you please; without any great trouble: Sc. Make a fire on that [...] line of the stone where you would have it crack; and after the stone is well heated, draw over a line with cold water, & immediately give a knock with a Smyths sledge, and it will break like the Collets at the Glass house.   Aubrey, quoted in Fowles & Legg (1980), 38

This was further elaborated by Stukeley, who not only recorded the fabric of the monument in painstaking detail, but also undertook a social-historical study of the stone breakers themselves, observing their practices, interviewing the chief architects and recording their motivations.

Disengaged, objective scientific observation was not for Stukeley; he formed alliances with local opponents of the stone breaking, such as the parish clerk Reuben Horsall, and owner of Avebury manor Sir Richard Holford, and campaigned vigorously for the destruction to stop (Burl 1979, 49). Drawing upon his observations and the testimonies of the stone-breakers themselves, Stukeley described the process of stone destruction in detail. First a pit was dug alongside the stone. Before it was toppled, large chunks of stone were placed in the base of the pit to support the sarsen when it fell, thus creating an airway beneath. Often the sheer bulk of the falling stone was sufficient to cause these supporting stones to break and shatter. In such cases enormous wooden levers were used to raise the stone to enable supports to be placed beneath. Once supported, loads of straw were placed beneath the stone and set light in order to heat it up, prior to the application of water and the sledge (Stukeley 1743, 15-16).

Archaeological evidence for stone destruction

Circumstantial evidence of stone burning can be found in the accounts of early antiquarian exploration of the site. For example, in his 1833 excavation at the Avebury Cove, Mr Browne of Amesbury noted that:

> Before the central one of the three, facing, (like the altar trilithon of Stonehenge) the north east, was placed the stone on which sacrifices were burnt. This I ascertained myself by digging, the place being still apparent where it lay, but now filled up with rubbish.   Long (1858), 17

143

While Browne mistook the remains of a stone destruction pit for a sacrificial altar, a more detailed and reasoned record comes from the excavations carried out by A.C. Smith and William Cunnington III between 29 September and 5 October 1865. In an attempt to elucidate the form and nature of the Cove setting, they dug a series of trenches around the surviving stones. Here they recorded a 'quantity of black charred matter' containing 'numerous large flakes and chips of sarsen, covered with black charred matter and burnt straw, or other material' (Smith 1867, 211). Further excavations around the site of the Obelisk revealed large quantities of the same. Unlike Browne, the excavators directly associated the burning deposits with the stone destruction episodes described by Stukeley (ibid., 211-13).

The best archaeological evidence for this episode of stone destruction comes from Alexander Keiller's excavations of the 1930s (Smith 1965), and from more recent work along the Beckhampton Avenue (Gillings et al. 2000, 2002) and at the Falkner's Circle (Plate XVI). During work on the West Kennet Avenue, Keiller excavated eight destruction features, two showing evidence of stone breakage through direct fracture and the remaining six through fire-setting. The latter were identified on the basis of 'the blackened sides of pits dug beneath the prostrate stones, burnt fragments of sarsen and even piles of charred straw' (Keiller & Piggott 1936, 419). Likewise, in the course of his excavations within the henge a total of 16 destruction features were excavated, nine of which produced evidence of burning (Ucko et al. 1991, 181). Here the burning pits were described as 'shallow scoops, just deep enough to permit straw to be shoved under the stone' (Smith 1965, 180). As with the West Kennet Avenue examples, the burning pits were found to contain masses of charred straw, flakes and 'scalings' of burnt sarsen, along with frequent finds of later seventeenth- and early eighteenth-century clay pipe (ibid.).

These rather simplified descriptions hide a variety of technological practices. The settings of the southern inner circle at Avebury perhaps provide the clearest illustration of variation in the techniques of stone breaking. Of the stones of the inner circle proper investigated by Keiller in 1939 (stones 101-9), three had been destroyed by fire: 104, 107 and 108. While employing a broadly similar methodology, in each case the burning pits displayed different characteristics. Pits were dug up against the outer faces of stones 104 and 107; that of the former being larger and more irregular than the latter, even though the stones must have been of comparable size. However, in the case of 108, a large, irregular pit was dug around the base of the stone leaving it more or less unsupported immediately prior to toppling (information from excavation records in Alexander Keiller Museum).

Of the smaller internal settings adjacent to the Obelisk, stone *i* was found to have been buried before being discovered and burned, perhaps around 1700-1710 (Smith 1965, 199). In keeping with the surviving stones of this setting and the overall size of the burial pit, this does not appear to have been a particularly large sarsen. However, to facilitate the burning of this stone a complex procedure had been adopted. It appears that a cavity some 0.34 m deep was dug beneath the stone as it lay in its burial pit, its bulk left supported on undug spurs of chalk. This void was then filled with straw and the stone burned. It is interesting to note that this approach mirrors that taken with the recumbent Longstones Cove stone described below, and with the Obelisk itself.

In contrast to the elaborate and carefully planned furnace constructed to destroy stone *i*, stones *ix*, *x* and *xi* were burned in a single communal burning pit centred upon stone *x*. This appears to have been an entirely pragmatic act. While digging the burning pit for stone *x* the burial pit for *ix* was discovered and the stone dug out and burned in the stone *x* pit. Stone *xi* was discovered likewise.

As if this was not variation enough, a final stone setting, stone *xii*, appears to have been broken up *in situ* using direct fracture instead of fire. This was suggested by the complete absence of any burning debris and a spread of 87 pieces of fractured sarsen covering an area of 2.5 x 1.5 m to the south of the stone socket (Keiller, unpublished notebooks). Far from forming a single coherent practice, it is clear from the destruction features within this relatively restricted area of the henge that a number of distinct strategies of stone breaking were employed.

Within the henge the majority of destruction pits were left open once stones had been removed (Smith 1965, 180; Ucko et al. 1990, 181). The recovery of horse bones from the upper fills of the multiple burning pit near the Obelisk suggests it had subsequently been used as a convenient receptacle for the dumping of refuse from the adjacent tanner's yard. Smith and Cunnington's excavation of the site of the Obelisk showed the pit had been left open to act as a repository for broken bottles from the nearby inn (Smith 1867, 212). Stukeley talked of 'nettles and weeds growing up' in the places where stones had been removed (1743, 22), and many destruction pits remain visible today as hollows (e.g. in the northern inner circle: Ucko et al. 1991, pl. 67) (Fig. 4B).

Recent excavations at Beckhampton and Falkner's Circle

Excavations undertaken on the line of the Beckhampton Avenue between 1999 and 2003 provided a unique opportunity to investigate in detail the archaeology of stone destruction. Of the 15 Beckhampton Avenue settings investigated, two had been dismantled in prehistory, four buried, eight fire-set and one initially buried and then subsequently dug up and presumably dragged away.

The majority of the burning pits were dug into the chalk in an expedient manner with sides and bases left uneven. Oval in plan, the pits ranged in maximum dimension from 1.8 m to 5.8 m, and were up to 0.95 m deep, their size seemingly a product of the dimensions of the stone and depth of ploughsoil through which they were cut. The destruction pit for one of the larger stones was cut from the south, sloping in a rather haphazard fashion down to the base of the stone. The resultant wedge-shaped profile seems designed to facilitate the removal of broken stone, while irregularity in the base of the cut could either reflect the employment of a rather *ad hoc* digging strategy, or a much more deliberate attempt to ensure a flow of air beneath the stone once firing had begun.

The basal fills comprised extensive spreads of flaked and burnt sarsen within a matrix of burnt straw and charcoal. Distinctive conchoidal fracture marks on the sarsen fragments suggest that *in situ* trimming of the blocks took place. In all instances the burning deposits on the bases of the pits were sealed by layers of ploughsoil containing sherds of medieval and early post-medieval pottery, occasional iron fragments and pieces of clay pipe. These upper fills seem to have formed slowly, perhaps as the result of repeated episodes of ploughing, meaning that, as at Avebury, the pits were effectively abandoned once the stone had been raked clear and roughly dressed.

In contrast to these simple burning pits, the destruction feature relating to the north-west stone of the Longstones Cove was markedly different (Plate XVII). Of the order of 50 tonnes, this stone had fallen at an early date, and lying recumbent posed particular problems for the stone-breakers. To enable the stone to be broken up they needed to create a sufficient space under it in order to pack straw and other fuel for the fire-setting and provide a free flow of oxygen. An elaborate, ingenious and rather dangerous solution was adopted. This involved the sinking of shafts into the solid chalk around the fallen stone deep enough and sufficiently wide for a person to stand upright in. These shafts provided the stone-breakers with sufficient working space to burrow horizontally beneath the bulk of the stone, allowing the chalk and earth supporting the sarsen to be mined away, leaving it supported on small un-dug spurs of chalk. In essence the pit became a furnace with the stone forming its 'lid'. In order to maximise the surface area of the fire, the shafts were partially backfilled up to the level of the mined central section, thus creating an even base on which to spread fuel for the burning. In this instance the destruction feature appears to have been too large to leave open, and as a result, following the burning the pit was partially backfilled with chalk rubble.

Stone breaking through fire-setting was also very much in evidence at the site of Falkner's Circle, a small late Neolithic setting of 12 stones, 800 m to the south-east of Avebury (Plate III). Excavations undertaken in 2002 revealed burning pits marking the positions of four stones of the southern and eastern arc of the circle. Two of these were shallow, cut largely into the topsoil. Of the remainder, one took the form of a shallow oval scoop, closely resembling the pits encountered on the line of the Beckhampton Avenue. The final pit was very different, being almost circular, some 3.6 m wide and 0.9 m deep. The base and sides of this feature were extensively fire-reddened, in some places firing the clayey sub-soil into brick-like lumps. Both the depth of the pit and its dished base suggest that it was cut *around* rather than *against* a standing stone. This certainly represents a more tidy technique than the usual practice of digging an extensive pit adjacent to the stone. However, it may not have been as economic; evidence for two separate firing episodes suggesting the process was less technologically efficient in distributing heat along the stone. In contrast to the pits at Avebury and Beckhampton, oak roundwood was used as the principal fuel for the firing at the Falkner's Circle instead of straw.

In a number of respects, the archaeological evidence from Avebury, the Beckhampton Avenue and Falkner's Circle conforms closely to Stukeley's account: pits were dug against the stones; smaller sarsen boulder 'supports' were occasionally used; and straw was the predominant fuel. Metal fittings from some of the pits could even derive from recycled structural timbers used as props, much as Stukeley displays in his drawings of fire-setting episodes (Piggott 1985, pl. 14). However, operating within this basic technology variability in practice can be found, generally resulting from the problems posed by the breaking-up of different megalithic settings, but perhaps also reflecting the experimentation and messiness of a nascent craft tradition.

It is, however, easy to overplay the role played by burning within the overall scheme of stone destruction. While the Falkner's Circle was almost totally destroyed by fire-setting, the stones of the Sanctuary were simply dragged away in the 1720s in order to provide the foundations for a barn. On the line of the West Kennet Avenue, of the 59 'missing' stone positions investigated, 14 had been buried (one of which had been subsequently discovered and broken up), six had been fire-set, two had been broken directly, and the remainder yielded no indication as to their ultimate fate except for their empty sockets (Smith 1965, 186). This suggests strongly that they had been dragged away, though perhaps before the time of the early antiquaries. It would appear that here burning accounted for the disappearance of relatively few of the settings.

A number of burning questions remain

With regard to the dating of these events and the motivations behind their enactment Stukeley was unequivocal. Through oral testimony he dated the beginning of this episode to around 1694 when 'Walter Stretch, father of one of the present inhabitants, found out the way of demolishing these stones by fire' (Stukeley 1743, 25). He was also wrong. As discussed earlier, Aubrey had recorded the same process in the 1660s; though some ambiguity remains over whether Aubrey was describing the breaking up of natural sarsens or megalithic settings.

In terms of archaeological evidence, the earliest stone burnings so far encountered are those at the Falkner's Circle. Here radiocarbon dating of roundwood charcoal from one of the destruction pits produced a date range spanning the early fifteenth to late seventeenth centuries, with the probability weighted towards the earlier part of the range. This pre-dates by a reasonable margin the destructions at Avebury recorded by Stukeley but is, interestingly, within or close to the time of Aubrey's account of stone breaking.

Some of the latest burning episodes took place at the Longstones Cove and along the line of the Beckhampton Avenue, when we know that stones recorded by Stukeley in the 1720s were subsequently burned and broken up. Sandwiched in between are a number of other Beckhampton Avenue destructions that can be dated on the basis of stamped clay pipes to the late seventeenth century, and those recorded by Stukeley at Avebury itself, taking place between the 1690s and 1720s (Stukeley 1743, frontispiece).

These dates are interesting since they indicate quite a long period of stone breaking, perhaps beginning as early as the late medieval period; and note should be taken here of the use of dressed sarsen within the fifteenth century rebuilding of the southern aisle of Avebury church (Freeman 1983, 103). There are some important implications that result from an awareness of the longevity of this stone breaking tradition. For instance, given the sixteenth- to seventeenth-century radiocarbon date for one of the stone burials along the Beckhampton Avenue, we must conclude that traditions of burial and burning were, for a time, coeval. It also makes the relatively short and intense episode of late seventeenth- to early eighteenth-century stone breaking within the henge itself and along the avenues all the more striking. Why had the stone-breakers suddenly focussed their activities on the remains of the monument complex, and why had fire-setting gradually replaced burial as the appropriate response to an unwanted standing stone? A different relationship now existed between the inhabitants of Avebury and the stones that surrounded them; no longer were sarsens merely hidden, they were now transformed into the very structures making up the fabric of the village.

Stone breaking could be a massive and expensive undertaking, involving a large amount of labour and materials. Indeed, the notorious stone-breaker Tom Robinson confessed to Stukeley that a stone burning could cost anywhere between 30 and 60 shillings, and noted that two stones had cost £8 to destroy (Stukeley 1743, 15-16, 25). Stukeley claimed that the chief motivation for stone destruction was a 'covetousness of the little area of ground, each stood on' (Stukeley 1743, 15). This implies that it was land that was of utmost importance rather than the stone itself.

There is certainly circumstantial evidence to support this interpretation. For example, it may be no surprise that the area of the West Kennet Avenue that was most degraded was that directly adjacent to the henge where intensive agricultural activity was taking place. However, in the case of Avebury itself we have seen that the majority of destruction pits were left open once the stones had been removed. If stone breaking was merely clearance for horticulture or agriculture, why was the debris left littered around and the pits themselves abandoned to accumulate nettles and rubbish? What is more, there is little evidence for intensive cultivation within the henge after the fourteenth century, and we know that the standing stones served as boundary markers in the organisation of the garden plots and orchards within the bank and ditch.

Another popular explanation for the spate of stone destructions focuses not upon the land occupied by the stones, but on the sarsen itself. Also rooted firmly within the economic sphere, this links the depredations to a general boom in building within the village during the late seventeenth and early eighteenth centuries (e.g. Malone 1989, 121-2; Ucko et al. 1991, 166). As with the issue of clearance, there is evidence to both support and challenge this claim. For example, Stukeley records how one of the Beck-hampton Cove stones was broken up to build part of the present Waggon and Horses Public House on the Calne-Marlborough road (Burl 1979, 51). Other buildings of this period, both houses and barns within and around Avebury, show the use of dressed sarsen blocks in their construction; one of the most elegant being Silbury House of *c.* 1700-1710 in the very centre of the henge. However, Stukeley also notes in detail the downside of such a strategy:

> They have sometimes us'd of these stones for building houses; but say, they may have them cheaper, in more manageable pieces, from the gray weathers [natural sarsens]. One of these stones will build an ordinary house; yet the stone being a kind of marble, or rather granite, is always moist and dewy in winter, which proves damp and unwholesome, and rots the furniture.
>
> Stukeley (1743), 16

Who were the stone-breakers?

In an attempt to shed further light on the question of motivation, let us look not at the destruction events themselves, but instead at the perpetrators. In his *Abury* Stukeley is clear as to who was responsible for the stone destruction, listing six 'cuvetous' local farmers whose names have since become synonymous with stone breaking: Tom Robinson, Farmer Green, John Fowler, Walter Stretch, Farmer Griffin and Richard Fowler. Their status as farmers and workers of the land lends some support to the economic arguments outlined above. However, as Peterson has shown (in Gillings et al. 2004), Stukeley's unpublished field notes tell a slightly different story, listing a further group of people who were equally responsible for the destruction of prehistoric monuments in the Avebury landscape: the lawyer Mr Smith, Mr Boak and the late parson of the local village of Winterbourne Monkton. He was also careful to exclude certain names from his published list of offenders. These included Caleb Baily, the owner of the nearby manor of Berwick Basset, and one of his professed fellow campaigners, Sir Richard Holford, who levelled parts of the bank of the henge. Indeed the former, Baily, was so prolific in his stone breaking that the Society of Antiquaries had written to him personally asking him to desist, and even commissioned a poet to attack him in verse (Gillings et al. 2004).

Not only does Stukeley firmly lay the blame at the feet of a small cabal of local farmers, he also appears to exaggerate their involvement in the breaking episodes, attributing to their actions a number of missing stones that we now know had been buried long before (Ucko et al. 1991, 210-11). These include several of the outer circle stones in the south-east quadrant which he claimed had been 'demolished by Tom Robinson Ao. 1700' (Stukeley 1743, frontispiece). He also placed an unreasonable emphasis upon Tom Robinson as the notional head of the group, singling him out for particular ire and going as far as to include a rather demonised portrait of him, replete with bat, in his *Abury* (ibid., 53, tailpiece) (Fig. 18). Even his identification of the men as 'farmers' was a gross simplification, for his group of stone-breakers included two publicans and two minor landowners (Gillings et al. 2004).

So why did Stukeley chose to focus his attack on these specific men? The difference between the two groups appears to be one of social class and standing: those excused blame by Stukeley were all *gentlemen*; the accused in contrast were, to use a term of Stukeley's, 'miserable farmers'. It can be argued that this may reflect a deliberate strategy on Stukeley's part to contrast 'ignorant destruction' with the 'educated appreciation' of the local gentry, when in reality a wide spectrum of the local community was involved in piecemeal destruction of the monument complex.

There is, however, a further dimension to the story. The later seventeenth and early eighteenth centuries were a period of frequently vociferous conflict between the established Anglican Church and sects of protestant non-conformity (for a detailed discussion in the context of Avebury, see Gillings et al. 2004). These conflicts resulted in tensions that were played out on both national and regional stages. Avebury is more or

18. William Stukeley's demonised portrait of Tom Robinson.

less equidistant between the towns of Marlborough, Devizes and Calne, and the Five-Mile Act, which prevented dissenting clergymen for preaching within five miles of an urban centre, resulted in numbers of non-conformists moving into the village during this period. In 1670 a non-conformist chapel was founded in Avebury, where a congregation of 25 met close to the centre of the henge in a group of cottages. In 1707 a purpose-built chapel was constructed opposite the original cottages, and by 1715 the congregation numbered some 130 (Dunscombe 1998, 3-8). What is of interest here is that the principal stone-breakers – Tom Robinson, Caleb Baily and John Griffin – were not only active non-conformists but closely involved with the construction of the chapel (Plate XXIII).

Peterson has noted how the monument itself may have become inexorably linked in the minds of the local populace to the established church, through feast and sports days, festivities and perhaps even the stone burials. Memories of the visit of Charles II to the site may also have served to consciously link the stones to the Anglican church in the minds of the non-conformists (Gillings et al. 2004). This may explain why the non-conformist chapel was not only constructed within the henge, and close to the site of the village maypole, but out of the very stones of the southern inner circle. This suggests that the decision to break the stones may have been a local reaction to wider events, and as much political and religious as it was economic. In this light it is interesting to note that those most vocal in their opposition to the stone-breakers were staunch Anglicans, such as the parish clerk Reuben Horsall and Stukeley himself – who was ordained in 1729 – a fact which may have fuelled the very fires they sought to extinguish.

While recognising how the practice was influenced by political and religious agendas, we are still left unclear as to why stone-breaking should have become preferred over burial or simple removal of the megaliths. The desire to create a usable building material is surely the driving factor, though like any form of technology, stone breaking was also embedded within contemporary social and cultural values. The seventeenth and eighteenth centuries represented a period of considerable social and ideo-logical transformation, which has been represented by some as marking the shift from a medieval to a 'Georgian' mindset (Deetz 1996). Johnson (1996) has characterised these changes as revolving around concepts of order, closure and commodification, and operating at several levels from the individual body to the landscape. Underpinning a 'rationalisation' of the agricultural landscape, as promoted by contemporary treatise on farming and estate management, were ideas surrounding the ordering of an unruly nature through processes such as enclosure (Johnson 1996, 72, 87), and of the moral and aesthetic 'improvement' inherent in these laboured practices.

One wonders whether Avebury's dissenting stone-breakers viewed their work as contributing to such an 'improved' social and physical landscape – clearing the land, but also removing stones tainted by tradi-tional superstition and associated in their minds with the dubious nature of Anglican values. As such, this work also facilitated an important *transformation* in the nature of these stones, from the material remains of an ungodly past into commodities in the making.

Although fire-setting was potentially more expensive and certainly involved greater risk than cold-working, it may have become the preferred technology of the stone breakers because of its highly visible nature, and because of the metaphoric connections that it could draw upon. Fire-setting of the larger stones must have provided a very public spectacle, especially when undertaken close to houses within the village. Its enact-ment would surely have recalled in people's minds the kinds of public bonfires popular during the period. Perhaps the use of fire was viewed as symbolically cleansing and apotropaic, in the same way that the common practice of lighting midsummer fires was intended to ward off evil and provide protection and blessing (Hutton 1996, 320-1). The burning of ungodly stones might therefore have been linked in the minds of non-conformists to the burning of papal or devil effigies as a part of Gunpowder Treason Day celebrations. These are just speculations, but they illustrate the potential cultural complexity of what, at first sight, might appear a relatively prosaic process. Of course there remain many ambiguities, and the archaeological evidence reminds us just how episodic, piecemeal and generally 'messy' the destruction of Avebury's megalithic monuments was.

Negotiating the remains of antiquity

It is clear that one of the most dramatic episodes in the long life of the Avebury monuments occurred during the seventeenth and early eighteenth centuries, when the stone settings of the henge, its avenues and other monuments in the immediate vicinity were simultaneously discovered and dismantled. As we have seen, it may not be entirely coincidental that the antiquarian recording of the monument occurred alongside an increase in the rate of its destruction. Unintentionally, academic interest transformed local understandings of the stones, which may previously have been considered little different to the natural 'grey wethers' forming the sarsen spreads in surrounding valleys. The stones now became the symbols of a politicised antiquity that pitched the interests of High Church antiquaries such as Stukeley against those of an increasingly non-conformist populace.

It is the records of Aubrey and, particularly, Stukeley that later generations of antiquaries and archaeologists have turned to when attempting to comprehend this episode of stone breaking. They, rather than the local inhabitants of the village, provided the written account of events, producing a somewhat single-sided perspective that has become the accepted narrative. There is no doubt that our understandings of this episode have been filtered through the lens of the antiquaries themselves. As has we have seen, while undoubtedly comfortable, the accepted view of enlightened scholarship on the one hand, and the forces of commerce pitted against the solidity of stone on the other, masks a much more complex, muddled and intriguing situation.

Furthermore, it can be argued that from the moment of its academic discovery a wholly new Avebury emerged – Avebury as an object, a curiosity; something precious to be preserved in a jar and pored over. This is an Avebury that could *only* be recognised by outsiders – by scholars like Aubrey and Stukeley. The monument now had a new material form, existing as a series of texts and manuscripts that served to represent the real physical entity within the Wiltshire landscape. Avebury could now be studied and consumed from afar in the comfort of private libraries and the rooms of learned societies. Elevated to the status of a canonical text, Stukeley's *Abury* in particular would leave a lasting legacy to be negotiated by successive generations of Avebury scholars.

9. An Emerging Discipline

Men of the greatest learning, and most subtle intellect have felt the difficulty, as well as importance of the subject: it has been acknowledged by
hundreds, who have started, full of energy, in the pursuit of their true
history, and have in the end wisely kept silence. ... And Stonehenge and
Abury continue as before, – apparently incapable of explanation: still inex-
pressibly awful, awfully majestic, in the now feebleness, so to say, of their
abused remains; fragments, rather than ruins; shadows of skeletons, rather
than presenting to the common observer even a rude outline of their original
structure; exciting a solemn veneration; raising up question after question,
theory upon theory; and still the same now as yesterday, – falling back into
the dark obscurity of a hundred generations.

Christian Remembrancer xii 1846,
cited in Long (1858), 52

The publication of Stukeley's *Abury* led to a flurry of academic interest in
the site, an interest that was to grow and develop throughout the course
of the nineteenth century. As early as 1858 the antiquarian William Long
was able to publish a detailed historiography charting the key moments
in Avebury's discovery, record and interpretation, and by 1901 the geologist W. Jerome Harrison could cite 105 references in his detailed bibliography of the site (Long 1858; Harrison 1901).

Yet Avebury's newly found fame was not restricted solely to the ivory
tower. A growing public curiosity is clear from the decision to include an
explicit reference to the 'stupendous remains of a Druid's Temple' in the
1748 edition of Daniel Defoe's popular and influential *Tour of Great
Britain* (Ucko et al. 1991, 56). Public interest was to grow during the
nineteenth century, Avebury appearing in a variety of guises within
contemporary travel literature. In 1862 *Black's Picturesque Tourist*
boasted 'the remains of one of the most gigantic druidical monument in the
world' (1862, 94), while the more sober *Baedeker* preferred to draw attention to Avebury's significance as the 'largest stone-circle in England' with
a special asterisk of commendation (1894, 108).

We have argued throughout this book that Avebury's sheer presence
has always demanded explanation. Generation after generation has con-
fronted the stones and earthworks and sought to account for them,
incorporating them into the fabric of their lived worlds. From the eight-

eenth century onwards, the explosion of academic and public interest was to lead new groups to encounter Avebury. However, in many ways this was a very different Avebury to any that had been encountered before. The early antiquaries had quite literally stumbled upon the site, their encounter being as physical and immediate as those who had grown up within its landscape. But this is where any similarity ends. Their understanding was that of the *outsider*, and their attempts to account for the monument drew not upon folklore, legend and social memory, but instead the frameworks of written history, the Bible and the scientific revolutions of the Enlightenment.

In time, a second group would also encounter Avebury, the first of what we would now recognise as scientific archaeologists. However, their encounter was different again, not so much physical as *literary*. The Avebury they came upon and debated was that described and evoked in the writings and drawn records of the antiquaries and chorographers who had preceded them.

As these researchers began to realise the extent of human antiquity and the depth and richness of Britain's prehistoric past, Avebury came to occupy a position at the forefront of debates – who built it, when, and for what purpose? Indeed Avebury's early-modern history can be read as a series of increasingly elaborate attempts by the first archaeologists to wrest answers from the frustratingly incomplete records and piecemeal remains that were deemed to have survived.

Of druids and Danish kings ...

It is important to realise that speculation on the origin and function of Avebury was not the sole preserve of the late eighteenth and nineteenth centuries. Attempts to *explain* the monument had accompanied and informed the very earliest episodes of concerted fieldwork at the site. For example, John Aubrey believed firmly that Avebury originated at a time before recorded history. Drawing on biblical accounts in the Old Testament, and widely held contemporary beliefs that the first pillared temples had replaced woodland groves as sites of worship, he equated stone circles with an archetypal form of religious structure. Noting the similarity between stone avenues and tree-lined walkways, he went on to interpret the former as a type of processional way leading up to the sacred precinct (Ucko et al. 1991, 70-3). As for who constructed it, Aubrey drew upon classical accounts to argue that it was an arch-temple of the druids, the most eminent of priests among the ancient Britons (Colt Hoare 1821, 60-1). Aubrey thus believed that Avebury was a pagan temple. In direct contrast, his contemporary and friend Walter Charleton believed that Avebury dated from the historic period and was not 'British' (i.e. pre-

155

Roman) but of Danish origin. Nor was it a temple. Building upon the work of Danish antiquarians such as Olaus Worm, Charleton believed that Avebury was instead a monument to a Danish king (Ucko et al. 1991, 19).

... celestial spheres and serpents

> ... throughout his annual visits to the site between 1719 and 1724, Stukeley's mind was awash with opinions about ancient religion, its structures and symbolism.   Ucko et al. (1991), 74

Although Piggott (1985) saw a strict separation between his fieldwork and theorising, Stukeley's entire recording project was intimately bound up with his developing interpretations and beliefs concerning the site. His changing ideas about Avebury were complex and deeply nuanced, intimately embedded within the contemporary political, religious and scientific debates of his day. As a result, it would take a book of its own to do them justice and we offer here only a brief sketch of his views and speculations. Fortunately, for readers keen to engage in more detail with Stukeley and his world, a number of excellent recent syntheses exist (particularly Ucko et al. 1991; Haycock 2002).

At a basic level, Stukeley accepted Aubrey's view that Avebury was a druidical monument. However, he sought to develop this through a detailed examination of the nature of druidical worship and religious practice. Drawing upon his keen interest in early religion, and wider renaissance concerns with Egypt, he identified the druids as practitioners of an early form of patriarchal Christianity, in effect as pre-Christian Christians (Haycock 2002, 11). To Stukeley the whole monument was soaked in symbolism, from the precise number of stones erected, to their geometrical proportions and orientation. A key aspect of his interpretation was the argument that rather than a series of temples and monuments, the whole was far more than the sum of its individual parts – a coherent, symmetrical form centred upon Silbury Hill, the mausoleum of its founder. Like Aubrey before him, he saw the stone circle as an archetypal form of temple. However, this was not one whose form echoed that of earlier woodland groves. Instead Stukeley's circles were modelled directly upon the shapes of the heavenly bodies. In his celestial scheme the inner circles at Avebury comprised temples to the Sun (south) and Moon (north) while the avenues served to link these in turn to temples of the earth (the Sanctuary) and the underworld (located at the terminus of the Beckhampton Avenue) (Stukeley 1743).

It has been argued that as his recording progressed, and despite concerted efforts in the field, his failure to identify the requisite temple at the end of the Beckhampton Avenue led Stukeley to rethink this interpretation (Ucko et al. 1991, 87-9). He was still convinced that the answer lay in the overall configuration of the monument complex that he had painstakingly identified and recorded. In an attempt to shed light upon what this pattern signified he turned to the study of Egyptian hieroglyphics, recognising in the symbol of the snake traversing a circle a possible explanation for the Avebury complex (ibid., 91). Removing explicit references to the Solar and Lunar temples, and the elusive shrine to the underworld originally thought to lie at the end of the Beckhampton Avenue, he argued that the snake and circle motif – a powerful symbol of the existence and creative power of God – could be overlain perfectly on to his symmetrical plan (ibid.). This, he argued, proved that Avebury was an archetypal form of druidical monument known as a *Dracontium* or serpent temple, the Sanctuary forming the head of the snake, the Beckhampton Avenue its tail.

As we noted in Chapter 8, while Stukeley was busy recording and interpreting *his* Avebury, Twining was identifying another. Once again the fieldwork was driven and informed by an underlying interpretation and for Twining, as for Stukeley, the key to understanding Avebury lay not in its constituent parts but instead in their interrelation with one another. Twining's Avebury was Roman in date, the layout of the monument complex not a hieroglyph or symbol, but a straightforward map of Roman *Britannia* (Twining 1723).

It is interesting to note that although common threads can be seen within many of these interpretations, whether in their emphasis upon druids, the presence of memorials to a great leader, or a reading of the Avebury complex as a vast pictogram, contemporary views rarely agreed. There was much debate and dispute. In the decades following these pioneering studies, debates were to grow in number and stature. The reasons for this appear relatively straightforward: as much of the fabric of the monument had been destroyed, there was less evidence for later observers to use to support any given case, let alone question the authority of those who had observed it apparently complete. It was their deep misfortune that these primary observers had themselves expressed so many conflicting opinions.

Stone destruction revisited

At this point it is important to acknowledge that widespread recognition of Avebury as an ancient monument did not signal an end to the destruction that had characterised the seventeenth and eighteenth centuries. While the tempo may have relaxed, we do not see an episode of 'ignorant' destruction giving way to a period of enlightened recording and speculation. Nothing is ever that neat at Avebury.

Stone breaking was continuing, albeit at a much reduced pace, and mainly (though not exclusively) focussed on fallen or part-broken stones. For example, between 1819 and 1859 four stones were removed from the henge, and one was blown up using gunpowder, the resultant explosion being big enough to send fragments of sarsen over a nearby barn. The motivations for these acts appear to have been largely utilitarian. One of the northern inner circle stones adjacent to the road was destroyed as it was deemed a hazard to road traffic, carters having repeatedly driven into it. The same was felt true of a large stone of the outer circle that stood adjacent to the northern entrance. This projected into the road and not only frightened horses, but caught on sacks of corn as loaded carts passed by. The northern inner circle stone destroyed so spectacularly by gunpowder met its fate as it was deemed to be blocking a rick-yard (Smith 1885, 141-2).

Such events were not confined to the henge. The Rev. Charles Lucas recorded a spate of late eighteenth-century destruction events along the avenues, noting how, on the instructions of his landlord, one Mr Nalder took stones of the West Kennet Avenue to build a farmhouse. In 1794, the owner of the same farmhouse himself destroyed up to nine avenue stones (Long 1878, 333). In 1878, William Long noted further depredations, recounting communications between the antiquary William Cunnington and Mr Butler of Kennet who had observed stone destructions taking place before 1873. These included the removal and burial sometime between 1807-9 of one stone that had stood stubbornly in the way of a proposed road, and the breaking up of a fallen megalith in 1824-5 to make a footpath (Long 1878, 330-1). In 1829, a further three stones of the West Kennet Avenue were removed by order of the Trustees of the turnpike road, as they had caused horses to shy and bolt at dusk (Long 1858, 23).

A landscape lost for ever

... it was prodigious to see how full the downes are of great stones; and all along the valley, stones of considerable bigness, most of them certainly growing out of the ground.   Pepys (1688), cited in Long (1858), 11

It was not only the stones of the Avebury monuments that witnessed destruction. In the High Wycombe area of Buckinghamshire a specialised industry had developed in the early nineteenth century centred upon the working of sarsen stone. Around 1850 one of the High Wycombe stone-masons, Edward Free, moved to the Avebury area looking for new markets to develop and exploit. He quickly established a very successful sarsen-cutting business, replacing the rather haphazard stone burning techniques with the more efficient tools and techniques that had been perfected by the High Wycombe masons.

The success enjoyed by Edward Free seems to have attracted other stone-masons to the area, creating an industry that was to continue well into the twentieth century. At its height in the 1890s, the local masons were supplying substantial quantities of cut sarsen for use as tramway supports, building stone and pavement kerbing, mostly to the rapidly expanding railway town of Swindon (King 1968).

With the widespread adoption of concrete the industry began to decline, closing as a concern in 1939. In its 80 years of operation, the industry completely altered the landscape of the north Wiltshire downs around Avebury, devastating the sarsen spreads that had covered the surrounding valleys and downland. Whole sarsen fields had been either completely or largely worked out, and areas of down had been cleared (ibid., 92-3). The unique landscape out of which Avebury had emerged had been obliterated, and the world of sarsen that had so moved Pepys had gone forever.

Canonical texts

As intimated earlier, one result of the flurry of stone destruction that characterised the early eighteenth century was a later reliance upon the records of Aubrey and more markedly Stukeley. Seen as a unique record of a monument now largely gone, their accounts were afforded considerable authority and provided a key point of departure for much of the work that followed. There were scholars such as Richard Colt Hoare who accepted the druidic *Dracontium* at face-value (Colt Hoare 1821). Others sought to re-interpret the evidence presented by Stukeley, or build upon it. Much of the fieldwork carried out in the nineteenth century was also driven by Stukeley's canonical text, designed either to confirm the more contentious aspects of his record or compare the contemporary state of the monument with that described by him.

The longevity and influence of Stukeley's account can perhaps best be illustrated by William Long's lament, some 145 years after the publication of *Abury*, that Stukeley's *Dracontia* was proving so persistent, when it should have been allowed to 'die out, never to be revived' long before (Long 1878, 334). Paradoxically, it was those researchers whose views broke most markedly from the Stukeley template that prompted the most challenging and informative fieldwork.

Wrestling with the serpent

In 1755 the Rev. William Cooke published what was for the most part an abridged version of *Abury*, in which he attempted to build upon Stukeley's ideas regarding patriarchal and druidic religion by proving that Avebury was in fact a temple dedicated to the Holy Trinity (Long 1858, 44-52).

The first attempt to reinterpret, rather than enrich, Stukeley's ideas was undertaken by Edward King in his *Munimenta Antiqua* of 1799. King explicitly set out to use the empirical record of the earlier antiquary while avoiding his conjectures. Accepting Avebury as a druidical monument, King used a particular reading of passages from the Bible to argue that rather than being temples, stone circles had served a variety of functions. These included memorialising great events, hosting courts, and variously acting as places for electing kings, holding councils, public games and spectacles, superstitious purposes and sacrifices (King 1799, 137). Applying his ideas to Avebury, he argued that the southern inner circle and Obelisk marked an area for councils and inaugurations. The key to the function of the northern inner circle was the Cove or 'cromlech'. This was seen as the 'remains of British Antiquity, so horrible, that I should wish to pass over the consideration of all that relates thereunto, with as much rapidity as possible' (ibid., 210): namely human sacrifice. The bank and outer circle provided a boundary for this special area, and linked to the circles by processional ways were altars of oblation at the site of the Sanctuary, and a more secluded cromlech for private sacrifice at the Longstones Cove (ibid., 222-3).

A very different interpretation was offered in 1801 by the oriental scholar, the Rev. Thomas Maurice. Once again happy to attribute the monument to the druids (whom he saw as descended directly from a tribe of Brahmins), he built upon his extensive knowledge of monumental structures in India to claim that the significance of Avebury was not serpentine but celestial. To Maurice, the number of stones making up the settings had a strong astronomical significance, and the Obelisk could be nothing other than the gnomon of a mighty megalithic sundial (Long 1858, 44-52; Harrison 1901, 91).

So far researchers had confined themselves to working solely with the information presented by Stukeley in his *Abury*. The first programme of new fieldwork at the site took place in 1812 as part of a pioneering survey of the antiquities of Wiltshire under the aegis of the prominent local antiquary Sir Richard Colt Hoare (Colt Hoare 1821). The work took the form of a measured survey carried out by Colt Hoare's surveyor, Philip Crocker, supplemented by a detailed written account of the monument. As well as providing a valuable check on Stukeley's earlier record, it also enabled Colt Hoare to chart the extent to which the monument had been further depleted since Stukeley's time; realising that of the 29 stones visible in 1722, only 17 remained by 1815 (ibid., 86). It is interesting to note that while he was sufficiently suspicious of Stukeley's recording to commission a wholly new survey, he was entirely happy to accept the earlier antiquary's interpretation without critical comment. This is particularly intriguing given his oft-stated motto 'We speak from facts, not theory'; but as Robinson has illustrated, Colt Hoare's approach mixed Baconian reasoning with a good dollop of romantic imagination (Robinson 2003). When it came to interpretation Colt Hoare deferred entirely to Aubrey and Stukeley, repeating large chunks of both Aubrey's *Templa Druidum* (the first volume of the unpublished *Monumenta Britannica*) and Stukeley's *Abury*. He concurred with Stukeley that the ditch and bank configuration proved that the site was religious rather than defensive, the bank acting as an amphitheatre for spectators watching the officiating druids. He also accepted not only that the serpent was venerated by ancient priests but that Avebury was indeed a serpent temple or *Dracontium* (Colt Hoare 1821, 57-96).

The first direct challenge to the druid hegemony (though not the serpent motif) came in 1823 with the publication of Henry Browne's *Origin and Character of the Serpent and Temple at Avebury*. In a thesis he was to develop in his later published work (1833) he attempted to shed light upon the motivations that lay behind serpent temples. Put simply, why choose the symbol of the snake? Rather than a place of druid worship, he argued that it was older – much, much older – in fact predating the biblical flood. Browne's Avebury was built under the direction of someone for whom the serpent had a particularly potent significance, Adam, to memorialise his experience in the garden of Eden (ibid., 35-6). Browne was convinced that the class of druidical temple recognised by Stukeley as *Dracontia* were merely later copies and appropriations of Adam's original handiwork. Of interest in Browne's account is the way in which geological discoveries of fossil animals were woven into his narrative (ibid.), with enormous antediluvian creatures presumed to be used by Adam as traction animals in a rather prescient anticipation of the techniques employed in Bedrock Quarry in the popular 1960s cartoon series *The Flintstones*.

It seems that in the early nineteenth century you couldn't keep a good druid down. They were to make a rapid comeback in the Rev. William Lisle Bowles' argument that Avebury was a druidic temple to the Celtic deity Teutates, a god who had been introduced to them by the Phoenicians. Bowles' scheme built upon the earlier suggestion of Maurice that the Obelisk acted as the gnomon of a sundial, suggesting that the stone settings of the circles formed a heavenly calendar, the whole designed to mark the passage of time. Beyond the immediate confines of the circles the 'serpent' defined by the avenues was seen as a potent symbol of rebirth and immortality, charting the course of the stars across the heavens. The final component was Silbury Hill, the platform upon which an effigy of the deity had once been placed (Bowles 1828; Long 1858, 46-7).

Fieldwork in the decades following the exertions of Colt Hoare was limited. In 1829, the antiquary and Presbyterian minister Joseph Hunter undertook a perambulation around the site, comparing his observations to

Stukeley's records and making a detailed note of any changes that had taken place since the publication of Crocker's 1812 survey. Although notable mainly for the detailed (and impassioned) record made of ongoing stone destructions, Hunter did speculate that the avenues, which were so integral to Stukeley's serpent temple, were later elaborations rather than a coherent part of a single grand design, equivalent, one imagines, to the formal drives built to lead visitors to a great house (Hunter 1829). The first recorded, if rather ad hoc, antiquarian excavation was undertaken by Henry Browne in 1833, in support of his antediluvian theory of Avebury's origin. As well as describing the surviving fabric of the monument, he dug within the area of the Cove in an attempt to locate an assumed altar stone (Browne 1833, 32-3). Although he claimed at the time to have discovered evidence of burnt sacrifice, he had in fact dug into a post-medieval stone-burning pit.

Dracontia, however, were never far away. As Browne was reiterating his claims regarding the antediluvian origins of Avebury, Mr Bathurst Deane was busy developing Stukeley's sinuous theme, arguing that Avebury was indeed some form of druidic serpent symbol, or hierogram, laid out across the landscape (Long 1858, 47; Deane 1833). One of the strongest challenges to the druid stranglehold came in 1839, with the publication of the statistician and antiquary John Rickman's attempt to establish a firm date for the construction of Avebury (Rickman 1839).

Rickman's argument hinged in part on the relationship between Avebury and the Roman road and the apparent way the otherwise rational Roman engineers had aimed a road at Silbury Hill 'merely for the sake of avoiding it' (ibid., 401). Thus Silbury Hill post-dated its construction, but not by much, its precise location in the landscape closely linked to the course of the road. That the entire complex was similarly Roman in date was suggested by the way in which the monuments appeared to be laid out using the Roman mile as the basic unit of measurement.

At Avebury itself, the internal ditch, circular form and four entrances could mean only one thing: it was a circus or amphitheatre for ceremonies and games, the avenues leading audiences from the road to it. Through a complex set of calculations Rickman showed that around 20 rows of spectators could be accommodated on the bank, each seating 2,400. This gave Avebury a total capacity of 48,000 spectators. By comparing this figure with population estimates for the Roman centres of London, Bath and Verulamium, along with other towns within an 80 mile radius, he argued (albeit in a rather circular fashion) that Avebury *had* to be Roman as prior to the Roman period there were simply not enough people to fill it, and who in their right mind would build a circus too big to fill? He thus dated the complex to the third century AD (ibid., 401-8).

Elsewhere new discoveries were being made on the ground. Some 800 m to the south-east of Avebury, in the broad, dry valley that runs from the henge to West Kennet, the Devizes antiquary Mr Falkner found another, previously unrecorded, stone circle. While riding along the West Kennet Avenue in 1840, he noticed a single standing stone, along with two fallen stones and nine hollows, that appeared to define a circle of twelve settings some 40 m in diameter. The circle was in a meadow that was subsequently brought under cultivation, nearly all traces of the monument being destroyed in the process of clearance (Long 1858, 39-40).

What is intriguing about Falkner's Circle is that neither Aubrey nor Stukeley made any mention of such a monument in their records; though the one remaining stone was well hidden in a hedgerow forming the tithing boundary between Avebury and West Kennet. This in turn suggested that contemporary understandings of the density and arrangement of megalithic monuments in the Avebury landscape, based solely on the work of the early antiquaries, were at best partial. However, it may have been precisely that lack of reference in the canonical text of Stukeley that meant that Falkner's putative circle made little impact on orthodox understandings of the Avebury complex. This is evident from the suggestions of the Rev. Edward Duke, who in 1846 claimed that Avebury was part of an enormous, albeit fixed, Orrery or Planetarium. This was centred upon Silbury Hill, which represented the earth, with the southern and northern inner circles at Avebury indicating the sun and moon respectively. The avenues marked the pathways of the celestial orbs and the precise number of stones present in each circle had complex calendrical significance (Long 1858, 48-50). There was clearly no room for Falkner's mysterious planet in Duke's complex schema.

The final key publication from the first half of the nineteenth century suggested that Avebury had little to do with druids. In his 1849 volume *Cyclops Christianus*, Algernon Herbert argued that Avebury post-dated the Roman period, labelling Stukeley's *Dracontium* a 'gross deception' (Herbert 1849, 104). His reasoning was twofold. First, as the classical writers had not deigned to mention it, Avebury must be much later than the Roman occupation. This was confirmed in his mind by the way in which the stone circles and avenues mirrored the oak groves of the druids and their pathways through the forest. Secondly, as the druid faith was dependent upon trees, and the stone monuments were erected in the open, it followed that this act of mimicry took place at a different time, marking an earlier forest-bound tradition in a now open landscape. The monuments were little more than an echo of earlier druidic traditions (ibid., 99-109).

The birth of a discipline

The object for which the great work at Abury was constructed will probably
ever be involved in mystery.   Long (1858), 43

By the early decades of the nineteenth century, antiquarian understandings of what we would now term 'prehistory' had reached something
of a stalemate, constrained as they were by their near total dependence
upon written records. For periods pre-dating the classical era the only
source of information was the Bible, with the entirety of prehistory
crammed into the period following Creation – an event that had taken
place on 23 October 4004 BC, according to the calculations of the seventeenth-century Archbishop James Ussher (Trigger 1989, 31). However, a
number of significant developments took place in the middle of the nineteenth century that would mark an important turning point both in the
development of scientific archaeology as a formal academic discipline, and
understandings of prehistoric monuments such as Avebury.

Various social, institutional and academic developments characterised
the period 1840-1860. A burgeoning middle class, educated and taking an
interest in the new sciences of archaeology, geology and natural history,
was instrumental in the creation of a number of very active county-based
archaeological societies during the 1840s. A desire to put archaeology onto
a more 'scientific' footing also led to a split within the ranks of the Society
of Antiquaries of London in 1843. This resulted in the formation of the
British Archaeological Association, a group disaffected with the antiquarian tradition and keen to promote scholarly research into the 'arts and
monuments of the early and middle ages' (Piggott 1991, 108-9).

The study of prehistory was furthered by a number of landmark publications, including the introduction of the Danish scholar Christian
Jürgensen Thomsen's three-age system into British archaeology. Developed from his work cataloguing the collections of the Danish National
Museum between 1816 and 1819, this gave a coherent framework to
prehistory for the very first time through the identification of successive
ages of stone, bronze and iron. His system was published in English in
1848, the first application coming shortly after in Daniel Wilson's 1851
book *The Archaeology and Prehistoric Annals of Scotland*, which also
marked the first use of the term 'prehistoric' within the discipline (Trigger
1989, 73-94; Chippindale 1988).

Outside archaeology, the publication of the geologist Charles Lyell's
Principles of Geology between 1830 and 1833 had established the antiquity
of the earth, providing a long timescale within which geological and
archaeological evidence could be placed. A visit in 1859 to excavations in
the Somme Valley by the Geological Society of London enabled Lyell, John

Prestwich and eminent archaeologists such as John Evans, to confirm the antiquity of human tools found in association with extinct animals (Trigger 1989, 93-4). The year 1859 also saw the publication of Charles Darwin's landmark *On the Origin of Species*, followed in 1863 by Lyell's *The Geological Evidences of the Antiquity of Man*.

In 1865 John Lubbock published his highly influential volume *Prehistoric Times*. A cultural evolutionist strongly influenced by the work of Darwin, he was the first to draw a distinction between an early (palaeo) and later (neo) stone age. No longer constrained by biblical and written sources, prehistory now had a considerable time-depth and a formal structure.

Closer to Avebury, 1853 saw the formation of the Wiltshire Archaeological and Natural History Society, which set out to collect and publish information on all matters connected with the archaeology of the county (Piggott 1991, 109). The inaugural meeting attracted 200-300 people and the Society boasted an early membership of some 200 individuals. From the outset it established a library and museum, and in 1854 published the first volume of the *Wiltshire Archaeological and Natural History Magazine* (ibid., 110-12). It was in the 1858 volume of this journal that William Long published his encyclopaedic historiography of Avebury, detailing the surviving physical fabric, and critically reviewing the antiquarian records and changing interpretations of its date and function (Long 1858). Long's survey was a benchmark document, and its value and importance to contemporary students of Avebury can be seen in the regular updates that were published to it (Long 1862; 1878). Indeed, it is still an invaluable document today, and has been drawn upon heavily in the writing of this chapter.

Despite the apparent 'opening up' of prehistory in the 1850s, the first major syntheses of Avebury to follow Long's careful review pursued an avowedly post-Roman agenda. Influential in this was the work of the historian J.M. Kemble, who in 1857 had speculated that:

> ... the avenue you see, which my friends the Ophites consider so mysterious was only a common stone row, and the 'temple' itself of the snake, the sun, the helio-Arkite cult, the mystic zodiac, and a number of other very fine things – so fine that one cannot understand them – is very probably, in the eyes of this dull dog of a surveyor, only a burial place.
>
> Kemble, quoted in Long (1858), 55

This rather prosaic claim was based upon a particular reading of a reference to a 'stone row' leading to a 'burial place' in an Anglo-Saxon boundary charter. Kemble linked this directly to the West Kennet Avenue and Avebury, arguing that the latter was little more than a cemetery. His work is important because his conclusions were taken up and developed by one of the most influential nineteenth-century scholars of Avebury. The latter was a man whose work not only led to the first formal campaigns of excavation within the henge, but who, unintentionally, did more than any other to establish its prehistoric date – James Fergusson.

Fergusson – many wrongs make a right

Fergusson's interests lay with megalithic monuments. Noting that little progress had been made in explaining such structures since the eighteenth century, he was particularly concerned that learned authors could not agree whether stone circles were temples, tombs or observatories, or whether they were of historic or prehistoric date. In much the same way as Rickman and Kemble before him, he believed that researchers such as Stukeley had been too imaginative in their interpretations – little more than 'speculative dreamers' forming a 'Druids and Dragons' faction all of their own (Fergusson 1872, 61). He also regarded the work of local antiquaries as being too parochial, based on a narrow foundation of fact and unaware of broader trends in the material under study. Fergusson set out to rectify this situation, basing his interpretation on a corpus of excavated evidence from around half the stone circles then known in the United Kingdom (ibid., 50).

At Avebury, he followed Herbert in dismissing any druid connection due to the lack of trees (which he deemed essential to druidical forms of worship), and the failure of any of the classical authors to mention such structures. He also criticised suggestions that Avebury was a temple or meeting place on the grounds that the site was simply too big and visibility in and across it was restricted, being broken up by the stone settings. He affirmed this in his usual dogmatic style: 'No place, in fact, can be so ill adapted for either seeing or hearing as Avebury; and those who erected it would have been below the capacity of ordinary idiots if they designed it for either purpose' (ibid., 67). Furthermore, he saw at Avebury no evidence of the progressive elaboration and enhancement one would expect in a temple. Instead Avebury was of one build, following a coherent design 'as would be raised by an illiterate army wishing to bury with honour those who had fallen in the fight' (ibid., 73).

Building upon the work of Kemble, he argued that while smaller stone circles were undoubtedly concerned with burial, larger examples such as Avebury acted instead as battlefield memorials or cenotaphs, the avenues memorialising the lines of the opposing armies as they were drawn up for battle. Avebury was then a military burial ground commemorating a specific battle. But given that Avebury was no ordinary monument, this could have been no ordinary battle. Fergusson argued that it was in fact

King Arthur's last conflict, the battle of Badon Hill, fought around AD 520. Silbury was raised in honour of the great leader, Arthur's key generals were buried within the two inner circles of Avebury, and his troops under the vallum, which was in effect a circular long mound. The remains of the defeated army were interred in the Sanctuary (Fergusson 1872, 61-89; Smith 1867, 216).

Fergusson first aired his controversial views in the *Quarterly Review* of 1860, repeating them in letters to the editor of the *Athenaeum* in 1865 and 1866 as part of a spirited debate on Avebury between himself, Sir John Lubbock and the physicist Professor Tyndal (ibid., 215-16). The most developed version of his argument was presented in his remarkable synthesis of megalithic structures, *Rude Stone Monuments*, published in 1872.

At this point readers may be wondering why Fergusson has been afforded such an influential status in our account. In an irony we can be quite confident Fergusson himself would not have enjoyed, he was influential not because his interpretations were *correct,* but because they were so profoundly *wrong.* It was not his ideas that advanced our understanding of the site, but the reaction they provoked from other archaeologists who sought to disprove them.

To his credit Fergusson was under no illusions that some of his theories would be controversial and would prompt others to carry out work expressly to prove him wrong. He was also supremely confident that he was correct in every detail. Central to his interpretation was the assumption that Silbury Hill was erected sometime around AD 520 and was thus later than the Roman road. In January 1866 he sent a letter to the editor of the *Athenaeum* suggesting that the Wiltshire Archaeological and Natural History Society (WANHS) settle the issue once and for all by undertaking a thorough excavation and survey to determine the relationship between the Hill and the road. In October 1867 they did just that, with Fergusson in attendance. In this pioneering piece of research-driven excavation no sign was found of the road beneath Silbury, instead its course was tracked some 28 m to the south (Wilkinson 1869).

Two years earlier, and unbeknown to Fergusson, a series of excavations had taken place at Avebury itself, prompted in large part by his claim that the site was an enormous burial ground. Directed by the Rev. A.C. Smith and William Cunnington III, both prominent local antiquaries and original officers of WANHS, these excavations are notable for the way in which they were carefully structured around a clear research question. Although 30 years earlier Browne had dug around the Cove, this was in a rather ad hoc fashion, the results going unrecorded. Other interventions that had taken place had been little more than chance observations, for example the note made by the antiquary John Thurnam in 1860 of the discovery of a buried stone on the line of the West Kennet Avenue, and the remains of a burning pit discovered during the burial of a horse (Long 1878, 331). In contrast, the work of Smith and Cunnington was designed to prove once and for all whether Avebury had been used for burial. In total, 14 areas were excavated, including trenches around the Cove and Obelisk, and into the bank. Needless to say, no human remains were found, and what Fergusson did not know while he was busy exhorting the Society to dig in order to prove his claims, was that they had already proved him wrong (Smith 1867).

Probings and soundings

The excavations stimulated by Fergusson heralded a much more proactive phase of fieldwork at the site, including more concerted attempts to confirm the antiquarian records. This is typified by the work of the Rev. W.C. Lukis, another original officer of WANHS. Following a further monitoring exercise carried out by Long in 1878, Lukis was commissioned by the Society of Antiquaries in London to produce a definitive measured record of the monument. In 1881, aided and abetted by A.C. Smith, he spent two months at Avebury undertaking a detailed survey of the site and making camera lucida portraits of each of the remaining upright stones.

With the help of five labourers, Lukis used iron bars to probe the vacant places in the outer and inner circles where the plans of Stukeley and Colt Hoare had indicated that stones once stood. This appears to have been tiring and frustrating work, but resulted in the discovery of 18 buried sarsens, two in the northern inner circle and 16 in the outer. Some of these were uncovered and measured, and all were marked with painted wooden pegs. This discovery was interesting for a host of reasons, not least because several buried stones in the outer circle corresponded to sarsens that Stukeley had claimed were removed by Tom Robinson around 1700. Lukis rather charitably assumed that the former antiquary had been misinformed. As well as the buried stones, the measured survey also identified a further 24 or so hollows indicative of former stone positions that had been missed by Crocker and Colt Hoare in 1812 (Lukis 1881-3, 151-3; Smith 1885, 139-42).

Smith's role in the study and interpretation of Avebury is an important one. An early member of the breakaway British Archaeological Association, he became familiar with the archaeology of the Avebury region after being appointed Vicar of Yatesbury in 1852, helping to inaugurate WANHS a year later. In much the same way as contemporaries such as William Long, he was acutely aware of the destruction of antiquities that was going on around him, through stone breaking and the gradual ploughing up of earthworks on surrounding downland. In 1880 the congress of the British Archaeological Association was held in Devizes, and as part of the proceedings Smith led members on a tour of the Avebury landscape. This prompted the Secretary of the society to encourage him to put together a record of the monuments for the benefit of other archaeologists, before they were completely ploughed away and dismantled (Smith 1885). Although a considerable task, this is exactly what he did, drawing upon his 30 years of familiarity of the downland environment.

His survey was published in 1885 as *A Guide to the British and Roman Antiquities of the North Wiltshire Downs*, an impressive folio volume comprising a series of detailed annotated maps and supporting text. Although similar in some respects to a modern Sites and Monuments Record, this work can also be seen as a continuation of the antiquarian landscape tradition of earlier workers such as Stukeley and Colt Hoare. Avebury lay quite literally at the centre of Smith's enterprise. His account of the monument drew not only upon the records and discussions of Aubrey, Stukeley and Colt Hoare, but those of William Long and his own fieldwork with Lukis (Smith 1885, pl. V). What makes his work so important was that for the very first time the records of the early antiquaries and later commentators were brought together with the results of contemporary survey and fieldwork in a unique attempt to shed light upon the wider archaeological landscape and Avebury's place within it.

Avebury preserved and pickled

In the late nineteenth century there was considerable pressure to remodel and develop the fabric of the monument, driven by the gradual expansion of the village. Between 1841 and 1871 Avebury's population had virtually doubled, and in 1872 an area of the circle was sold as part of a proposed programme of house building (Burl 1979, 55). The planned development seems to have been the final straw in pushing the archaeological lobby from merely lamenting and recording acts of destruction to taking positive action to prevent them. This took the form of a combination of on-the-ground protest by local enthusiasts and, perhaps more tellingly, purchase of the contested ground by Sir John Lubbock in 1871, who had long been concerned by what he saw as the wanton destruction of Avebury (Lubbock 1865, 53).

Influenced by developments at Avebury, Lubbock was later instrumental in the introduction of legislative protection for ancient monuments; the Ancient Monuments Act of 1882 being largely a product of his efforts. Providing the first schedule of 28 monuments deemed to be of national importance, the Act took almost a decade to reach the Statute Book (Bowden 1991, 95). Although it now became a criminal offence to deface or injure any one of the 'scheduled' monuments, the Act was initially very permissive, requiring the consent of the landowner for a site to be included on the list (ibid.). It is fitting that for his efforts as a politician and scholar, Lubbock would later take the title Lord Avebury.

Among those sites on the first schedule were Avebury, the West Kennet Avenue, the Longstones at Beckhampton, and Silbury Hill. As a result of the Act, subsequent impacts to the fabric of the monument were only those that had been sanctioned by the government, rather than at the whim of farmers or speculative developers. However, while it seemed as though the process of piecemeal destruction that had begun in the early medieval period was finally being halted, there were still appreciable impacts being made on the stones and earthworks, though this time they came from archaeologists.

In 1894 a trench was excavated through the henge bank to the level of the old ground surface on the orders of Sir Henry Meux (Passmore 1935). The results of this were never published in detail, and as such it might be regarded as little different from earlier acts of more utilitarian bank levelling. Of more value was the campaign of excavation carried out by Harold St. George Gray, driven not by a desire to check the validity of earlier records, but instead addressing a pressing scientific question.

The Age of Stone Circles

In 1899, the British Association for the Advancement of Science formed a committee whose remit was to address the 'Age of Stone Circles'. They duly commissioned Harold St. George Gray, then curator of Taunton Museum, to undertake excavations on their behalf. Gray had earlier worked as secretary to the pioneering field archaeologist General Pitt-Rivers, and it was under the General that he learned the craft of methodical excavation (Bowden 1991, 106-7), making him one of the most competent field archaeologists of his day.

After campaigns in Derbyshire and Cornwall that did little to shed light upon the dating of these monuments, Gray finally turned his attentions to Avebury in 1908 (Gray 1935). With a team of labourers and assistance from his wife and young son, Gray undertook short excavation seasons in 1908, 1909, 1911, 1914 and 1922, with a phase of detailed survey in 1912 (Plate XVIII). During the same period Gray was also engaged in the excavation of the Neolithic henge and Roman amphitheatre of Maumbury Rings, Dorchester (Bradley 1975), though curiously he never seems to have made a real connection between this site and the Avebury henge.

Excavation at Avebury focussed upon the ditch and bank, with only cursory work around a single prostrate stone of the southern inner circle and a partly buried stone in the northern. Confined to the southern half of the earthwork, he dug five trenches through the ditch, one partway into the bank and a series of narrow slots across the southern entrance causeway (Gray 1935) (Plates XX, XIX). The sheer scale of the excavated cuttings was impressive, the full depth of the ditch being revealed for the very first time, some 6 m below the level of the modern silting (Gray 1935, pl. XLIV) (Plate VI). Gray also succeeded in his principal aim of dating the construction of the monument, recovering Neolithic pottery from the ground surface beneath the bank and late Neolithic and Bronze Age sherds from the lower fills of the ditch (Piggott, in Gray 1935).

Avebury resurrected – seeds are sown

It is worth noting that this period in Avebury's long history is notable for witnessing the beginning of a strategy that was to completely dominate approaches to the site during the first half of the twentieth century. Having arrested the process of decay, archaeologists now sought to *reverse* it, and for the first time since the early Bronze Age stones were beginning to go up instead of come down.

This process began on the morning of 2 December 1911, when Adam, one of the stones of the Longstones Cove, fell with what one imagines was an almighty thump. In January of the following year the Wiltshire Archaeological and Natural History Society decided that the remains of the stone setting should be investigated and the sarsen raised and reset. Between May and August 1912 the prominent Wiltshire archaeologists Maud and Benjamin Cunnington duly excavated the socket, discovering the remains of an adjacent Beaker burial in the process, and supervised the resetting of the stone in a concrete base. Lifting the stone up proved to be a complex and hazardous operation, but was eventually achieved using jacks borrowed from the Great Western Railway yard at Swindon (Cunnington 1913). While the re-erection was taking place the Society also decided to raise a stone of the West Kennet Avenue that had fallen sometime around 1899 (ibid.). As we will see in Chapter 10, this process of piecemeal restoration was to gain considerable momentum in the following decades.

Parasites, dull swains and clouted shoons

Oh! let not the rude and ignorant demolish what is still left of these venerable piles, these truly precious relics of antiquity.

Browne (1833), 38

... the pretty little village of Abury, like some beautiful parasite, has grown up at the expense, and in the midst, of the ancient temple.

Lubbock (1865), 53

This chapter has, by necessity, proceeded at a rather breakneck pace in its attempt to chart a coherent course through the swarm of ideas and gallons of academic ink spilt in the name of Avebury during the nineteenth century. However, one important aspect of Avebury has, until this point, been largely absent. That is the village itself. With Avebury more firmly recast as a unique object of learned study, the village became little more than an intrusion and obstruction, a 'vile hamlet' at the root of all of Avebury's problems and depredations (e.g. Hunter 1829, 4). It could be argued that it is at this point that commentators began to consider Avebury as a miraculous curiosity fouled by the mundane and domestic. This trend was to reach its height during the first half of the twentieth century.

What we hear of the inhabitants of Avebury is largely filtered through the perceptions of the learned commentators, appearing only as an anonymous workforce, an inconvenience, or source of mischief, driven by 'ignorance and avarice' (Browne 1833, 36). For example, in the early nineteenth century Hunter recorded how two fallen stones had been broken up by tenant farmers, lamenting that 'Such an unparalleled remain may be in little esteem with the dull swain, who treads on it daily, with his clouted shoon' (Hunter 1829, 6). Where the locals were named it was only as architects of destruction, as is the case of Mr Naldy, who ordered a labourer to destroy three stones of the northern inner circle that were standing 'inconveniently to him in his husbandry arrangements' (ibid.). That tensions were developing between the population of Avebury and the growing coterie of archaeologists and learned men attracted to it is suggested by the following tale recounted to Cunnington by Mr Butler:

> While this work of destruction was going on, two gentlemen from London, in a post chaise, saw the men thus engaged. They drew up and expressed their disapproval in warm language; one of them winding up by telling the foreman that a man who would undertake such work, ought not to die in his bed. The man's name was Shipway, he lived at Avebury; and, added Mr. B(utler)., the saying of the gentleman was fulfilled, for the man hung himself.   Long (1878), 330-1

If we look beyond these accounts, the villagers were going about the business of everyday life in much the same way as they had always done. The village was certainly growing, but that does not mean that the henge and stone settings ceased to be an integral part of village life. The annual fête was held in the area of the southern inner circle and children still played by making models of the circles out of small stones and chunks of broken brick (Smith 1885, 142; Lukis 1881-3, 153).

What the early archaeologists and learned commentators failed to grasp was that their perceptions were profoundly those of the outsider. The villagers were neither ignorant nor wilfully malicious, they simply saw Avebury in a wholly different way. To those dwelling in and around the monument Avebury was not special or extraordinary: it had always been there and always would, a familiar part of their everyday dwelling and deeply entwined within their lives and memories. This is perhaps most clearly illustrated by the experiences of Gray, returning to Avebury after the First World War. In an experimental mood, Gray had left one of his ditch cuttings open at the end of the 1914 season in an attempt to monitor the degree to which it would naturally silt-up before he could resume digging. When he was finally able to return in 1922 he found that several tons of domestic rubbish had been thrown in, learning that the open trench had become something of a convenient amenity for the village and beyond (Gray 1935, 124, 132n1).

As the twentieth century progressed all this was to change, as attempts were made to transform Avebury from a living village to a representation of the prehistoric monument. The 'disempestring' effected by Aubrey, Stukeley and the antiquaries that followed them had been carried out using parchment, paper and ink. From the 1930s onwards it was to involve forcible relocation, mechanical excavators and concrete.

10. Resurrecting Avebury

The marmalade man cometh

Gray's work at Avebury concluded in 1922, the final report on his excavations being published 13 years later in the journal *Archaeologia* (Gray 1935). By this time Gray had had quite enough of the Avebury landscape (see below) and had returned to his post as curator of Taunton Museum, turning his attentions to the excavation of prehistoric and Roman sites in Somerset (Bowden 1991, 164). Though Gray's report was thorough and invaluable with regard to the data it contained, its publication had a muted impact upon general understandings of the Avebury complex. This may have been due in part to the emphasis he had placed upon the excavation of the henge ditch, at the expense of the stone circles, avenues and other settings. It was also rapidly over-shadowed by a new campaign of excavation that had begun a year before Gray's publication under the aegis of one of the most influential and important of Avebury's archaeological admirers, Alexander Keiller. As we will see, this latter programme of work had its sights set squarely upon the stone settings.

Some three years after Gray's workmen had backfilled their final ditch sections and abandoned Avebury once more to the village, the debonair Keiller arrived (one imagines with the screech of burning rubber) in the Avebury landscape. The contrast between the two men could not have been greater. Gray was an Edwardian and archaeologist of the old school; an excavator and museum curator who had learned his craft under General Pitt Rivers, and continued the great man's traditions of excavation and recording throughout his working life (Bowden 1991, 63). In a world of rapidly developing methodology, Gray never altered his digging style or embraced new ideas, leading Mortimer Wheeler to describe his approach to the Meare Lake villages in Somerset during the 1950s as like the digging of a cabbage patch (Coles 1987, 15). Put simply, while of a high standard in 1908, by the 1930s his field methodology was that of an earlier age of investigation.

The same could not be said of Keiller, whose life was one of extreme wealth, with archaeology one of a number of obsessions that included skiing, flying, fast cars, sexual experimentation and witchcraft (Murray 1999). His interests in archaeology were characterised by a continual drive towards methodological and procedural perfection. Whether this was through meticulous survey, the pioneering use of cine film, or schemes to employ a Zeppelin to facilitate an aerial survey of Britain (Piggott, in Smith 1965, xix-xx), Keiller appears to have craved innovation.

Rebel with a cause

Keiller's interests in archaeology, and in particular megaliths, developed during the 1920s when he undertook preliminary surveys of the stone circles of Aberdeenshire and Kincardineshire (Smith 1965, xxiii). His first tentative connection to the archaeology of Wiltshire came in 1922 when he wrote a letter to *The Sunday Observer* offering to sponsor a survey of Wessex. This was in response to an article by the pioneering field archaeologist O.G.S. Crawford extolling the virtues of aerial photography. The result was a collaborative aerial survey undertaken in 1924 by Crawford and Keiller, and funded by the latter. The results of this were published as *Wessex from the Air* in 1928, and included the first aerial photographs of Avebury; a series of three verticals covering the henge and the postulated course of the Beckhampton Avenue (Crawford & Keiller 1928, pls XXXVI-XXXVIII).

Keiller and Crawford were to develop a highly productive, if largely professional, relationship. Keiller used his considerable financial reserves to support a number of Crawford's schemes, including the founding of the journal *Antiquity*, and the purchase of land around Stonehenge (Murray 1999, 46-9). In 1923 the two joined forces to prevent the erection of a radio mast by the Marconi wireless company on Windmill Hill to the north of Avebury (ibid., 23-4; Whittle et al. 1999, 1-4). The importance of the site had been realised by Crawford in the same year when he visited the excavations that were being conducted there by H.G.O. Kendall, the rector of nearby Winterbourne Bassett. Kendall had dug a section through the outer ditch of the earthwork in 1922-3, recovering Neolithic pottery and worked flint from its lower fills. That such a monument could be Neolithic in date was a revolutionary concept in the early 1920s, and Crawford was quick to spot the potential of the site and the impact it might have on any understanding of nearby Avebury (Murray 1999, 27; Whittle et al. 1999, 1-2).

The threat from the Marconi company soon passed, and in 1924 Keiller purchased a large chunk of Windmill Hill after Crawford had alerted him to its upcoming sale. The following year Keiller began to organise excavations on his newly acquired land, at first unaware that the monument was scheduled (Whittle et al. 1999, 2). Opposition to Keiller's proposals appears to have come thick and fast, emanating chiefly from the formidable Maud Cunnington, wife of the curator of the Wiltshire Archaeological and Natural History Society's museum at Devizes.

Along with her husband Benjamin, Maud had (and was) excavating widely within Wiltshire when Keiller purchased his way on to the scene. While the Cunningtons had been highly influential in opening up and popularising the archaeology of the county, they were also ferociously parochial, regarding Wiltshire as their stamping ground, and exerted what has been described as a 'stranglehold' over Devizes Museum (Roberts 2002, 57). Wiltshire's archaeological establishment were clearly uncomfortable with the idea of a wealthy outsider (and what is more one lacking in any archaeological pedigree) excavating a site as potentially important as Windmill Hill. Keiller's playboy lifestyle appears to have exacerbated the situation, jarring with the inherent conservatism of the Cunningtons (ibid.).

In an attempt to resolve any potential conflict, Crawford arranged for Harold St. George Gray to act as nominal director of any excavations on Windmill Hill until Keiller had demonstrated his archaeological capabilities (Murray 1999, 39; Whittle et al. 1999, 2). With a solid track record of excavation and publication, Gray was initially acceptable to both parties. As a direct consequence of the Cunningtons' proprietary attitude to Wiltshire's archaeology, these two unlikely bedfellows – the conservative Edwardian and the progressive playboy – found themselves thrown together on Windmill Hill. It is perhaps not surprising that they quickly fell out.

Keiller came to the site as a novice excavator, but his skills and confidence developed rapidly. He possessed an enthusiasm for precision and technique that manifested itself in the development of new excavation and recording strategies (Whittle et al. 1999, 24-5). Gray, by contrast, refused to move beyond the techniques he had learned at the turn of the century. Personal philosophies, lifestyles and contacts within archaeological circles also set Keiller and Gray apart. The former was connected with influential contemporary figures in archaeology, such as Gordon Childe, Crawford and Charles Peers (then President of the Society of Antiquaries). He also offered patronage to the young rising stars of British prehistory such as Stuart Piggott, Grahame Clark and Leslie Grinsell. Gray was of another generation, looking back rather than forward, and taking his inspiration from earlier researchers such as Pitt Rivers.

The conflict between the old and new lasted for almost three seasons, Gray departing for good halfway through the 1927 excavation (Whittle et al. 1999, 2). It appears that the perfectionist in Keiller could no longer stomach Gray's seemingly lax techniques of excavation, finds recovery and recording. One of his first acts following the expulsion of Gray was to initiate the re-excavation of ditch sections dug during 1925 and 1926 (ibid.).

Some flavour of the ill-feelings Keiller held towards Gray and the

Cunningtons, whom he no doubt blamed for the imposition, can be gained from a series of limericks ridiculing Gray (e.g. Murray 1999, 43-4) and in comments in his personal correspondence. In a letter to his foreman, W.E.V. Young, he lamented 'I wish that you and I had lived twenty-five years hence, or that Gray and Mrs Cunnington had expired a quarter of a century ago' (quoted in Roberts 2002, 54). Indeed, in his diary Young was to note that 'It is part of AK's childish manner that he cannot write a letter on any archaeological matter without making some caustic remark about Mrs. Cunnington. It has become quite a mania with him, and ... it's quite evident he is on the borderline of insanity in this respect' (quoted in Murray 1999, 108). Keiller's obsessions clearly extended beyond methodological concerns and it may have been more than a question of exactitude that prompted him to pointedly 'rectify' the setting of a fallen West Kennet Avenue stone that had been re-erected by Maud Cunnington in 1912, claiming it was not only in the wrong position, but upside down (Keiller & Piggott 1936, 418).

With Gray gone, Keiller continued the direction of the Windmill Hill excavations himself, the final season taking place in 1929. Further excavation may have been planned, but in July that year Keiller was badly injured in a car accident in Savernake Forest (Murray 1999, 54), and this forced a temporary break from fieldwork that was to last several years.

Despite the untimely end to Keiller's Windmill Hill excavations, work at the site would prove instrumental in developing an understanding of Neolithic material culture sequences and economies, at a time when a full and proper understanding of this period was only just emerging. With the success of this work widely acknowledged, by this stage Keiller clearly felt himself 'proven' with respect to the Cunningtons and the Wiltshire establishment. However, tensions were to remain. In 1930 Maud Cunnington located and excavated the timber and stone circles at the Sanctuary on Overton Hill (Cunnington 1931). Keiller appears to have been deeply frustrated at being beaten to the site by Cunnington, and appealed for information on the progress of work from W.E.V. Young, who at various times acted as foreman on both parties' excavations (Pitts 2001, 16).

The best book about Avebury never written

From the mid-1920s, and stimulated by the purchase of many of Stukeley's manuscripts at a sale of the family papers in 1924, Keiller was to share with O.G.S. Crawford a passionate interest in the antiquary's work at Avebury. However, it was Crawford who first began work on a book dedicated to the site. To this end he undertook research between 1920 and 1927, making observations on surviving remains and attempting to relate these to the antiquarian archives (Ucko et al. 1991, 242). Although the book was never completed, the painstaking notes he compiled provided a valuable resource for later scholars, being drawn upon extensively by Keiller and also by the current authors in their work on the course of the Beckhampton and West Kennet Avenues.

Crawford's notes remain in the Alexander Keiller Museum; the ghost of a book that never was. However, a distilled version of his ideas about the monument complex was published in *Wessex from the Air* (Crawford & Keiller 1928, 210-13). Here he reconstructed the henge with a single entrance to the south, and the West Kennet Avenue leading to the stone circles of the Sanctuary. An analogy was drawn with early Bronze Age disc barrows, following a belief that the 'plan of Avebury resembles, in stone, the plan of those disc-barrows with two burial-mounds in them' (ibid., 213). In a distant resonance of Fergusson's cemetery hypothesis, Crawford saw Avebury's purpose as primarily funerary, with the Cove containing a burial, and a second cove with another interment on the site of the Obelisk (ibid., 213). At the time of writing, what Crawford could not have envisaged was the radical transformation in knowledge about Avebury that was to occur within the next decade.

The remaking of Avebury

In 1933 Keiller offered employment to the young archaeologist Stuart Piggott, the two having met and become friends some five years earlier (Piggott, in Smith 1965, xx). Like Crawford before them, both men shared an interest in Stukeley's records of the Avebury landscape. When Piggott made the tentative suggestion that useful additional information could be gained through excavation of the West Kennet Avenue (ibid.) it set in motion a chain of events that would radically re-define the monument and contemporary understandings of it. It is perhaps illustrative of Keiller's character that the following year, late one evening in the Red Lion Public House at Avebury, he announced to Piggott his plan to:

> acquire the whole of the land on which the main monument of Avebury lay, and as much of the West Kennet Avenue as possible; to devote himself to its excavation and judicious restoration; and since there was a possibility of renting, and ultimately acquiring the Manor House as well, of leaving London and transferring his library, drawing offices, and museum to Avebury as an archaeological institute to carry out this task.
>
> Piggott, in Smith (1965), xxi

Thus the Morven Institute of Archaeological Research was formed. Keiller's goal was quite clear: drawing upon Stukeley's records, and his vast financial resources, he intended to excavate the whole site and restore the monument to its 'former glory'.

Between 1934 and 1935 excavations took place on the northern third of the West Kennet Avenue with the aim of determining its precise course and restoring the stone settings. Before the excavations commenced all that remained visible of the Avenue were three standing and nine fallen stones, along with the standing stone that had been re-erected by Cunnington in 1912 (Plate XXI above). Excavation proceeded from a point some 840 m to the south of Avebury working northwards towards the henge (Keiller & Piggott 1936, 418). Using the surviving stones to provide an estimate of the longitudinal and transverse stone spacing, a median line was established for the notional course of the avenue and a 24 m wide strip was centred upon this. In practice the full strip was not excavated, efforts being confined to two parallel 6 m wide ribbons at either edge with extensions where the actual line and estimated line deviated. As the excavations approached Avebury, and first-hand experience of actual stone spacing was gained, the continuous strips were replaced by targeted trenches (Smith 1965, 185-6) (Plate XXI below).

During the course of these excavations Keiller uncovered both avenue stone sockets and an area of earlier (mostly middle Neolithic) occupation marked by a dense artefact scatter, pits and post-holes (ibid., 210-16). He also found crucial evidence for the acts of stone burial and destruction described in earlier chapters. This included burning pits with piles of charred straw and shattered sarsen, and 13 stones lying within their burial pits (ibid., 186). In the case of fallen and buried stones, the sarsens were carefully re-erected in their original locations and fixed in place with concrete. To mark the sites of destroyed stones distinctive triangular concrete markers were manufactured and set in place. Gradually the Avenue was resurrected.

Excavations within Avebury itself began in 1937. Keiller adopted a similar methodology to that employed during the last two seasons at Windmill Hill – though here dealing with stone settings rather than ditches – working anti-clockwise around the circuit of the outer stone circle (Plate XXII above). Work started with the north-western quadrant in 1937, then the south-western in 1938, opening a series of contiguous strips along the arc of the circle (Smith 1965, 188-90). Small cuttings were made into the bank and the top of the ditch, but an investigation of the earthwork was not regarded as a priority. He began with the north-western sector in response to the 'indescribable squalor and neglect' encountered there in the form of refuse piles, trees and choking undergrowth (Keiller 1939, 223).

As with the precedent set on the West Kennet Avenue, where buried stones were encountered they were carefully excavated and re-erected into beds of concrete (Plate XXII below). Burning pits likewise were excavated and the location of stone sockets marked with distinctive concrete pillars. During the course of this reconstruction work in the north-western quadrant a boundary wall that followed the arc of the outer circle was dismantled, revealing the broken remains of six stones embedded within it (Smith 1965, 188). Where fragments like this were found, plaster casts of the broken surfaces were taken and used to identify conjoining fragments which were reattached using iron rods and cement.

The work was like a megalithic jigsaw puzzle, with Stukeley's records providing the picture on the box. As work progressed on the stone settings of the outer circle, trees and bushes were removed from the bank; stubborn tree-roots being removed with the assistance of explosives, and the rubbish that had accumulated in the ditch was machined away to the level of the natural silting (ibid., 225-8).

There was an abrupt change in Keiller's methodology in 1939 when he turned his attention to the excavation of stone settings in the south-eastern quadrant, focussing first on the southern inner circle (ibid., 190-1). Rather than simply following the arc of the outer circle and plotting in trenches with a theodolite, Keiller adopted a strategy of excavating an open area made up of contiguous squares on a 50 foot (15 m) grid, each further subdivided into four quarters. This proved highly successful, particularly in revealing the plan of the complex internal features around the Obelisk, and in locating the isolated stone D.

The adoption of this new excavation strategy may have been dictated by the anticipated complexity of the stone settings here. However, it is equally likely that influence came from elsewhere, perhaps even from Gerhard Bersu's pioneering excavations at Little Woodbury, near Salisbury, which had begun in 1938 (Bersu 1940). An importation of German open-area excavation techniques, these revealed for the first time Iron Age post-built structures and finally dispelled the notion of pit dwellings which had been so prevalent in the literature on prehistoric Britain (Evans 1989). Piggott worked at Little Woodbury during the 1938 and 1939 seasons (Piggott 1983, 32), and perhaps he and Keiller hoped to find similar traces of timber structures at Avebury. Although originally planned to last for 12 years, this was to be the last season of work undertaken by Keiller at Avebury, the outbreak of war putting paid to further excavation. In 1941 he closed down his research institute, citing financial worries, and in 1943 Avebury was sold to the National Trust for the agricultural price of the land (Murray 1999, 106-7).

Keiller's work was notable for its methodological rigour and the attention paid to the later archaeology encountered. A detailed pre-excavation survey plan of the south-eastern quadrant was undertaken (Ucko et al. 1991, pl. 52), medieval ditches and other features were carefully excavated, and finds dating to the medieval and early post-medieval periods were retained. This would not have happened on the majority of excavations on prehistoric sites during this period. Indeed, by the standards of the day this was a very competent and rigorous excavation. While this was driven largely by Keiller's methodological zeal and perfectionism, it also reflected the sense of competition Keiller and Piggott felt with respect to Mortimer Wheeler's contemporary work at Maiden Castle – the other 'big show' (letters in Alexander Keiller Museum). This rigour did not, however, extend to publication. Keiller was clearly driven more by the *process* of excavation, the academic context for much of his work coming from colleagues such as Piggott. Commissioned by Keiller's widow, the synthesis of his work at both Windmill Hill and Avebury was finally prepared for publication by Isobel Smith after his death (Smith 1965).

His painstaking attention to detail and constant revisions effectively hindered the publication process. However, this reluctance to publish may also have been due in part to a feeling that resurrecting the monument was an end in itself: Avebury being allowed to tell its own story rather than through the filter of the archaeologist. Indeed, it is important to acknowledge that the impact of Keiller's ambitious programme of excavation preceded publication. A museum was opened in the former stable block of Avebury Manor in 1938 to showcase the finds recovered from the excavations, receiving a positive write-up in *The Times* and 6000 visitors in its first five months (Murray 1999, 90). During the course of the excavations themselves visitor numbers to the site swelled from 100-200 per week to around 1000-1500 (Keiller 1939, 229, 233). The site also came back into prominence in the archaeological literature. The henge merited only a short paragraph in Kendrick and Hawkes' influential survey of British archaeology published in 1932, which made brief reference to the work of Gray (Kendrick & Hawkes 1932, 96-7). By contrast, there is extended discussion of the monument in Grahame Clark's *Prehistoric England* of 1940, the book even opening with an aerial photograph of the henge in which the white chalk of the newly restored north-western quadrant shines brightly (Clark 1940).

Keiller's work, as a self-sponsored and entirely independent venture, was the last big excavation of its kind, marking the end of a certain phase of archaeological investigation. In an irony both Maud Cunnington and Gray would have undoubtedly enjoyed, its inception and funding perhaps had more in common with the work of Pitt Rivers than contemporaries such as Wheeler. It might even be argued that Keiller's achievements at Avebury were more the product of money and single-minded vision than academic insight and endeavour. Indeed, in retrospect even his employee and colleague Stuart Piggott referred dryly to Keiller's work as verging on an act of 'megalithic landscape gardening' (Piggott 1983, 32).

Avebury

The enforced separation of village and circle

> Avebury was a village with a living and thriving community. It had all the
> accoutrements of the imagined quintessential English village, with a large
> number of people living their lives around their church, chapels, hall, social
> club, sports clubs, shops, guest houses, hotel, pub, farms, garages, butchers,
> bakers, and even saddlemakers. Edwards (2000), 67

Integral to Keiller's vision of a pristine Avebury was the 'disempestring'
that Aubrey and Stukeley had struggled to achieve through survey and
drawing. Reconstruction also necessitated deconstruction, and Keiller's
ambitious project involved more than the removal of stubborn tree-
stumps, rubbish and field-walls. In 1937 a cow-byre in the north-western
quadrant was demolished with permission of its owner 'in the interest of
the monument'. This was followed in 1938 by the demolition of two derelict
cottages, their outbuildings and a modern stable in the south-western
sector (Keiller 1939, 225, 230). Rawlins' Garage, built against the western
stone of the Cove, was also demolished, and at Keiller's expense new
premises were constructed immediately outside the northern entrance
(Rawlins 1999, 44). Put simply, the village and the monument were
forcibly disentangled (Plate XXIV).

The work of demolition did not stop with Keiller's departure. Further
buildings within the confines of the henge were selectively demolished in
the two decades following the transfer of ownership of the property to the
National Trust. Although ostensibly directed at removing modern and
unsightly structures, a number of early post-medieval buildings, which
would now be considered as of historic value, were torn down. These
included the late eighteenth-century Rawlins' Cottages fronting the Swindon Road, which by the 1950s were deemed insanitary and in a poor state
of repair.

The impact of these demolitions on the inhabitants of Avebury has
escaped comment until very recently, when social historians began to
explore the toll exacted on the everyday lives of those dwelling in Avebury
as houses were pulled down, the garage relocated, and trees and hedgelines rooted up. Indeed, many villagers were also uprooted and relocated
to a new housing development at Avebury Trusloe, 1.6 km to the west of
the village. But while houses moved, amenities did not, and a dislocation
was created between the villagers and their familiar focal places such as
the church, pub, shops and school (Pitts 1996; Edwards 2000). Excavations
and building removal combined, this was one of the most dramatic periods
in the recent history of the henge and village.

Keiller's work could, therefore, be seen to have set in train a shameless
process of demolition and relocation that seriously affected the traditional

life of the village (Rawlins 1999, 43). However, his excavations provided much needed paid labour, especially during the Depression years, and he appears to have taken a genuine and active part in village life during his time in residence at the Manor (Murray 1999, 83). In a recent interview one of his original workmen commented that he had 'never heard anyone complaining about him. He would always buy everyone a drink and was a bit of an eccentric, a bit of a rogue and a great ladies man' (quoted in Johnston 2000).

In some senses Keiller 'made' the Avebury we see today, and it is his facsimile that has proven such an effective focus for neo-pagans, archaeologists, dowsers, new-age pilgrims and heritage managers alike. This was one person's notion of what a pristine, original Avebury would have looked like, albeit filtered through excavation and the records of Stukeley. As we hope readers will acknowledge from the preceding chapters, it is very hard to identify an 'original' Avebury. Efforts to fossilise the monument deny the inherent energy and dynamism that have made it the unique place it is today. Indeed we have argued throughout that rather than being executed according to a single, coherent plan, Avebury is the product of process, slowly taking shape through myriad negotiations, additions and alterations. Building upon this, it could be argued that Keiller's efforts marked the *only* point in time where a predetermined design was imposed upon the monument.

Keiller's Avebury is then very much an Avebury of the 1930s rather than the late Neolithic period he sought to bring vividly to life. There is certainly an Art Deco feel to the concrete blocks used to mark the positions of missing stones, and to the 'Egyptian' style of Rawlins' new garage. But as well as materialising a very specific vision of the henge, Keiller's work also generated (consciously or not) a tourist industry to go with it, raising public awareness to new heights and pushing forward the issues of conservation and management that so dominate the life of the monument today.

Excavations after Keiller

Excavation within the henge did not stop with Keiller, but the work that has followed has been small in scale and driven either by localised development, conservation needs, or very specific research questions. A good example of the latter is the excavation undertaken by Stuart Piggott in the north-eastern quadrant in order to assess the existence, or otherwise, of a third inner stone circle as originally suggested by Keiller (Piggott 1964). The results were negative. Research-driven excavations like this have unfortunately been rare, with most work taking place in advance of development and the creation and maintenance of service facilities. Instances include the excavations by W.E.V. Young on the line of the West Kennet Avenue, prompted by road-widening and the digging of drains (Young 1959, 1961), and Faith and Lance Vatcher's numerous unpublished rescue excavations in the 1960s and 1970s. During their time as curators of the Alexander Keiller Museum, the Vatchers recorded a buried stone of the Beckhampton Avenue, and directed a large excavation at the Avebury School site which included a cutting through the bank of the henge (Pollard & Reynolds 2002, 198-9). Another opportunity to examine the bank and the pre-henge buried soil came in 1982 when alterations were made to the north wing of the Great Barn. Despite the small scale of this work, amounting to no more than six square metres of excavation, useful environmental evidence was obtained (Evans et al. 1985).

Few of the stone settings within the henge have been excavated since Keiller's time, but in recent years a stone-hole belonging to the southern inner circle was recorded in a service trench adjacent to the Chapel (Anon. 2003, 229), and in 2003 the writers were commissioned by English Heritage and the National Trust to carry out an excavation in advance of the stabilisation of the remaining Cove stones. Limited though these excavations have been, they have provided an opportunity to recover environmental samples and materials for radiometric dating – techniques that Keiller could not have envisaged during the 1930s. Other work, at various locations in the village in advance of building extensions, has largely encountered medieval and post-medieval deposits (e.g. Harrington & Denham 1986).

If the scale of excavation within the henge has diminished greatly since Keiller's campaigns, the same cannot be said of work within the environs of Avebury. Development-led excavations since the 1970s have, for example, encountered traces of the early Anglo-Saxon settlement beneath the main tourist car park (Pollard & Reynolds 2002, 192-8), and a buried sarsen of the Beckhampton Avenue in Butler's Field (Wessex Archaeology 1998, 10). However, it is the concerted programme of research-driven excavation on Neolithic sites that has had the greatest impact upon our understanding of region's prehistory and, by implication, the context of the Avebury henge. All the key elements of the late Neolithic complex have been targeted since the late 1960s.

The first of these projects involved digging a tunnel into the centre of Silbury Hill. Sponsored by the BBC, this was styled largely as an exercise in presenting archaeology to the public, but behind it lay a tacit expectation that spectacular discoveries might be made (Whittle 1997a, 11).

Altogether more successful was Alasdair Whittle's programme of fieldwork conducted between 1987 and 1993, which set out to enhance knowledge of the Neolithic sequence, its environment, monuments and settlement (Whittle 1993). This included an extensive investigation of the

West Kennet palisaded enclosures, a monument complex that had re-mained largely hidden and neglected up to that date (Whittle 1997a).

More recently, Mike Pitts has re-excavated part of the Sanctuary with the aim of evaluating the quality of the Cunningtons' 1930 investigation (Pitts 2001); while the authors have focussed attention on testing the veracity of earlier antiquarian observations through the excavation of the re-discovered Beckhampton Avenue, Longstones Cove (Gillings et al. 2000, 2002) and Falkner's Circle (Plate II). Such work has radically altered our vision of the prehistoric landscape, even though much remains still to be done.

Explaining Avebury: big men and astronomer-priests

Keiller died in 1955 and the results of his excavations were eventually published by Isobel Smith a decade later (Smith 1965). *Windmill Hill and Avebury* was a seminal volume, and appeared at a time when there was renewed interest both in the British late Neolithic and in henge monu-ments in particular. Impetus came from a new campaign of fieldwork conducted on a scale Keiller would have approved, and, somewhat contro-versially at the time, making extensive use of earth-moving machinery. Directed by Geoffrey Wainwright, this series of state-funded excavations took place on the analogous Wessex 'henge enclosures' of Durrington Walls, Mount Pleasant and Marden between 1966 and 1971. Wainwright's work radically transformed contemporary understanding of these enig-matic sites: providing a cultural context in the form of a re-evaluated 'Rinyo-Clacton' or 'Grooved Ware culture'; highlighting the range of prac-tices associated with henge enclosures; and revealing complex timber counterparts to the stone settings at Avebury (Wainwright 1971; 1979; Wainwright & Longworth 1971).

In the mainstream of prehistoric studies, Avebury lost its individuality, being subsumed within a general category of 'henge enclosures'. Its crea-tion was seen as a by-product of increasing social complexity and the emergence of hierarchical forms of power during the late Neolithic of Wessex (Renfrew 1973b; Wainwright 1979, 237). Avebury was merely one piece of evidence for broader social transformations, specifically the emer-gence of chiefdoms and defined territorial units. Unsurprisingly, this rather cold relegation of Avebury to the status of a 'henge enclosure', produced through abstract conceptualisations of social power, did little to capture the public imagination. However, other strands were developing that did. Working within the general theme that monuments such as Avebury were indeed a direct manifestation of an increasingly hierarchi-cal society, these focused upon astronomy and religion rather than labour estimates and Thiessen polygons. This was epitomised by the work of an engineering professor, Alexander Thom, who claimed that megalithic monuments such as Avebury were laid out using precise geometry and a standardised measurement – the 'megalithic yard' – and were utilised for high precision astronomical observations (e.g. Thom 1967). In the 1970s the archaeologist Euan MacKie drew heavily on Thom's findings to argue that such monuments were the manifestation of a religious revolution, where a set of theocratic ideals originating in the Near East were spread throughout later Neolithic Britain by a caste of professional astronomer-priests (MacKie 1977).

Huffety, puffety ring-stone round

At the same time other interpretations were gaining currency that stressed Avebury's uniqueness and individuality. In these schemes the henge and its surrounding landscape were once again interpreted as a pictogram or 'working model' in the manner of Stukeley, Bowles and Bathurst Deane. In *The Silbury Treasure* (1976) and *The Avebury Cycle* (1977), a former lecturer in the History of Art, Michael Dames, offered a compelling blend of folklore and myth, mixed with a heady confection of anthropological, historical and archaeological information, to argue that Avebury and surrounding monuments were a symbolic representation of the annual agricultural round – the myth-cycle of a notional Great Neolithic Goddess writ large upon the landscape. Both books proved extremely influential among the general public and those seeking alternative interpretations. Such work, with its presentation of Avebury as a gigantic puzzle with a single, unambiguous meaning waiting to be unlocked, sparked public interest in a way that contemporary archaeological texts could not.

Along with the work of Thom and MacKie, Dames' narratives also meshed well with a growing number of independent strands of interpretation that operated beyond the bounds of the archaeological establishment. Beginning with long established techniques such as dowsing and the formal 'recognition' and study of so-called ley-lines in the 1920s, approaches began to develop that sought to shed light on the Avebury 'puzzle' through such diverse strands as earth powers, supposed archaic religious practices, cerealogy (the study of crop-circles) and lost ancient sciences.

1978 saw the publication of Tom Graves' influential *Needles of Stone*, a book that attempted to introduce some coherence into the burgeoning field of earth-mysteries and their study (Graves 1978) and the continued and enduring popularity of such musings is evident in the wealth of books, videos and websites seeking to explore Avebury and explain what is perceived as its singular mystery. These far outweigh archaeological texts on the subject.

It could be argued that this presentation of Avebury as a puzzle that could, given the right approach, be decoded or unravelled generated far more public interest than the campaigns of excavation undertaken by the likes of Gray and Keiller. This is not only evident in the tide of publications that followed the work of individuals such as Dames, Graves and Thom, but also in a number of fictional television series that appeared in the second half of the 1970s that drew directly upon the work of these authors (Jones 2001).

One of the most influential was a children's television series set within a thinly disguised Avebury. Broadcast in 1976, Harlech Television's *Children of the Stones* depicted the Avebury circles as a place oozing with serpents, folklore, mysterious earth energies and sinister astronomical alignments. What is admirable is the ingenious way in which the writers wove together aspects of Avebury's history with these alternative approaches to its interpretation. It was also downright scary and, along with the ominous role attributed to stone circles in the series *Quatermass* broadcast in 1979, certainly had a stimulating effect on the imaginations of the current writers.

Archaeologists and monuments

The twin paths charted by the archaeological establishment and those commentators keen to offer alternative explanations continued to drift apart throughout the 1970s and much of the 1980s, with mutual suspicions and misunderstandings being the order of the day. Interestingly, over the last 15 or so years there has been a subtle convergence, with dialogue and exchange replacing accusations of stuffiness and wild speculation. This has been in part due to changes in the way archaeologists themselves have begun to approach the task of understanding the past, and a growing openness to other views and perspectives (e.g. Bender 1998). It may also be in part due to increased media coverage, reflecting a growing awareness by those outside the profession of what it is that archaeologists do.

As a result, there is perhaps more in common between the general themes explored by contemporary prehistorians on the one hand, and by Dames and fellow 'alternative' commentators on the other, than at any point since the 1970s. Working within various strands of what has become known as 'Post-Processual' archaeology, academic studies of monumentality now place emphasis upon themes such as symbolism, memory, myth, and the importance of human movement and engagement (e.g. Barrett 1994; Bradley 1998, 2000, 2002b; Tilley 1994; Watson 2001). Indeed, many of these themes are drawn upon in the opening chapters of this book. This is not to acknowledge a complete openness on the part of archaeologists to all alternative and New Age readings, but simply reflects a common interest in the meanings and ontological significance of monuments like Avebury, and a desire to explore the multiple and sometimes conflicting viewpoints that have emerged through the influence of post-modern philosophies.

A site of international importance (Avebury in aspic?)

In 1986 Avebury and Stonehenge were designated as a single World Heritage Site, one of several hundred cultural monuments and landscapes deemed to be of truly international importance. As a result, the concerns of preservation and tourism have dominated the agenda throughout the 1990s and into the twenty-first century. Following a number of management initiatives encouraged by English Heritage in the early 1990s, Avebury now has its own Archaeological and Historical Research Group (AAHRG) – a forum for archaeologists, managers, historians and the public to discuss research and management issues – a formal Management Plan (English Heritage 1998) and a Research Agenda (Chadburn & Pomeroy-Kellinger 2001).

Driven by an ethos that seeks to restrict further changes to the monument and village, increased management means that further excavation on any large scale within the henge is unlikely, at least in the foreseeable future. While Avebury has its own research agenda, this advocates an explicit policy of 'preserving maximum rather than minimum remains (although some excavation may be desirable), [and] encouraging the use of non-invasive techniques' (ibid., 3). There is no doubt that the latter have proved invaluable, as shown by the results of recent programmes of geophysical and aerial survey, which continue to hint at the structural complexity of the monument (e.g. Ucko et al. 1991; Bewley et al. 1996). However, it does restrict the range of questions that might be addressed, and portrays excavation as a form of controlled destruction rather than creative knowledge production. This acknowledged, the benefits of a management regime are clear, in terms of the need to preserve archaeological deposits for future investigation, and to negotiate the wishes and demands of tourism, education and the village's inhabitants.

The 'running' of Avebury has become a labour-intensive task, with the National Trust alone employing several individuals in the capacity of property managers, site wardens, and museum, shop and café staff. Visitor numbers are now estimated to be in the order of 400,000-600,000 a year (Cleal 1996, 194), many of whom come to Avebury because of a feeling that the site has a 'special and personal meaning' to them (Pitts 1996, 123). Among these are various New Age and religious groups, some the legacy of Stukeley's earlier druidical interpretations and inventions. In 1993 an

10. Resurrecting Avebury

Avebury Order of Bards, or the *Gorsedd Caer Abiri*, was founded, resulting in a meeting on the autumn equinox of the following year of such diverse parties as King Arthur's Warband, The Secular Order of Druids, The Insular Order of Druids, and The Order of Bards, Ovates and Druids (ibid., 125). Avebury has now been appropriated by druids of various factions, one of whom currently acts as an unofficial Keeper of the Stones.

In a reversal of fortunes, it is now the village itself which is suffering, rather than the henge. Ostensibly a working agricultural community, this is arguably one whose heart has been removed. The remaining buildings have become prestigious and desirable properties, their value inflated by their location in a heritage hotspot. This has put them beyond the reach of many of those whose families have lived in Avebury for generations, creating a village as artificial as the circle within which it is located (Edwards 2000, 72). Planning fiascos, further National Trust purchases of land, and tensions between the locals and the Trust have done little to help (Pitts 1996).

Management agendas might seek to slow down the rate of change, but the dynamism of Avebury continues. While we may never witness changes or developments on the scale of those during the early to mid-twentieth century, it is unlikely that Avebury will stay still for long. Indeed, tensions are never far from the surface, and Avebury will continue to confront and be negotiated for centuries to come.

Epilogue

Avebury today is a place of contrasts and tensions, simultaneously the stuff of committees and management plans, academic interest, worship and reverence. It is home to a new generation of antiquaries seeking to construct their own chorographies of this unique place (e.g. Cope 1998), and a focus for New Age pilgrims, archaeologists and the merely curious, drawn by a sense of mystery that has recently been woven around the stones and earthworks. However, people hug the stones unaware that much of what they are encountering is a simulacrum – stone plugged not into mystical currents of earth power but large dollops of 1930s concrete. Credulity is commonplace, and it is surely very telling that when the British television company Channel 4 concocted an elaborate UFO hoax during the summer of 2003, Avebury was chosen as the ideal place to launch it. Reflecting a process of continual re-contextualisation that we have charted throughout this book, the site has now gained a mystique that it has never otherwise had in its post-Roman history.

Here we have sought to tell Avebury's story from an explicitly archaeological perspective. In so doing, it will no doubt have become clear that archaeological knowledge about the site contains many ambiguities, and that there is an inherent slipperiness and contingency to many of the interpretations tendered. Like the Aveburys of Stukeley, Browne, Rickman, Fergusson, Keiller, Smith and Burl, *our* Avebury remains an interpretation, open to challenge, revision and review. What is more, it is no less a product of its time than any of the works explored in the later chapters here, perhaps destined eventually to find itself tucked away in a short paragraph highlighting the follies of the early twenty-first century archaeological narrative. Whatever its ultimate fate, we hope that it has gone some way to justify Stukeley's claim that Avebury is 'the most extraordinary work in the world'.

Dramatis Personae

Some of the key historical players in our little drama.

John Aubrey: Pioneering antiquary who first 'discovered' Avebury.

Caleb Baily: Gentleman, non-conformist and prolific destroyer of stones. Targeted for poetic attack by the Society of Antiquaries.

The Barber-surgeon: Or was he a tailor? Avebury's enduring mystery – squashed beneath a falling stone or murdered and hidden there?

Walter Charleton: Friend of John Aubrey and early recorder of Avebury.

James Fergusson: Antiquary notable not for getting things right, but for spurring others into action by getting them wrong.

Richard Fowler: An active stone-breaker referred to by Stukeley as 'that destroyer'.

Harold St. George Gray: An Edwardian through and through, Gray undertook the first major campaign of excavations within the henge.

Farmer Griffin: Active non-conformist responsible for destroying much of the Sanctuary

Sir Robert Holford: Pragmatic gentleman who opposed stone destruction while simultaneously demolishing parts of the earthwork.

Reuben Horsall: Parish Clerk of Avebury who vociferously opposed the stone destruction.

Alexander Keiller: Playboy and marmalade magnate who undertook the excavation and restoration of large portions of the site in the 1930s.

William Long: Compiled the first detailed history of antiquarian work at Avebury.

Sir John Lubbock: Otherwise known as Lord Avebury, a prominent archaeologist who campaigned successfully for statutory protection for the monument.

W.C. Lukis: Antiquary who along with A.C. Smith undertook the first detailed programme of excavation at the site.

Rev. A.C. Smith: Local clergyman and founding member of the Wiltshire Archaeological and Natural History Society who did much to record the archaeology within and around Avebury.

Tom Robinson: Active non-conformist and stone-breaker who 'made cruel havoc of the place'.

Walter Stretch: Stone destroyer who reputedly developed the technique of stone burning.

William Stukeley: Antiquarian polymath who undertook copious, detailed records of Avebury and chronicled its destruction.

Thomas Twining: Author of the first published work on Avebury, unfortunately attributing it to the Romans.

Appendix

Summary of key published dating schemes for the Avebury henge

Smith (1965) – short shronology (unitary)

Component	Date
Main earthwork	
Outer circle	
Inner circles	
Inner settings	
Avenue	1850 BC
Stone-hole D in southern inner circle	Later – ?1700 BC

Based upon ceramic typology and structural relationships with the Sanctuary. Other assumptions based upon lower chalk sarsen packing thought to be derived from the digging of the ditch and the overall morphology of the ditch line and outer circle.

Burl (1979, 166) – short chronology (essentially unitary)

Component	Date
Inner circles and settings	2600 BC
Third inner circle begun (abandoned)	2500 BC
Earthworks, outer circle, avenues begun	2400 BC
Avenues completed	2300 BC

Malone (1989, 14-15) – short chronology (essentially unitary)

Component	Date
Earthworks	2600 BC
Stone settings	2400 BC
Avenues	2400-2300 BC
Avebury completed	2300 BC

Also regards odd stones such as the Ring-stone as earlier because of the presence of lower chalk packing. This is the opposite view to that taken by Smith who saw the stone settings that did not seem to 'fit' the suggested structural patterns as being later.

Appendix

Pitts & Whittle (1992) – long chronology (spanning a millennium)

Component	Date
Inner circles	prior to 3490-3280 BC
Primary bank	3490-3280 BC
Main earthwork	3150-2630 BC
Outer circle	2840-2230 BC

The first phase is based upon analogy, the remainder C14 determinations on material derived from the Gray and Keiller excavations. The West Kennet Avenue only discussed insofar as it being regarded as perhaps coming early in the sequence, marking a pre-Avebury routeway. C14 ranges quoted to 1 sigma.

Burl (2000, 319) – long chronology (spanning a millennium)

Component	Date
Obelisk and Cove settings	3400-3200 BC
Settlement around Cove	3000 BC
Inner circles erected	2800 BC
Earthwork and outer circle	2600 BC
Avenues	2400 BC

Based in part upon C14 determinations.

Pitts (2000, 279) – long chronology (spanning a millennium)

Component	Date
Old land surface under primary bank	3633-3104 BC; 3345-2879 BC
Primary ditch fills	3304-2625 BC
Old land surface under later bank	3007-2495 BC
Outer circle settings	2906-2466 BC; 2575-2039 BC

Based entirely upon C14 determinations. The C14 ranges quoted here are calibrated (95% confidence limit).

Bibliography

Anon., 'Excavation and fieldwork in Wiltshire 2001' *Wiltshire Archaeological and Natural History Magazine* (2003) 229-37.

Arnold, C.J., *An Archaeology of the Early-Saxon Kingdoms* (Routledge, 1997).

Ashbee, P., 'Fussell's Lodge long barrow excavations, 1957' *Archaeologia* (1966) 1-80.

Ashbee, P., Smith, I.F. and Evans, J.G., 'Excavation of three long barrows near Avebury, Wiltshire' *Proceedings of the Prehistoric Society* (1979) 207-300.

Ashbee, P., 'Early ditches, their forms and fills' in R. Cleal and J. Pollard (eds) *Monuments and Material Culture: papers on Neolithic and Bronze Age Britain in honour of Isobel Smith* (Hobnob Press, 2004) 1-14.

Austin, P., 'The emperor's new garden: woodland, trees and people in the Neolithic of southern Britain' in A.S. Fairbairn (ed.) *Plants in Neolithic Britain and Beyond* (Oxbow, 2000) 63-78.

Baedeker, K., *Great Britain: a handbook for travellers* (Baedeker, 1894).

Barclay, A., Gray, M. and Lambrick, G., *Excavations at the Devil's Quoits, Stanton Harcourt, Oxfordshire, 1972-3 and 1988* (Oxford Committee for Archaeology, 1995).

Barclay, A. and Halpin, C., *Excavations at Barrow Hills, Radley, Oxfordshire*, vol. 1: *The Neolithic and Bronze Age monument complex* (Oxford University Committee for Archaeology, 1999).

Barclay, A., Lambrick, G., Moore, J. and Robinson, M., *Lines in the Landscape: cursus monuments in the Upper Thames Valley* (Oxford Archaeology, 2003).

Barker, C., 'The long mounds of the Avebury region' *Wiltshire Archaeological and Natural History Magazine* (1985) 7-38.

Barrett, J., Bradley, R. and Green, M., *Landscape, Monuments and Society: the prehistory of Cranborne Chase* (Cambridge University Press, 1991).

Barrett, J., *Fragments from Antiquity: an archaeology of social life in Britain, 2900-1200 BC* (Blackwells, 1994).

Barrett, J. and Fewster, K.J., 'Stonehenge: is the medium the message?' *Antiquity* (1998) 847-52.

Barrett, J., 'The mythical landscapes of the British Iron Age' in W. Ashmore and A.B. Knapp (eds) *Archaeologies of Landscape* (Blackwells, 1999) 253-65.

Barth, F., *Cosmologies in the Making* (Cambridge University Press, 1987).

Basso, K.H., 'Wisdom sits in places: notes on a western Apache landscape' in S. Feld and K.H. Basso (eds) *Senses of Place* (School of American Research Press, 1996) 53-90.

Bayliss, A., Bronk Ramsey, C. and McCormac, G., 'Dating Stonehenge' in B. Cunliffe and C. Renfrew (eds) *Science and Stonehenge* (British Academy, 1997) 39-59.

Bender, B., *Stonehenge: making space* (Berg, 1998).

Bersu, G., 'Excavations at Little Woodbury, Wiltshire, part 1' *Proceedings of the Prehistoric Society* (1940) 30-111.

Bewley, R., Cole, M., David, A., Featherstone, R., Payne, A. and Small, F., 'New features within the henge at Avebury, Wiltshire: aerial and geophysical evidence' *Antiquity* (1996) 639-46.

Black, A. and Black, C., *Black's Picturesque Tourist and Road and Railway Guidebook through England and Wales* (Adam and Charles Black, 1862).

Bloch, M., *From Blessing to Violence: history and ideology in the circumcision ritual of the Merina of Madagascar* (Cambridge University Press, 1986).

Bloch, M., 'People into places: Zafimaniry concepts of clarity' in E. Hirsch and M. O'Hanlon (eds) *The Anthropology of Landscape: perspectives on place and space* (Oxford University Press, 1995) 63-77.

Boardman, J., *The Archaeology of Nostalgia: how the Greeks re-created their mythical past* (Thames & Hudson, 2002).

Bowden, M., *Pitt Rivers: the life and archaeological work of Lieutenant-General Augustus Henry Lane Fox Pitt Rivers* (Cambridge University Press, 1991).

Bowen, H.C. and Smith, I.F., 'Sarsen stones in Wessex: the Society's first investigation in the evolution of landscape project' *Antiquaries Journal* (1977) 185-96.

Bowles, W.L., *Hermes Britannicus* (J.B. Nichols & Sons, 1828).

Bradley, R., 'Maumbury Rings, Dorchester – the excavations of 1908-13' *Archaeologia* (1975) 1-97.

Bradley, R., *The Passage of Arms: an archaeological analysis of prehistoric hoard and votive deposits* (Oxbow, 1990).

Bradley, R., 'The excavation of an Oval Barrow beside the Abingdon Causewayed Enclosure, Oxfordshire' *Proceedings of the Prehistoric Society* (1992) 127-42.

Bradley, R. and Edmonds, M., *Interpreting the Axe Trade: production and exchange in Neolithic Britain* (Cambridge University Press, 1993).

Bradley, R., *Altering the Earth: the origins of monuments in Britain and continental Europe* (Society of Antiquaries of Scotland, 1993).

Bradley, R., *The Significance of Monuments* (Routledge, 1998).

Bradley, R., *The Good Stones: a new investigation of the Clava Cairns* (Society of Antiquaries of Scotland, 2000a).

Bradley, R., *An Archaeology of Natural Places* (Routledge, 2000b).

Bradley, R., *The Past in Prehistoric Societies* (Routledge, 2002).

Brooke, J.W. and Cunnington, H., 'Excavation of a Roman Well near Silbury Hill' *Wiltshire Archaeological and Natural History Magazine* (1896) 166-71.

Brooke, J.W., 'The excavation of a Roman well nr. Silbury Hill, October 1908' *Wiltshire Archaeological and Natural History Magazine* (1910) 373-75.

Brown, A.G., 'Floodplain vegetation history: clearings as potential ritual spaces?' in A.S. Fairbairn (ed.) *Plants in Neolithic Britain and Beyond* (Oxbow, 2000) 49-62.

Browne, H., *An Illustration of Stonehenge and Abury, in the County of Wilts, pointing out their Origin and Character, through considerations hitherto unnoticed* (Smith and Greaves, 1833).

Brück, J., 'Monuments, power and personhood in the British Neolithic' *Journal of the Royal Anthropological Institute* (2001) 649-67.

Burl, A., *Prehistoric Avebury* (Yale University Press, 1979).

Burl, A., *Megalithic Brittany* (Thames & Hudson, 1985).

Burl, A., 'Coves: structural enigmas of the Neolithic' *Wiltshire Archaeological and Natural History Magazine* (1988) 1-18.

Burl, A., *From Carnac to Callanish: the prehistoric stone rows and avenues of Britain, Ireland and Brittany* (Yale University Press, 1993).

Burl, A., *The Stone Circles of Britain, Ireland and Brittany* (Yale University Press, 2000).

195

Burnham, B. and Wacher, J., *The 'Small Towns' of Roman Britain* (Batsford, 1990).

Case, H.J. and Whittle, A., *Settlement Patterns in the Oxford Region: excavations at the Abingdon causewayed enclosure and other sites* (Council for British Archaeology, 1982).

Chadburn, A. and Pomeroy-Kellinger, M., *Archaeological Research Agenda for the Avebury World Heritage Site* (Wessex Archaeology, 2001).

Chippendale, C., 'The invention of words for the idea of "Prehistory"' *Proceedings of the Prehistoric Society* (1988) 303-14.

Clare, T., 'Towards a re-appraisal of henge monuments' *Proceedings of the Prehistoric Society* (1986) 281-316.

Clare, T., 'Towards a re-appraisal of henge monuments: origins, evolutions and hierarchies' *Proceedings of the Prehistoric Society* (1987) 457-77.

Clark, J.G.D., *Prehistoric England* (Batsford, 1940).

Clarke, D.L., *Beaker Pottery of Great Britain and Ireland* (Cambridge University Press, 1970).

Clarke, D.L., 'Archaeology: the loss of innocence' *Antiquity* (1973) 6-18.

Clarke, S., 'Abandonment, rubbish disposal and "special" deposits at Newstead' in K. Meadows, C. Lemke and J. Heron (eds) *TRAC 96: Proceedings of the Sixth Annual Theoretical Archaeology Conference* (Oxbow, 1997)

Clarke, S., 'In search of a different Roman period: the finds assemblage at the Newstead military complex' in G. Fincham, G. Harrison, R. Rodgers Holland and L. Revell (eds) *TRAC 99: Proceedings of the Ninth Annual Theoretical Roman Archaeology Conference* (Oxbow, 2000) 22-9.

Cleal, R., Walker, K. and Montague, R., *Stonehenge in its Landscape: twentieth century excavations* (English Heritage, 1995).

Cleal, R., 'Interpreting Avebury: the role of the Alexander Keiller Museum' in D.M. Evans, P. Salway and D. Thackray (eds) *'The Remains of Distant Times': archaeology and the National Trust* (Boydell, 1996) 192-7.

Cleal, R. and Pollard, J., 'Dating Avebury' in R. Cleal and J. Pollard (eds) *Monuments and Material Culture: papers on Neolithic and Bronze Age Britain in honour of Isobel Smith* (Hobnob Press, 2004) 120-9.

Coles, J.M., *Meare Village East: the excavations of A. Bulleid and H. St. George Gray 1932-1956* (Somerset Levels Papers, 1987).

Colt Hoare, R., *The Ancient History of North Wiltshire* (Lackington, Hughes, Harding, Mavor and Jones, 1821).

Connerton, P., *How Societies Remember* (Cambridge University Press, 1989).

Cope, J., *The Modern Antiquarian: a pre-millennial odyssey through megalithic Britain* (Thorsons, 1998).

Corney, M., 'New evidence for the Romano-British Settlement by Silbury Hill' *Wiltshire Archaeological and Natural History Magazine* (1997a) 139-50.

Corney, M., 'The origins and development of the small town of Cunetio' *Britannia* (1997b) 337-49.

Corney, M., 'The Romano-British nucleated settlements of Wiltshire' in P. Ellis (ed) *Roman Wiltshire and After* (Wiltshire Archaeological and Natural History Society, 2001) 5-38.

Corney, M. and Walters, B., 'Romano-British' in A. Chadburn and M. Pomeroy-Kellinger (eds) *Archaeological Research Agenda for the Avebury World Heritage Site* (Wessex Archaeology, 2001) 24-6; 47; 68.

Crawford, O.G.S. and Keiller, A., *Wessex from the Air* (Clarendon Press, 1928).

Bibliography

Cummings, V. and Whittle, A., 'Tombs with a view: landscape, monuments and trees' *Antiquity* (2003) 255-66.

Cunliffe, B., *Wessex to AD 1000* (Longman, 1993).

Cunnington, W., 'Notes on a long barrow on Oldbury Hill' *Wiltshire Archaeological and Natural History Magazine* (1872) 103-4.

Cunnington, M.E., 'The re-erection of two fallen stones, and discovery of an interment with drinking cup, at Avebury' *Wiltshire Archaeological and Natural History Magazine* (1913) 1-11.

Cunnington, M.E., *The Early Iron Age Inhabited Site at All Canning's Cross Farm, Wiltshire* (Simpson, 1923).

Cunnington, M.E., 'The "Sanctuary" on Overton Hill, near Avebury' *Wiltshire Archaeological and Natural History Magazine* (1931) 300-35.

Dames, M., *The Silbury Treasure* (Thames & Hudson, 1976).

Dames, M., *The Avebury Cycle* (Thames & Hudson, 1977).

Dark, K., 'Roman-period activity at prehistoric ritual monuments in Britain and in the Amorican Peninsula' in E. Scott (ed.) *Theoretical Roman Archaeology: first conference proceedings* (Avebury, 1993) 133-46.

Darvill, T., 'Ever increasing circles: the sacred geographies of Stonehenge and its landscape' in B. Cunliffe and C. Renfrew (eds) *Science and Stonehenge* (British Academy, 1997) 167-202.

David, A. and Payne, A., 'Geophysical surveys within the Stonehenge landscape' in B. Cunliffe and C. Renfrew (eds) *Science and Stonehenge* (British Academy, 1997) 73-113.

David, A., Field, D., Fassbinder, J., Linford, N., Linford, P. and Payne, A., ' "A family chapel ... to an archdruid's dwelling": an investigation into the stone circle at Winterbourne Bassett, Wiltshire' *Wiltshire Archaeological and Natural History Magazine* (2003) 195-205.

Deane, B., *The Worship of the Serpent Traced Throughout the World; Attesting the Temptation and Fall of Man by the Instrumentality of the Serpent Tempter* (J.G. Rivington, 1833).

Deetz, J., *In Small Things Forgotten: an archaeology of early American life* (Anchor, 1996).

Denison, S., 'Lost skeleton of "barber-surgeon" found in museum' *British Archaeology* (1999) 4.

Douglas, M., *Purity and Danger: an analysis of concepts of pollution and taboo* (Routledge, 1966).

Dovey, K., *Framing Places: mediating power in built form* (Routledge, 1999).

Dunscombe, H., *Avebury, a five mile chapel: the story of three hundred years of life and worship in a congregational country Chapel* (Avebury Chapel, 1998).

Eagles, B.N., 'Pagan Anglo-Saxon burials at West Overton' *Wiltshire Archaeological and Natural History Magazine* (1986) 103-19.

Eagles, B.N., 'The archaeological evidence for settlement in the fifth to seventh centuries AD' in M. Aston and C. Lewis (eds) *The Medieval Landscape of Wessex* (Oxbow, 1994) 13-32.

Eagles, B.N., 'Anglo-Saxon presence and culture in Wiltshire' in P. Ellis (ed.) *Roman Wiltshire and After* (Wiltshire Archaeological and Natural History Society, 2001) 199-233.

Edmonds, M., *Ancestral Geographies of the Neolithic* (Routledge, 1999).

Edwards, B., 'Avebury and other not-so-ancient places: the making of the English heritage landscape' in H. Kean, P. Martin and S.J. Morgan (eds) *Seeing History: public history in Britain now* (Francis Boutle, 2000) 64-79.

English Heritage, *Avebury World Heritage Site Management Plan* (English Heritage, 1998).

Evans, C., 'Monuments and analogy: the interpretation of causewayed enclosures' in C. Burgess, P. Topping, C. Mordant and M. Maddison (eds) *Enclosures and Defences in the Neolithic of Western Europe* (British Archaeological Reports, 1988) 47-73.

Evans, C., 'Archaeology and modern times: Bersu's Woodbury 1938 & 1939' *Antiquity* (1989) 436-50.

Evans, C., Pollard, J. and Knight, M., 'Life in woods: tree-throws, "settlement" and forest cognition' *Oxford Journal of Archaeology* (1999) 241-54.

Evans, J.G., *Land Snails in Archaeology* (Seminar Press, 1972).

Evans, J.G. and Smith, I.F., 'Excavations at Cherhill, North Wiltshire, 1967' *Proceedings of the Prehistoric Society* (1983) 43-117.

Evans, J.G., Pitts, M. and Williams, D., 'An excavation at Avebury, Wiltshire, 1982' *Proceedings of the Prehistoric Society* (1985) 305-10.

Evans, J.G., Limbrey, S., Mate, I. and Mount, R., 'An environmental history of the Upper Kennet Valley, Wiltshire, for the last 10,000 years' *Proceedings of the Prehistoric Society* (1993) 139-95.

Evans, J.G. and O'Connor, T., *Environmental Archaeology: theory and methods* (Sutton, 1999).

Fairbairn, A., 'On the spread of crops across Neolithic Britain, with special reference to southern England' in A. Fairbairn (ed.) *Plants in Neolithic Britain and Beyond* (Oxbow, 2000) 107-21.

Fergusson, J., *Rude Stone Monuments in all Countries: their age and uses* (Murray, 1872).

Fielden, K., 'Avebury saved?' *Antiquity* (1996) 503-7.

Fowler, P., *Landscape Plotted and Pieced: landscape history and local archaeology in Fyfield and Overton, Wiltshire* (Society of Antiquaries, 2000).

Fowler, P.J., 'Wansdyke in the Woods: an unfinished Roman military earthwork for a non-event' in P. Ellis (ed.) *Roman Wiltshire and After* (Wiltshire Archaeological and Natural History Society, 2001) 179-98.

Fowles, J. and Legg, R., *John Aubrey's Monumenta Britannica, parts 1-2* (Dorset Publishing,1980).

Freeman, J., 'Selkley Hundred: Avebury' in D.A. Crowley (ed.) *Victoria County History of Wiltshire,* vol. 12 (Oxford University Press, 1983) 86-104.

Frere, S., *Britannia* (Routledge, 1974).

Geddes, I., *Hidden Depths: Wiltshire's geology and landscapes* (Ex Libris, 2000).

Gibson, A., 'Excavations at the Sarn-y-bryn-caled cursus complex, Welshpool, Powys and the timber circles of Great Britain and Ireland' *Proceedings of the Prehistoric Society* (1994) 143-223.

Gibson, A. and Kinnes, I., 'On the urns of a dilemma: radiocarbon and the Peterborough problem' *Oxford Journal of Archaeology* (1997) 65-72.

Gibson, A., *Stonehenge and Timber Circles* (Tempus, 1998).

Gillings, M. and Pollard, J., 'Non-portable stone artefacts and contexts of meaning: the tale of Grey Wether (museums.ncl.ac.uk/Avebury/stone4.htm)' *World Archaeology* (1999) 179-93.

Gillings, M., Pollard, J. and Wheatley, D.W., 'The Beckhampton Avenue and a "new" Neolithic enclosure near Avebury: an interim report on the 1999 excavations' *Wiltshire Archaeological and Natural History Magazine* (2000) 1-8.

Gillings, M. and Pollard, J., 'A Roman shrine at Beckhampton?' *Current Archaeology* (2002) 453.

Bibliography

Gillings, M., Pollard, J. and Wheatley, D.W., 'Excavations at the Beckhampton Enclosure, Avenue and Cove, Avebury: an interim report on the 2000 season' *Wiltshire Archaeological and Natural History Magazine* (2002) 249-58.

Gillings, M., Peterson, R. and Pollard, J., 'The destruction of the Avebury monuments' in R. Cleal and J. Pollard (eds) *Monuments and Material Culture: papers on Neolithic and Bronze Age Britain in honour of Isobel Smith* (Hobnob Press, 2004) 139-63.

Gingell, C., *The Marlborough Downs: a later Bronze Age landscape and its origins* (Wiltshire Archaeological and Natural History Society, 1992).

Gingell, C., 'Avebury: striking a balance' *Antiquity* (1996) 507-11.

Gosden, C. and Lock, G., 'Prehistoric histories' *World Archaeology* (1998) 2-12.

Gow, P., 'Land, people and paper in Western Amazonia' in E. Hirsch and M. O'Hanlon (eds) *The Anthropology of Landscape: perspectives on place and space* (Oxford University Press, 1995) 43-62.

Grahame, M., 'Redefining Romanisation: material culture and the question of social continuity in Roman Britain' in C. Forcey, J. Hawthorne and R. Witcher (eds) *TRAC 97: Proceedings of the Seventh Annual Theoretical Roman Archaeology Conference* (Oxbow, 1998) 1-10.

Graves, T., *Needles of Stone* (Turnstone, 1978).

Gray, H.S.G., 'The Avebury excavations 1908-1922' *Archaeologia* (1935) 99-162.

Green, M., *A Landscape Revealed: 10,000 years on a chalkland farm* (Tempus, 2000).

Griffiths, N., 'The Roman army in Wiltshire' in P. Ellis (ed.) *Roman Wiltshire and After* (Wiltshire Archaeological and Natural History Society, 2001) 39-72.

Grimes, W.F., *Excavations on Defence Sites, 1939-45. 1, Mainly Neolithic-Bronze Age* (Ministry of Works, 1960).

Hamerow, H., *Excavations at Mucking*, vol. 2: *The Anglo-Saxon settlement* (English Heritage, 1993).

Harding, A. and Lee, G.E., *Henge Monuments and Related Sites of Great Britain: air photographic evidence and catalogue* (British Archaeological Reports, 1987).

Harding, J., *Henge Monuments of the British Isles* (Tempus, 2003).

Harrington, P. and Denham, V., 'Excavations at Avebury 1982' *Wiltshire Archaeological and Natural History Magazine* (1986) 217-21.

Harrison, W.J., 'A bibliography of the great stone monuments of Wiltshire – Stonehenge and Avebury' *Wiltshire Archaeological and Natural History Magazine* (1901) 1-169.

Haselgrove, C., 'Iron Age brooch deposition and chronology' in A. Gwilt and C. Haselgrove (eds) *Reconstructing Iron Age Societies* (Oxbow, 1997) 51-72.

Haycock, D.B., *William Stukeley: science, religion and archaeology in eighteenth-century England* (Boydell Press, 2002).

Healy, F., 'Hambledon Hill and its implications' in R. Cleal and J. Pollard (eds) *Monuments and Material Culture: papers on Neolithic and Bronze Age Britain in honour of Isobel Smith* (Hobnob Press, 2004) 15-38.

Helms, M., *Craft and the Kingly Ideal: art, trade and power* (University of Texas, 1993).

Herbert, A., *Cyclops Christianus* (John Petheram, 1849).

Hill, T., *The Love of Stones* (Faber & Faber, 2001).

Holgate, R., *Neolithic Settlement of the Thames Basin* (British Archaeological Reports, 1988).

Hope-Taylor, B., *Yeavering: an Anglo-British centre of early Northumbria* (HMSO, 1977).

Hunter, J., 'Present state of Abury, Wilts' *The Gentleman's Magazine* (1829) 3-7.

Hutton, R., *The Stations of the Sun: a history of the ritual year in Britain* (Oxford University Press, 1996).

Johnson, M., *An Archaeology of Capitalism* (Blackwells, 1996).

Jones, B. and Mattingly, D., *An Atlas of Roman Britain* (Oxbow, 1990).

Jones, S., *The Archaeology of Ethnicity* (Routledge, 1997).

Jones, L.E., 'Everybody must get stoned ...: megaliths and movies' *Third Stone* (2001) 6-14.

Jones, O. and Cloke, P., *Tree Cultures: the place of trees and trees in their place* (Berg, 2002).

Jope, E.M., 'The Saxon and medieval pottery from Alexander Keiller's excavations at Avebury' *Wiltshire Archaeological and Natural History Magazine* (1999) 60-91.

Jundi, S. and Hill, J.D., 'Brooches and identities in first century AD Britain: more than meets the eye?' in C. Forcey, J. Hawthorne and R. Witcher (eds) *TRAC 97: Proceedings of the Seventh Annual Theoretical Archaeology Conference* (Oxbow, 1998) 125-37.

Kahn, M., 'Stone-faced ancestors. The spatial anchoring of myth in Wamira, Papua New Guinea' *Ethnology* (1990) 51-66.

Kahn, M., 'Your place and mine: sharing emotional landscapes in Wamira, Papua New Guinea' in S. Feld and K.H. Basso (eds) *Senses of Place* (School of American Research Press, 1996) 167-98.

Keiller, A. and Piggott, S., 'The recent excavations at Avebury' *Antiquity* (1936) 417-27.

Keiller, A., 'Avebury: summary of excavations 1937 and 1938' *Antiquity* (1939) 223-33.

Kendrick, T. and Hawkes, C., *Archaeology in England and Wales 1914-1931* (Methuen,1932).

King, E., *Munimenta Antiqua* (G. Nicol, 1799).

King, B., 'Avebury – The Beckhampton Avenue' *Wiltshire Archaeological and Natural History Magazine* (1879) 377-83.

King, N.E., 'The Kennet Valley sarsen industry' *Wiltshire Archaeological and Natural History Magazine* (1968) 83-93.

Kirby, J.L., 'Alien houses: the Priory of Avebury' in R.B. Pugh and E. Crittall (eds) *Victoria County History of Wiltshire*, vol. 3 (Oxford University Press, 1956) 392-93.

Kirk, T., 'Constructs of death in the early Neolithic of the Paris Basin' in M. Edmonds and C. Richards (eds) *Understanding the Neolithic of North-western Europe* (Cruithne Press, 1998) 102-26.

Last, J., 'Out of line: cursuses and monument typology in eastern England' in A. Barclay and J. Harding (eds) *Pathways and Ceremonies: the cursus monuments of Britain and Ireland* (Oxbow, 1999) 86-97.

Last, J., *Avebury Southern Car Park (Glebe Field): a desk-based assessment* (English Heritage, 2002).

Laurence, R., *The Roads of Roman Italy: mobility and cultural change* (Routledge, 1999).

Laurence, R., 'The creation of geography: an interpretation of Roman Britain' in C. Adams and R. Laurence (eds) *Travel and Geography in the Roman Empire* (Routledge, 2001) 67-94.

Leland, J., *Itinerary* (Bell, 1907-10).

Long, W., *Abury Illustrated* (Wiltshire Archaeological and Natural History Society, 1858).

Long, W., 'Facsimiles of Aubrey's Plan of Abury' *Wiltshire Archaeological and Natural History Magazine* (1862) 224-7.

Long, W., 'Abury Notes' *Wiltshire Archaeological and Natural History Magazine* (1878) 327-35.

Loveday, R., 'Double entrance henges – routes to the past?' in A. Gibson and D. Simpson (eds) *Prehistoric Ritual and Religion* (Sutton, 1998) 14-31.

Lubbock, J., *Pre-Historic Times, as Illustrated by Ancient Remains, and the Manners and Customs of Modern Savages* (Williams & Norgate,1865).

Lukis, W.C., 'Report on the prehistoric monuments of Stonehenge and Avebury' *Proceedings of the Society of Antiquaries of London* (1881-3) 141-57.

MacKie, E., *Science and Society in Neolithic Britain* (Paul Elk, 1977).

Malone, C., *Avebury* (Batsford, 1989).

Margary, I. D., *Roman Roads in Britain* (J. Baker, 1967).

Meyrick, O., 'The Broadstones' *Wiltshire Archaeological and Natural History Magazine* (1955) 192-3.

Millett, M., *The Romanization of Britain* (Cambridge University Press, 1990).

Millett, M., *Book of Roman Britain* (Batsford, 1995).

Montgomery, J., Budd, P. and Evans, J., 'Reconstructing the lifetime movements of ancient people: a Neolithic case-study from southern England' *European Journal of Archaeology* (2000) 370-85.

Murray, L.J., *A Zest for Life: the story of Alexander Keiller* (Morven Press, 1999).

Oswald, A., Dyer, C. and Barber, M., *The Creation of Monuments: Neolithic causewayed enclosures in the British Isles* (English Heritage, 2001).

Parker-Pearson, M. and Ramilisonina, 'Stonehenge for the ancestors: the stones pass on the message' *Antiquity* (1998) 308-26.

Passmore, A.D., 'The Meux excavation at Avebury' *Wiltshire Archaeological and Natural History Magazine* (1935) 288-9.

Patton, M., 'Megalithic transport and territorial markers: evidence form the Channel Islands' *Antiquity* (1992) 392-5.

Peterson, R., *Neolithic pottery from Wales: traditions of construction and use* (Archaeopress, 2003a).

Peterson, R., 'Thomas Twining's Roman Avebury' *Wiltshire Archaeological and Natural History Magazine* (2003b) 210-13.

Piggott, S., 'Destroyed megaliths in North Wiltshire' *Wiltshire Archaeological and Natural History Magazine* (1955) 390-2.

Piggott, S., *The West Kennet Long Barrow: excavations 1955-56* (HMSO, 1962).

Piggott, S., 'Excavations at Avebury 1960' *Wiltshire Archaeological and Natural History Magazine* (1964) 28-9.

Piggott, S., 'Archaeological retrospect' *Antiquity* (1983) 28-37.

Piggott, S., *William Stukeley: an eighteenth-century antiquary* (Thames & Hudson, 1985).

Piggott, S., 'The background and beginnings of the Wiltshire Archaeological and Natural History Society' *Wiltshire Archaeological and Natural History Magazine* (1991) 108-15.

Pine, J., 'The excavation of a Saxon settlement at Cadley Road, Collingbourne Ducis, Wiltshire' *Wiltshire Archaeological and Natural History Magazine* (2001) 88-117.

Pitts, M. and Whittle, A., 'The development and date of Avebury' *Proceedings of the Prehistoric Society* (1992) 203-12.

Pitts, M., 'The vicar's dewpond, the National Trust shop and the rise of paganism' in D.M. Evans, P. Salway and D. Thackray (eds) *'The Remains of Distant Times':* *archaeology and the National Trust* (Boydell, 1996) 116-31.

Pitts, M., *Hengeworld* (Century, 2000).

Pitts, M., 'Excavating the Sanctuary: new investigations on Overton Hill, Avebury' *Wiltshire Archaeological and Natural History Magazine* (2001) 1-23.

Pitts, M., Bayliss, A., McKinley, J., Buyhton, A., Budd, P., Evans, J., Chenery, C., Reynolds, A. and Semple, S., 'An Anglo-Saxon decapitation and burial at Stonehenge' *Wiltshire Archaeological and Natural History Magazine* (2002) 131-46.

Pollard, J., 'The Sanctuary, Overton Hill, Wiltshire: a re-examination' *Proceedings of the Prehistoric Society* (1992) 213-26.

Pollard, J., 'Inscribing space: formal deposition at the later Neolithic monument of Woodhenge, Wiltshire' *Proceedings of the Prehistoric Society* (1995) 137-56.

Pollard, J. and Gillings, M., 'Romancing the stones: towards a virtual and elemental Avebury' *Archaeological Dialogues* (1998) 143-64.

Pollard, J., 'These places have their moments: thoughts on settlement practices in the British Neolithic' in J. Brück and M. Goodman (eds) *Making Places in the Prehistoric World: themes in settlement archaeology* (UCL Press, 1999) 76-93.

Pollard, J. and Ruggles, C., 'Shifting perceptions: spatial order, cosmology, and patterns of deposition at Stonehenge' *Cambridge Archaeological Journal* (2001) 69-90.

Pollard, J., 'The aesthetics of depositional practice' *World Archaeology* (2001) 315-33.

Pollard, J. and Reynolds, A., *Avebury: the biography of a landscape* (Tempus, 2002).

Pollard, J., 'Memory, monuments and middens in the Neolithic landscape' in G. Brown and D. Field (eds) *The Archaeology of the Marlborough Downs* (Oxbow, in press).

Powell, A., Allen, M. and Barnes, I., *Archaeology in the Avebury Area* (Wessex Archaeology, 1996).

Proudfoot, E., 'Bishop's Cannings: Roughridge Hill' *Wiltshire Archaeological and Natural History Magazine* (1965) 132-3.

Rawlins, M., *Butcher, Baker, Saddlemaker: village life in Avebury from 1920 to 1974* (Antony Rowe, 1999).

Renfrew, C., *Before Civilization* (Penguin, 1973a).

Renfrew, C., 'Monuments, mobilisation and social organisation in neolithic Wessex' in C. Renfrew (eds) *The Explanation of Culture Change* (Duckworth, 1973b) 539-58.

Reynolds, A.J., 'Later Saxon and medieval' in A. Chadburn and M. Pomeroy-Kellinger (eds) *Archaeological Research Agenda for the Avebury World Heritage Site* (Wessex Archaeology, 2001a) 28-34.

Reynolds, A.J., 'Avebury: a late Anglo-Saxon *burh?*' *Antiquity* (2001b) 29-30.

Richards, C. and Thomas, J., 'Ritual activity and structured deposition in later Neolithic Wessex' in R. Bradley and J. Gardiner (eds) *Neolithic Studies* (British Archaeological Reports, 1984) 189-218.

Richards, J., *The Stonehenge Environs Project* (English Heritage, 1990).

Richards, C., 'Monuments as landscape: creating the centre of the world in late Neolithic Orkney' *World Archaeology* (1996a) 190-208.

Richards, C., 'Henges and water' *Journal of Material Culture* (1996b) 313-36.

Richards, J. and Whitby, M., 'The engineering of Stonehenge' in B. Cunliffe and C. Renfrew (eds) *Science and Stonehenge* (British Academy, 1997) 231-56.

Bibliography

Rickman, J., 'On the antiquity of Abury and Stonehenge' *Archaeologia* (1839) 399-419.

Roberts, J., ' "That terrible woman': the life, work and legacy of Maud Cunnington' *Wiltshire Archaeological and Natural History Magazine* (2002) 46-62.

Robertson-Mackay, M.E., 'A "head and hooves" burial beneath a round barrow with other Neolithic and Bronze age sites, on Hemp Knoll, near Avebury, Wiltshire' *Proceedings of the Prehistoric Society* (1980) 123-76.

Robinson, D., ' "A feast of reason and a flow of soul": the archaeological antiquarianism of Sir Richard Colt Hoare' *Wiltshire Archaeological and Natural History Magazine* (2003) 111-28.

Robinson, P., 'Religion in Roman Wiltshire' in P. Ellis (ed.) *Roman Wiltshire and After* (Wiltshire Archaeological and Natural History Society, 2001) 147-64.

Roe, D. and Taki, J., 'Living with stones: people and the landscape in Erromango, Vanuatu' in P.J. Ucko and R. Layton (eds) *The Archaeology and Anthropology of Landscape* (Routledge, 1999) 411-22.

Semple, S., 'A fear of the past: the place of the prehistoric burial mound in the ideology of middle and later Anglo-Saxon England' *World Archaeology* (1998) 109-26.

Sharples, N., 'Aspects of regionalisation in the Scottish neolithic' in N. Sharples and A. Sheridan (eds) *Vessels for the Ancestors: essays on the Neolithic of Britain and Ireland* (Edinburgh University Press, 1992) 322-31.

Simmons, I.G., *The Environmental Impact of Later Mesolithic Cultures: the creation of moorland landscape in England and Wales* (Edinburgh University Press, 1996).

Smith, A.C., 'Excavations at Avebury' *Wiltshire Archaeological and Natural History Magazine* (1867) 209-16.

Smith, A.C., *British and Roman Antiquities of North Wiltshire* (Wiltshire Archaeological and Natural History Society, 1885).

Smith, I., *Windmill Hill and Avebury: a short account of the excavations 1925-1939* (The Clover Press, 1959).

Smith, I., *Windmill Hill and Avebury: excavations by Alexander Keiller, 1925-1939* (Clarendon Press, 1965).

Smith, I. and Simpson, D., 'Excavation of three Roman tombs and a prehistoric pit on Overton Down' *Proceedings of the Prehistoric Society* (1966) 122-55.

Smith, R.W., 'The ecology of Neolithic farming systems as exemplified by the Avebury region of Wiltshire' *Proceedings of the Prehistoric Society* (1984) 99-120.

Smith, R.W., Healy, F., Allen, M., Morris, E., Barnes, I. and Woodward, P., *Excavations along the Route of the Dorchester By-pass, Dorset, 1986-8* (Wessex Archaeology, 1997).

Soffe, G. and Clare, T., 'New evidence of ritual monuments at Long Meg and her Daughters, Cumbria' *Antiquity* (1988) 552-7.

Startin, W. and Bradley, R., 'Some notes on work organisations in prehistoric Wessex' in C. Ruggles and A. Whittle (eds) *Astronomy and Society in Britain during the Period 4000-1500 BC* (British Archaeological Reports, 1981) 289-96.

Stukeley, W., *Abury, a Temple of the British Druids* (London, 1743).

Taçon, P.S.C., 'The power of stone: symbolic aspects of stone use and tool development in western Arnhem Land, Australia' *Antiquity* (1991) 192-207.

Tarlow, S., 'Scraping the bottom of the barrow: metaphors and Neolithic/Bronze Age burial mounds' *Journal of Theoretical Archaeology* (1995) 123-44.

Thom, A., *Megalithic Sites in Britain* (Clarendon Press, 1967).

Thomas, N., 'A Neolithic pit on Waden Hill, Avebury' *Wiltshire Archaeological and Natural History Magazine* (1955) 167-71.

Thomas, J., *Rethinking the Neolithic* (Cambridge University Press, 1991).

Thomas, J., 'The politics of vision and the archaeologies of landscape' in B. Bender (ed.) *Landscape: politics and perspectives* (Berg, 1993) 19-48.

Thomas, J., *Time, Culture & Identity* (Routledge, 1996).

Thomas, J., *Understanding the Neolithic* (Routledge, 1999a).

Thomas, J., 'An economy of substances in earlier Neolithic Britain' in J. Robb (ed.) *Material Symbols: culture and economy in prehistory* (Southern Illinois University Press, 1999b) 70-89.

Thorpe, I.J., 'Ritual, power and ideology: a reconstruction of earlier Neolithic rituals in Wessex' in R. Bradley and J. Gardiner (eds) *Neolithic Studies: a review of some current research* (British Archaeological Reports, 1984) 41-60.

Tilley, C., *A Phenomenology of Landscape: places, paths and monuments* (Berg, 1994).

Tipper, J., *Grubenhäuser: pitfills and pitfalls* (unpublished PhD thesis, 2000).

Trigger, B., *A History of Archaeological Thought* (Cambridge University Press, 1989).

Turnbull, D., *Masons, Tricksters and Cartographers: comparative studies in the sociology of scientific and indigenous knowledges* (Routledge, 2000).

Twining, T., *Avebury in Wiltshire, the remains of a Roman work, erected by Vespasian and Julius Agricola, during their several commands in Brittany* (J. Downing, 1723).

Tylden-Wright, D., *John Aubrey: a life* (Harper Collins, 1991).

Ucko, P.J., Hunter, M., Clark, A.J. and David, A., *Avebury Reconsidered: from the 1660s to the 1990s* (Unwin Hyman, 1991).

Vatcher, F.d.M., 'Avebury: Beckhampton Avenue' *Wiltshire Archaeological and Natural History Magazine* (1969) 127.

Vatcher, F.d.M. and Vatcher, L., *The Avebury Monuments* (HMSO, 1980).

Wainwright, G.J. and Longworth, I.H., *Durrington Walls: excavations 1966-1968* (Society of Antiquaries of London, 1971).

Wainwright, G.J., 'The excavation of a Late Neolithic enclosure at Marden, Wiltshire' *Antiquaries Journal* (1971) 177-239.

Wainwright, G.J., *Mount Pleasant, Dorset: excavations 1970-1971* (Society of Antiquaries of London, 1979).

Wainwright, G.J., *The Henge Monuments: ceremony and society in Prehistoric Britain* (Thames & Hudson, 1989).

Waterson, R., *The Living House: an anthropology of architecture in south-east Asia* (Oxford University Press, 1990).

Watson, J.L., 'Of flesh and bones: the management of death pollution in Cantonese society' in M. Bloch and J. Parry (eds) *Death and the Regeneration of Life* (Cambridge University Press, 1982) 155-86.

Watson, A. and Keating, D., 'Architecture and sound: an acoustic analysis of megalithic monuments in prehistoric Britain' *Antiquity* (1999) 325-36.

Watson, A., 'Composing Avebury' *World Archaeology* (2001) 296-314.

Webster, J., 'Interpretatio: Roman word power and the Celtic Gods' *Britannia* (1995) 153-61.

West, S.E., *West Stow, the Anglo-Saxon village* (East Anglian Archaeology 24,1985).

Wheatley, D.W. and Earl, G., 'Virtual reconstruction and the interpretative process: a case-study from Avebury' in D.W. Wheatley, G. Earl and S. Poppy (eds) *Contemporary Themes in Archaeological Computing* (Oxbow, 2002) 5-15.

Whitley, J., 'Too many ancestors' *Antiquity* (2002) 119-26.

Whittle, A., 'A model for the Mesolithic-Neolithic transition in the Upper Kennet Valley, North Wiltshire' *Proceedings of the Prehistoric Society* (1990) 101-10.

Whittle, A., 'The Neolithic of the Avebury area: sequence, environment, settlement and monuments' *Oxford Journal of Archaeology* (1993) 29-53.

Whittle, A., Rouse, A.J. and Evans, J.G., 'A Neolithic downland monument in its environment: excavations at the Easton Down Long Barrow, Bishops Cannings, north Wiltshire' *Proceedings of the Prehistoric Society* (1993) 197-239.

Whittle, A., 'Excavations at Millbarrow chambered tomb, Winterbourne Monkton, north Wiltshire' *Wiltshire Archaeological and Natural History Magazine* (1994) 1-53.

Whittle, A., *Europe in the Neolithic: the creation of new worlds* (Cambridge University Press, 1996).

Whittle, A., *Sacred Mound, Holy Rings – Silbury Hill and the West Kennet palisade enclosures: a late Neolithic complex in north Wiltshire* (Oxbow, 1997a).

Whittle, A., 'Moving on and moving around: Neolithic settlement mobility' in P. Topping (ed.) *Neolithic Landscapes* (Oxbow, 1997b) 15-22.

Whittle, A., 'Remembered and imagined belongings: Stonehenge in its traditions and structures of meaning' in B. Cunliffe and C. Renfrew (eds) *Science and Stonehenge* (British Academy, 1997c) 145-66.

Whittle, A., 'People and the diverse past: two comments on "Stonehenge for the ancestors"' *Antiquity* (1998) 852-54.

Whittle, A., Pollard, J. and Grigson, C., *Harmony of Symbols: the Windmill Hill causewayed enclosure, Wiltshire* (Oxbow, 1999).

Whittle, A., Davies, J., Dennis, I., Fairbairn, A. and Hamilton, M., 'Neolithic activity and occupation outside Windmill Hill causewayed enclosure, Wiltshire: survey and excavation 1992-93' *Wiltshire Archaeological and Natural History Magazine* (2000) 131-80.

Wilkinson, P., 'A report on diggings made in Silbury Hill and in the ground adjoining' *Wiltshire Archaeological and Natural History Magazine* (1869) 113-18.

Williams, H., 'The ancient monument in Romano-British ritual practices' in C. Forcey, J. Hawthorne and R. Witcher (eds) *TRAC 97: Proceedings of the Seventh Annual Theoretical Archaeology Conference* (Oxbow, 1998a) 71-86.

Williams, H., 'Monuments and the past in early Anglo-Saxon England' *World Archaeology* (1998b) 90-108.

Witcher, R., 'Roman roads: phenomenological perspectives on roads in the landscape' in C. Forcey, J. Hawthorne and R. Witcher (eds) *TRAC 97: Proceedings of the Seventh Annual Theoretical Archaeology Conference* (Oxbow, 1998) 160-70.

Woodward, A. and Woodward, P., 'The topography of some barrow cemeteries in Bronze Age Wessex' *Proceedings of the Prehistoric Society* (1996) 275-91.

Yorke, B.A.E., *Wessex in the Early Middle Ages* (Leicester University Press, 1995).

Young, W.E.V., 'The West Kennet Avenue' *Wiltshire Archaeological and Natural History Magazine* (1959) 229-30.

Young, W.E.V., 'The West Kennet Avenue' *Wiltshire Archaeological and Natural History Magazine* (1961) 30.

Index

Figure and plate numbers appear in bold type. Figures are in Arabic numbers, plates in Roman.